9 TROOP IN THE FALKLANDS

For Mum and Dad
and
Dawn, Fern, Joss, Tom and Will

9 TROOP IN THE FALKLANDS

A Royal Marine Fighting Troop in 1982

CHRIS PRETTY

Pen & Sword

MILITARY

AN IMPRINT OF PEN & SWORD BOOKS LTD.
YORKSHIRE - PHILADELPHIA

First published in Great Britain in 2024 by
PEN AND SWORD MILITARY
An imprint of
Pen & Sword Books Limited
Yorkshire – Philadelphia

ISBN 978 1 39900 805 1

Typeset in Times New Roman 11.5/14.5 by
SJmagic DESIGN SERVICES, India.
Printed and bound in the UK by CPI Group (UK) Ltd.

Pen & Sword Books Limited incorporates the imprints of Atlas, Archaeology,
Aviation, Discovery, Family History, Fiction, History, Maritime, Military,
Military Classics, Politics, Select, Transport, True Crime, Air World, Frontline
Publishing, Leo Cooper, Remember When, Seaforth Publishing, The Praetorian
Press, Wharncliffe Local History, Wharncliffe Transport, Wharncliffe True Crime
and White Owl.

For a complete list of Pen & Sword titles please contact
PEN & SWORD BOOKS LIMITED
George House, Units 12 & 13, Beevor Street, Off Pontefract Road,
Barnsley, South Yorkshire, S71 1HN, England
E-mail: enquiries@pen-and-sword.co.uk
Website: www.pen-and-sword.co.uk

or

PEN AND SWORD BOOKS
1950 Lawrence Rd, Havertown, PA 19083, USA
E-mail: uspen-and-sword@casematepublishers.com
Website: www.penandswordbooks.com

Contents

Author's Note   vi

Acknowledgements   x

Introduction   xi

Chapter 1   A Call to Arms   1

Chapter 2   Blue Beach and Blue Sky   39

Chapter 3   Move to Wreck Point – Backwards   90

Chapter 4   We'll Be Home by Christmas   112

Chapter 5   At Last! Forward to the Front Line – Terra Incognita   126

Chapter 6   Battle Preparation and Scary Monsters   148

Chapter 7   Sapper Hill – A Fight for Our Lives   165

Chapter 8   Coda – A Reflective Future   206

Postscript   211

Appendix A: Alejandro Koch   213

Appendix B: Charlie Company Nominal Roll   221

Author's Note

There was once a happy girl called Alice. Everyone in the village knew her name, and could see she knew right from wrong. One cold winter she noticed people were muttering in the church and shop. They seemed to be saying bad things. When spring arrived, a blight came and spread through the orchard trees. For the first time, the apples and pears completely failed to blossom. As she walked alone in the meadow, she saw there were many more rabbit holes than normal. She could also see rabbits huddled in twos and threes, weeping and swaying, doing nothing. This day, a mad plan popped into her mind, and she ran all the way home. This Alice, you see, decided to send us down a rabbit-hole ...

Some of this is true ... the good parts anyway.

This story has been waiting to be told since 1982. By both sides. Some forty years or so and in which time it has never been fully told, in public and very rarely in private. It will not even be fully told here. As a renowned poet once said regarding his service in the First World War that it might be 'A preface for a tale I have never told'.[1] Ultimately it is the story of two peoples, initially a world apart, both of whom had lived their independent lives but were now set on an unseen collision course. One people from Great Britain and one people from Argentina. The characters are much the same age and reflect the generational nationalistic traits of the 1970s and early 1980s. They differ in their

---

1. Geoffrey Bache Smith, June 1918

military training somewhat but that is their biggest difference, probably. Their most significant exception is that the British came from an anarchic and monochromatic 1970s counterculture and the Argentinians from an undemocratic and authoritarian society, shall we politely say. We were all young. We were all oblivious and in our ignorant youth thought we were indestructible. Many of us had no experience of war. Maybe that is the best way to see war. Napoleon Bonaparte, who also spent some time in the South Atlantic, said, 'To understand the man you have to know what was happening in the world when he was twenty.' Most of us were 20, or very close, and this would prove to be our particular defining moment. Mostly, however, this story is about fellowship and friendship. The most important things in life.

The idea of the content of this book has existed since 1990 and has remained quietly undisturbed until today, when you are reading it now. The world has changed and many new technologies have appeared since that decade. They significantly contributed to the construction of this story. Modern social media is mostly a wonderful thing that allowed me to be introduced to, and then make friends with, Marcos Basavilbaso, an Argentine military historian. The complex idea of combining these two people's stories then really became a shared possibility. A shared voice. It may even elevate itself to being an opus. Maybe too pompous. For all its efforts though, it is probably the best approximation of the truth that can be currently made.

It is the very nature of books about war that they usually tell the story of only one side: the winner. This often seems to end up with a heroically jaundiced, jingoistic and sometimes cynical view of what truthfully happened. I generously use the word 'often', but other words could be applied that would be far more accurate. War books should probably never be one sided should you wish to portray the best approximation of that truth and to give fair voice to all participants. There are always two sides to any conflict. Hopefully this story gives some small voice to both. It is a book very much about journeys, adventures, voyages, friendships and ultimately returning home to a new land. A land that had perceivably changed, but probably less than we had changed.

In fact, the land had not changed but clearly we had. Coming home can be a traumatic event and the subsequent overcoming of the monsters of war that we encountered, and which we unknowingly brought home, is a very private journey and will therefore mostly mercifully remain untold. Most of these new monsters are encountered when alone, very alone, and there is no one else there to help you. Some monsters are much bigger, more malignant and unbearable than others. Some of these monsters mercifully disappear in the mists of time and some linger longer like irritating demons and refuse to be shifted, no matter what we seem to do, or neglect to do. This book is not written to put any demons to rest; I have no skill to do this, and it is not the remit of this writing to suggest otherwise. It is just a simple recognition that the demons are very real. Maybe. Maybe they are something quite different, but this word is socially understandable, so we shall use it. Please remember PTSD/PTS was not recognised in the UK at the time.

Demons, by their very nature, are very individual. Time, however, is universal, so we are all led to believe. However, time is a slippery eel. Sometimes it seems to speed up and sometimes it seems to slow down. It is probably something to do with the matter of relativity, generally speaking. Mr Einstein in 1905 proposed that there could be such a thing as spacetime. This may account for the disturbing experience of time speeding up and slowing down when in moments of extreme danger. Maybe the 'space' is the place we inhabit at that time. This spacetime has a tangible and logical link to the 'Alice model' and the 'rabbit hole' proposed throughout the story. This is also a social common myth. What may be relative in time to one person may not be the same to another person who has a distinctly different experience of that shared time and space, relatively speaking. There may be a more accurate adaption that has been described as time dilation. Slippery time.

Slippery time is that time when nothing seems to fit. A second may feel like an hour. The converse may also be true. This seems to happen in war. Slippery time dilation. It is not exclusive to war.

Our 9 Troop story is simple and universal to soldiers. We trained hard, very hard, and we sailed to war on a comfortable civilian cruise liner. We landed on D-Day, we fought hard and lived very fast, but this may be that same relativity. Maybe we lived slow. Some lived faster than others and saw more than they should have. Some got wounded and some of our friends were killed and never got home. Individually and collectively, we played a very small part in an international situation and we came home, bringing our new demons with us. Our new demons; maybe they are old demons but just given more teeth and claws and ascribed more power. Many are still here as I have said, and mine is beside me right now as I write this, paying full attention to what I do, and will probably be searingly critical of these observations that I will make to you. My demon loves to highlight 'imposter syndrome'.

The Argentine story has disturbing similarities but is obviously extremely different in its conclusion. But young men we were and old men we are now. The journey progresses but age does not seem to have dimmed those days.

Initially the text is very descriptive. This allows for a detailed understanding of 'the Troop' and its peculiar military ways. It also allows for the story to be told later without the complications of interrupting descriptions of process and particular military detail.

The stage is set and the players are absolutely not ready. In fact, they are spread around the world. They have not read their lines, and this could all go very wrong. In fact, there are no lines. No perfect end state to work towards. No final lines and no final curtain. The actors do not even know each other. The people in the audience don't even know what they are watching, and the players are making it up as they go along. The curtain is unstoppably going up and the first scene must start. The show must go on, as they always say. However, the show is someone else's show and we all have a bit part in it. Some have speaking parts, but most do not. Like I said, no one has any lines yet. We will all make it up as the play progresses. A true adventure at sea and in the mountains of far-off shores at the end of the world. Both voices are mighty.

Both sides have kindly contributed text to this story. Their words are included unaltered and unchanged. This is of paramount importance to the story, to retain the authenticity of these contributors. It is also polite. It may be difficult to understand some text, but I have resisted the urge to grammatically tidy anything up. This 'confusion' you will discover is part of the fog of war. The Latin adverb *sic* would need to be presumed and applied in all cases. Inappropriate words have been altered.

Stage lights lower and there is darkness. Some low mist drifts across the stage. Eight thousand miles away the fog of war is descending. We will sail to this strange land at the end of the world. Our ignorance and youth will be our main weapon. Actually, our ignorance, our youth and our friends are our main weapons. War has come to our generation, my generation.

Acknowledgements

First, I would like to thank Marcos Basavilbaso for his professional help with this book. I know he worked hard to trace the Argentine soldiers of 1982. It is appreciated. Thanks also to Alejandro Koch, who was the 'Jefe de Grupo' for sharing his memories. Thank you also for permission to reproduce the photographs.

Second, I would like to thank 9 Troop for just being themselves. Particular thanks go to Jono, Terry, Graham, Carl, Rick, Alex, Ged and Vince of 9 Troop who shared their thoughts with me. For their encouragement too. Also, to Andy Pillar.

To Terry and Ged for their photographs and their permission to reproduce them.

Tony Wright, my longest-term oppo, for his unceasing encouragement in the project.

Jules, my brother and my best friend, for his professional expertise and encouragement in the production of the text. And for being my brother.

Adrian and Emily Brown, who encouragingly sat through long discussions about the subjects and their relevance to a modern audience. Adrian for his photographs and for his permission to reproduce them.

To Beth Winch, a young author of the future.

Introduction

Two Voices are these; one is of the sea,
One of the mountains; each a mighty Voice ...

Wordsworth

So ... Sapper Hill. This almost insignificant hill rises almost insignificantly out of the back of Port Stanley and is just under a mile or so to its south. Port Stanley was a colourfully placid place with about 1,000 inhabitants in 1982. Standing peacefully on the summit of the hill on a clear bright day, with a breeze from the west and the sun in your face, the world stretches out forever before you. From this summit the hill overlooks the small town and the long, low bay to the north and then further on to Murrell and more low hills in the distance. Turn around and it overlooks Mullet Creek and Seal Point to the south, then as far as the eye cannot see it stretches away to an unseen Antarctica over a luminous horizon. To the right and to the west is Mount William some two miles away and then Mount Harriet, Tumbledown, Two Sisters and Mount Longdon. Further are the lofty heights of Mount Kent at 1,093 feet (333.14 metres). Further still and across the sea are the shores of Argentina and Rio Gallegos. Turn around again and face east and you see Stanley Common, which is a small peninsula, and then five miles away at its point is the sea at Rookery Bay. After the bay there is nothing, nothing at all, just sea, all the way round the globe until you reach Estrecho Nelson (Nelson Strait) in Chile in South America again. That sea brings a wildness and a brutality at these latitudes, but it also brings magnificent, tranquil beauty. At 453 feet (138 metres) elevation Sapper Hill is not a mountain; no one could rightfully claim that. More of a large hill. Maybe not even a large hill, but it is significant in the local landscape. Its importance may be a paradox. Paradoxically the sun still rises in the east and sets in the west, but the sun is seen to the north when in the southern hemisphere. A paradox, but a logical paradox. If you stand on either Mount Kent or Sapper Hill for a few days, you will feel the anger of this lower world.

Sapper Hill is a gently rising hill from the town aspect, covered with peat, deep peat. From the south it is craggy and with more complex ground that gives out to the peat plains and on to Mullet Creek. There is a particular rocky spine on the southern side that runs from east to west and if looked at from the south is a high, craggy, impenetrable wall. Local children have always known that the rocky outcrops and the crags have caves in them. Play among these crags was child's play to many generations of Islanders. The many peat cuttings to the north of this spine would probably indicate decades of farming to heat the houses of the small, colourfully painted South Atlantic town sitting at the end of nowhere, on the edge of the world. Terra Incognita.

Apparently, the hill is named after some British Army sappers who were living at Moody Brook in some past century. It is located close by, but not on the hill itself. Local knowledge says that they installed 6-inch guns here in the previous wars and local people came here to look at the English fleet and the German fleet in the Great War. Although insignificant in height, it dominates an extremely large geographical landscape. The openness is breathtaking. In many ways.

Moody Brook became the home of the Royal Marine Detachment NP8901 (Naval Party 8901). Moody was the name of a sapper army officer who felt it necessary, in a zeitgeist kind of way and within the accepted customs of the time, to name the hill after himself. Brook, or stream, seems self-explanatory and indicates wet ground, generally at low level. This wet ground is universal down here.

Tony Smith is a Stanley local and an expert and local guide on the war of 1982. He confirms that 'Sapper Hill was named after Governor Moody's men of the Corps of Sappers and miners whilst establishing the town of Stanley in the early 1840s. In July 1865 a tall stone cairn was erected on the hill by members of the Royal Marines Light Infantry, as a landmark for people to find their way back to the settlement in poor weather conditions'. Poor weather conditions may have been exacerbated by the imbibing of malted beverages and its own subsequent induced conditions. The cairn was useful. In 1914 a lookout post was sited on

Sapper Hill and manned by members of the Falkland Islands Volunteer Force, one of whom spotted the German fleet approaching on a summer's day on the 8th of December before the sea battle that took place that day. In 1932 the 6-inch naval gun from HMS *Lancaster* was sited on Sapper Hill. It was only fired once from that position, on Sunday, February 12 1933 to mark the Falkland Islands centenary celebrations, probably after church. In 1939 the gun was moved approximately 5 miles overland by 500 men of the West Yorkshire Regiment based in Stanley at that time. It went to Canopus Hill, which was much nearer the coast and thereby increased the useful range of the gun against any possible approaching enemy ships. One 6-inch gun should deter a battleship. Canopus Hill is 50 feet above sea level and is on the island where the airport is now. As it happened, thankfully no enemy came anywhere near the Falklands during the Second World War. This little hill, Sapper Hill, has some history and it will gain some more very soon.

On a luminous and still summer's day it's the kind of hill where you should find rabbit holes. Even though there are none. Rabbits only exist on one of the small islands of the Falklands archipelago. Although conveniently there is a place named Rabbit Cove just across Stanley Harbour to the north about 15 miles away. Maybe there are old rabbit holes there.

Personally speaking, if this had been my perfectly gentle rural home village of Blundeston, this area would have been covered in rabbit holes. Warrens. Here, at this far end of the Earth though, you are more likely to run into penguins than rabbits. Penguins also inhabit holes, similar habits to rabbits. Similar habits to Hobbits and rabbits. But sadly, penguins do not live here either. They have, however, been reported at Yorke Bay just south of Rabbit Cove – peculiarly ironic. Coincidently and utterly inconsequentially, Blundeston lies longitudinally at 52° north of the equator and Port Stanley is 52° south of the equator, approximately, and almost equal. However, anything but similar. Relatively. Some 7,948 miles as an unladen European swallow might fly, supposing it would fly in a straight line, of course.

The Falkland Islands are not big, but they are not small either. They have a rare feeling of the 'end of the world' types of places: barren, desolate, wet, very windy, mountainous, and utterly and stunningly beautiful. Allegedly T. E. Lawrence said that 'the desert is the Sun's

Anvil'. Clearly the Falklands is the anvil for the southern hemispheric winds. The general geography of the Falkland Islands is disturbingly like that found in the Hebridean Islands of Scotland and of Devonian Dartmoor. Many people have said it is also like the Brecon Beacons and Sennybridge, but there are no real rocky outcrops and ridges in Sennybridge that present themselves as the archetypal rocky tors on Dartmoor and the rocky mountaintops, spines and ridges of the Falklands. Any high ground in the Falklands is topped with rugged outcrops of mangled and wind-beaten ancient rock, like spines. The land seems to have been lifted until it ripped and burst and the rock ridges are the result of the extrusion, like open, swollen wounds on a stegosaurus's back. Nothing lives here. Why would it? The oldest rocks are Proterozoic, about 1,000 million years old, mostly formations of rough, worn granite and gneiss. These are the harsh places we would inhabit. As usual, as soldiers, we find these places to be our homes, trained into us to be places of comfort, both physical and psychological. These are places we are happy in. We inhabit the Earth, like Hobbits.

The British Army mainly trains on Sennybridge if they want it rough, and the Royal Marines do some of their training there too. Sennybridge is tough; however, in my personal experience Dartmoor is tougher. It seems as though there is a brooding, moribund malevolence in Dartmoor and I say 'in' rather than 'on' because you feel more 'in' in Dartmoor than ever on it. It always seems ready to do you harm, even when it is smiling at you and holding out its hand on a warm, sunny day and the heat reflects off the scented gorse; it broods and plans your ultimate destruction. Much like the Falkland Islands, really. All these places are very wet and very windy. Consequently, there are many 'babbling brooks' in both landscapes due to the waterlogged nature of these places. Turn your back for a second and it will brew up a storm that will utterly ruin your day, and probably spill your cup of tea. However, like many places in the world, it has every season in one day; just wait a little bit longer, is what we always say. The wet and the wind and the wide-open spaces of these places make them utterly beautiful. Just the mention of these places can send a shudder up the spine of all infantrymen.

The Royal Marines do their basic commando training on Dartmoor and memories linger of the wet, the wind, deep snow, penetrating cold, ice inside your sleeping bag and the long, dark nights, carrying cripplingly heavy loads through marsh and bog to reach another windswept tor, just to repeat the process again to another insignificant tor, and repeat ad infinitum. Repeat and beast. And all while dealing with that dark, brooding malevolence of the moor. I remember on one significant 'yomp' (Marine slang for a very long painful march with very heavy painful loads) across Dartmoor standing halfway up a hill facing the summit. I stamped my foot very hard on the ground. I was curious. This caused a 100-metre-plus ripple effect across the hill, which rolled and roiled it was so waterlogged … and waterlogged on an angle, how does that work! The Islands had a very similar feel except they had that added exciting feeling of being at the end of the world. It was pure adventure. High adventure. With a high probability of misadventure. People just don't go to these extraordinary places, the places where soldiers go. We may well have been the first people to walk in many places on the Islands during the war of 1982. They say training in harsh environments makes fighting in them more acceptable and easier. This is an inconvenient truth.

After completion of both Royal Marine and then commando training, when you 'go to your unit' you continue to train on Dartmoor and you get very used to its violent weather ways. Its very nature becomes a friend. It becomes a friend and like good friends the company is easy. In 1982 42 Commando and 40 Commando were based in Plymouth and used Dartmoor and Norway as their training areas. 45 Commando was Arbroath-based and used Scotland and Norway. 42 and 45 were Arctic commandos and did three months at the start of each year in Norway training to fight the Soviet hordes that would inevitably spill over the top of Norway. Most Marines in the 1970s and 1980s were Arctic trained.

Then, 40 was known as a 'sunshine commando'. Its remit was in more temperate climates … generally. You would therefore think that 40 would be a soft touch but it is a curious ability that the British military has perfected the ability to always find the coldest, hottest, wettest, driest, most unforgiving and most unbearable terrain wherever it goes. That is where it will do its training, and it will make you suffer. Whatever happens, it will make you suffer. Of that you can be sure. There is another saying in the military that says that the military will train you to do all sorts of adventurous things and then it will thoroughly put you off doing them ever again. This has many truths in it. Climbing, parachuting, diving, anything. Suffering was trained into us. So much so that it was peculiarly enjoyable. 'Train hard, fight easy' is another military maxim. This may be adapted to 'Train hard, fight harder'. That inconvenient truth again.

Being 'drafted' in the Corps was a lottery. We do not call it the Royal Marines. To Marines it is 'The Corps'. Officially, you had three choices of draft. In order of preference. However, you always seemed to get the one you did not want. So, invert your choices was the simplistic logic, but somehow, they always knew. Marines spent two years in each draft and then moved on. Hence most Marines had completed Arctic training. Swap drafts were possible with similarly disgruntled Marines from other units. This is very unlike army battalions where a soldier might stay his whole career in one battalion, thus maintaining continuity. The Corps kept its Marines moving around and most Marines had served in other commando units or specialisations before the Falklands 'party' came along. I do not belittle the 'conflict' or 'war' status but it was a 'bit of a ding dong' (please read this with a Terry Thomas voice).

I had served in 42 and at RM Poole before going to 40. In the Marines we talk like this. It is never talked about as 40 Commando or 42 Commando: not 'Forty-Two' Commando, it's just Four Two Commando, or Four Two). 40 Commando is 'Forty'. Or as I was introduced to her by Corporal Nellie Davis as 'The 40th Regiment of Her Majesty's Maritime Foot', because mostly it was just funny to play with words and also not to take it terribly seriously, even though we were intensely serious, with a wry smile on our faces and a mischievous twinkle in our eyes.

* * *

1982 started much as any other year started in the Corps. Nothing indicated that by spring we would be off on an adventure that would influence and dominate many of our lives up until today.

However, very importantly, it must be remembered that this story is written nearly forty years after the events of 1982. There may be danger in this expiration of time. That is a longer period than the Second World War books we read back in those days. It is a very long time, and yet it is a blink of an eye. Curious and becoming curiouser. Clearly there are some acceptable major recollection issues with this. Looking backwards is so utterly dangerous for accuracy. So utterly dangerous. At this stage, as the reader, you will need to prepare yourself for some conflicting memories by those within the story and you will need to prepare yourself to forgive any such conflicts of ability to remember correctly. This is the point. I repeat, this is the point. I have decided to keep the conflicts of memory in the text; I think this is extremely important to illustrate the fragility of memory and how selective our memory is and was at the time. In this sense writing memories forty years later ensures they were abiding memories and not 'passing ships' of memories, even though they could be incorrect anyway. Shakespeare said it is like holding a mirror up to nature. What did he know.

There is another obvious issue that was brought up by Jono. At one reunion when we discussed this book he joked, 'Why don't we just make it all up, no one will know.' No one would. But be assured we have not done that. I will say that again … we have NOT done that. The moral compass remains intact. In society there is also the accepted term of 'the older we get, the better we were'. I am aware of this and I am hoping that this does not inhabit the text either. Therefore, what is written is mostly corroborated memories of that time. It would be too embarrassing to fabricate situations for one's own glory and then be found out. Surely nobody does that, surely no soldier has ever done that. Also, and most critically, we only saw what was immediately around us; we had no awareness of the overall picture, none at all. Our world was microscopic. This is a vital part of understanding war from an infantryman's point of view.

To substantiate this, Rifleman Harris fought in the Peninsula War against Napoleon and wrote an accepted version of his experiences approximately 170 years before ours. He very eloquently said in his book, *The Recollections of Rifleman Harris*: 'all I can do is tell the things which happened immediately around me, and that, I think, is as much as a Private soldier can be expected to do.' I totally agree with him and find it strangely comforting that he experienced it in the same way we did.

If you have ever been on a live military operation of any sort, then you are fully aware that you are only fully aware of what is going on in your immediate circle, and that circle is very small. Much smaller than you think. Whatever you are thinking now, well it's much smaller than that. Probably only up to five people at a time, maximum. Probably and more realistically it would be three. War films portray soldiers always being aware of what is going on over the hill and of strategic objectives (the big picture). This is rarely true and a soldier lives a perfectly tactically microscopic and myopic life with his immediate friends. We call these friends 'oppos' in the Marines, those who are closest to you at any one given moment. This can go further, and if you truly like the man you can elevate your relationship to have 'bezzie oppos'; these are the best of your oppos and are clearly extremely close to you and remain so forty years later. These friendships survive the years easily and with no dramas and are comfortable relationships. 9 Troop still exhibits this.[1]

Information in war is limited and myopic. The information is passed down in the form of daily briefings on a 'need to know basis' and mostly it's on the 'need to know basis, and you don't need to know' basis. Disseminated information. These briefings are when you get to hear what other units are doing. These are formal and dry and steeped in military tradition. There is an alternative as always. This being the inevitable 'buzz' and this is the 'real stories' being passed around mouth to mouth throughout units, and these tend to move very fast; they are often incorrect, embellished or changed and adapted by individuals just to spice things up and just for a laugh. Information is limited in times of war. You only need to know what you need to know. You know.

So just to clarify. Our ability to accurately remember may be muddled, and probably is at this distance. We recognise this. However, significant personal incidents are not muddled at all but are clear as vodka even after so many years. Clear as vodka with gold in it. There is clarity but the gold are the memories that cannot be forgotten. It is very complex, but very simple. Also, and most importantly, we may have been in the very same situation, seen the same thing but interpreted them totally differently. This is human and quite normal, they say.[2] Prepare to forgive old men their memories please.

---

1. My 'bezzie oppos' were many and I was lucky. So many, I could not mention them here. But you are fully aware of who you are.
2. I'm not totally sure who 'they' or 'them' or 'those' are. But it is said, and it is generally accepted.

So, this small, small world of war, the wet windy world, and the possibility of a never-ending war was our lot in 1982, handed to us by chance of birth only. This is also a curious situation of time management and time consciousness, and probably luck. Time shoehorning its way into it again. Time is curious. I still don't really understand it. Its ability to stretch and contract still fascinates me. Normally on a peacetime exercise when the commando unit goes into the field the end date is often known; in fact it is definitely known. In Northern Ireland your tour of duty was usually six months with an end date, but could be up to one year or two years, but still with an end date. Always an end date. This puts a finite amount of time on how long you need to suffer. And suffering was our lot. This finite possibility was not the case 'down south'. Down south is the term used by those who attended this little party/ding dong/adventure, and it means 'The Falkland Islands War 1982' where once landed we had no idea how long it would take for this to conclude; it was infinite. For the first time ever, it was infinite. Unfortunately for some it was infinite, or more accurately, finite. I do remember people saying it would 'be over by Christmas', but I had heard that in films about the world wars and we were in the middle of the early southern hemisphere autumn, so surely this would be over by then ... but maybe not. John Mills, Jack Hawkins or Donald Sinden must have said that so many times in their films. Having no end date meant every day was dealt with as an individual day with an actual individual unknown ending, which would probably come, but no promises. A new day would mean just that: a whole new day, and a whole new world of suffering, and fun possibilities. Anything could happen and often it did. Infinity is a strange sensation in war. The infinity of time and the infinity of possibilities. It was clear we were not personally in charge of this infinity, in any way. We could influence the infinite nature, but it was unlikely. Just be ready for anything and everything and prepare to suffer every day, indefinitely and infinitely. I use the word suffering quite a lot, but it wasn't all suffering; most of it was laughing and admin and a considerable amount of fun. Sort of a monotonous languor.

Royal Marine basic training lasts for thirty-two weeks. They say it takes this long to make a Marine. I think they take thirty-two weeks to make you comfortable with suffering the worst cold and wet a human can endure and then they teach you to laugh at that pain and poke fun at it. This helped 'down south' in the constant wind and lashing rain and snow of the South Atlantic. They say pain is a passing thing, kind of finite, but that's not helpful when you are in the middle of that perceived infinite pain, but laughing at it really helps, and fills a moment. It is a hard lesson to learn. It is a hard lesson hard won. In this we were very well trained. Pain, suffering and laughing. Not necessarily in that order.

The Corps has an ethos, in fact, unsurprisingly, several, being a series of beliefs instilled into recruits during commando training. These are termed as core values or Royal Marines Values & Standards. It is essential that every man exhibits them. They run in a conventionally accepted order but I write them in a different order at different times. They are excellence, integrity, self-discipline, humility, courage, determination, unselfishness and cheerfulness. A massive sense of humour is probably first in my mind. These are also expressed as the 'commando spirit': courage, determination, unselfishness and cheerfulness in the face of adversity. Laughing in the face of adversity is essential: 'I laugh in the face of danger'. These are the tenets of the commando. Of being a commando. There are many words here and much to aspire to. Many words and many meanings, maybe too many words for a Marine and maybe very difficult to train into a human. Maybe you must have some of these traits in your bank before turning up for basic training.

Marines will usually say that the Corps is a family. It is true, quite probably. Why is it a family many will ask. Marines train all day together, eat together, drink together and sleep in the same room, often showering together when water is limited. We share everything, everything. We are never out of immediate proximity of each other. This creates a cohesive bond that modern sports teams might aspire to. This also allows for 'the team' to function at a very high level with no visible strain. In my experience this is true of the Marines and the Paras. Shared experiences. Shared pain. Shared humour. Shared.

I will say this only once. There is a classical myth in the British military world, and a perceived military sticky issue. Perceived by many to be a major issue and one I am sure some readers have been looking forward to. This is the subject of the Paras and the Marines – or more incorrectly 'Paras vs Marines'. I personally prefer Paras *and* Marines; there is no 'versus'. I will discuss this supposed rivalry here and then never mention it again in this story. It is irrelevant. I will mention them when they come into our very limited view on the Islands only. We were *all* tasked with taking back the Islands. 3 Commando Brigade is small and had to have the army along; of course, they have skills that the Marines needed and lacked, and the Commando Brigade was not big enough to do the job itself, no matter what any of them may say. Personally, I was very pleased it was the Paras. I had done my para course and one of my best friends from school, Roger Dunridge, was a Para and was even on my para course, among some significant others. One of whom was Captain John Hamilton SAS. We became firm friends/bezzie oppos and laughed and giggled our way through the course together much to the RAF's disgust and annoyance. I presumed he was at the 1982 party but I did not see him. Also, I could not predict what would happen to him during the war. Sadly, he found infinity.

The Paras were tough enough and we often exercised and competed against each other. If anyone could function well and suffer well, it was them; they were good sufferers, they were trained sufferers like us. I was confident in their certainty and never had an issue with them. I remember when I was told they were coming and thinking, 'Thank f*** it's them' and not some other regiment. Personally, Denzil Connick, another bezzie oppo, of 3 Para says he felt the same way; he suffered in a unique way from significant injuries on Mount Longdon. His stoicism is legendary. I do not particularly admire people who compare the two; it is wasted energy and quite unprofessional. We do completely different jobs but with remarkably similar standards. Unfortunately, we are too similar, and that similarity causes friction as individuals desperately seek to identify an imaginary difference to evaluate and then to potentially elevate themselves. Talking to Denzil ,we agreed it could be because the very reason we joined such units was that we are genetically competitive, and that competitive spirit is always there. We are the type of people who compete over the smallest issue. Coincidentally, we have a similar historical Second World War commando lineage anyway. Good lads one and all, probably *emperors*.

* * *

40 Commando was our home and 9 Troop was our life. 9 Troop had a history. Marines would come and go as they went to other units or

specialisations; this was normal for a rifle company troop of the time. This meant there was a steady turnover of personnel. But I had always heard of the 9 Troop in 40 and Marines seemed inordinately proud of being in it or having been in it … or even near it. 9 Troop was thirty-two guys. But it was more than that. 9 Troop may have been a 'thought', much more than the sum of its parts. It lived even without us, despite who belonged to it. It had its own life, its own existence. We do not personally select a troop. We cannot request to be in a particular troop; it does not work like that. You are assigned to a troop and that is where you go. I guess I was very lucky. In fact, we all count ourselves lucky to this day. There is a rumour that Bill Howie, the Company Sergeant Major (CSM), selected the Marines he wanted for Charlie Company measured by a physical fitness criterion, his personal exacting criteria. Mostly boxing, but always physical prowess. A very high standard set by a man of extremely high physical, personal and military standards. A man we all came to love.

9 Troop was made up of these 32 individual Marines: one officer (Troop Biff/Boss), one sergeant (Troop Stripey), three corporals (Full Screws), three lance corporals (Lance Jacks, or Lance Commicals) and 24 Marines. The troop was the equivalent size of an army platoon. Each troop had three sections. Each section consisted of nine people and had one corporal as a section commander, one lance corporal as a section second-in-command (2IC or 2 Ice Cream) and seven Marines, five of whom were riflemen or 'Gravs'. The remaining two Marines manned the General-Purpose Machine Gun (GPMG) commanded by the 2IC.

In 1982 a commando unit (called a commando or affectionately termed 'The Unit' by its Marines) had nine fighting troops. 40 Commando had three companies – Alpha Company (The Saints), Bravo Company and Charlie Company – which had three fighting troops each. 40 also had an HQ Company and a Support Company. Alpha Company was the first company. Its troops were numbered 1, 2 and 3; Bravo had 4, 5 and 6; Charlie had 7, 8 and then the infamous 9 Troop. Infamy, infamy, everybody's got it in for me.

There are three sections per troop. The first section in the unit ORBAT (order of battle) is 1st Section 1 Troop Alpha Company and therefore has a callsign of 11A (One One Alpha) and this ran logically all the way through the Commando to the 3rd section in 9 Troop in Charlie Company, at the end, the last, which had a callsign of 33C. 33C was my section, or more correctly the section I was 2IC in. A callsign is exactly that; it is your callsign on the radio net: Three Three Charlie.

Our troop officer was Second Lieutenant Carl Bushby and he says that:

> With more combined casualties suffered by British and Argentinean forces than the then Falkland Islands population, freedom came at a cost. For me, what started as a great adventure, as a young recently trained Second Lieutenant RM heading south on the 'great white whale' SS *Canberra*, ended more with a sense of relief than euphoric victory. My memories of events and conversations have dulled over time, many locked away by the harsh realities of the conflict, not helped by the significant intake of alcohol enjoyed on the return trip home! However, I do remember the feeling of overwhelming helplessness when caught in a minefield, combined with sadness which rapidly changed to anger having seen the helicopter casevac off two comrades. Then, the faces of Argentinean soldiers taken prisoner by 9 Troop at Mount Harriet: some young and frightened, some relieved but many bitter and belligerent. Finally, the stoic calmness of my fellow Royal Marines as we flew towards Sapper Hill on that final day. Would I do it all again: Umm … probably not but, if I had to, there would be two conditions: first, I'll need my younger body back as; although the 'State of Mind' remains unchanged, my body certainly has not! But, most important of all, I need those other thirty-one Royal Marines of 9 Troop to be on my left and right, not only for their banter and camaraderie but also their professionalism, trust and unflinching resolve, including 6ft 9in Mountain Leader Sergeant Nick Holloway for his guidance and support …

We all thought very highly of him, and still do. He was, and remains, our Boss.

This was the ORBAT for 9 Troop in early 1982 and these are the main players in this adventure.

---

9 TROOP ORBAT

TROOP HQ
2Lt Carl BUSHBY RM
Sgt Nick HOLLOWAY RM
Neil PLEASANCE (Radio Operator)
Si POOLE (84mm No1, weapon not taken)
Craig BROOKS (84mm No2)

33A	33B	33C
Cpl George PORTHOUSE	Cpl Ian (Jono) JOHNSON	Cpl Damian (Dee) IRVING
Pete PETERS	Simon (Sponner) HALL	Steve (Paddy) PORTER
Paul (Griff) GRIFFITHS	Steve PRITCHARD	Terry BARNES
Steve (Spud) MURPHY	Sam SAMPSON	Paul (Buck) ROGERS
Gary (Gaz) MCCONVILLE	Ricky MILLER	Graham (Pusser) HILL
Gary (Gaz) WESTERN	Gary (Gaz) PINCHES	Mick THORBURN
LCpl Alex HEPBURN	LCpl Andy GAUNT	LCpl Chris PRETTY
Colin (Skin) GALLAGHER (G)	Vince COMB (G)	Brian EDMUNDS (G)
Mark (Taff) NICOLLS (No2G)	Neil (Mac) MCFARLANE (No2G)	Ged HERD (No2G)

Each section has a gun team. These are the three Marines at the bottom of each section listed above. The gun teams are commanded by the section 2ICs, Andy, Alex and me. One Marine carries the gun and is the gunner (G). The gun by itself weighs 24lb.[3] His responsibility is to fire the weapon. The second is the number 2 on the gun (No2G),

---

3. Technical details taken from: *Infantry Training Volume 1*. Pamphlet no. 6. The General Purpose Machine Gun. 1966. MOD.

who manages the gun with ammunition, spare barrels and other duties). The 200-round belt is 12lb and the tripod is 30lb. His job is to always support the gunner. If there are heavy loads to be carried, then he does that too. In my section (33C) I had Brian on the gun and Ged as the second. Andy had Vince on the gun and Mac as second, and Alex had Skin and Taff respectively. The sight range is between 200 and 1,800 metres. The cyclic rate of fire is 600–1,000 rounds per minute.

In the Royal Marines it is the general career path that once you have 'passed out' of training at Lympstone, you are drafted to your unit and then to a rifle company and you become a rifleman within a section. This is where you cut your teeth on the skills of your craft of soldiering. As I have said, in 1982 this rifleman was the 'Grav'. Probably from 'Gravel Belly', which informs you of the position riflemen always find themselves in, lying down in the puddle or the gorse for hour after hour and moving forward on your belly. It's a squirming thing. It is a term of endearment. It has a proud connotation of being a grafter and a sufferer. Once you have successfully done your time in a rifle company you can specialise by applying for one of the many Corps specialisations. This would often take you away from the 'Grav' situation and for some this was the preferred option as soon as possible. For others the daily tough grind of fighting troop life was the preferred option and as a troop we were lucky with the Marines of 9 Troop. We had a very good officer, sergeant and set of corporals in the Troop at this time and this imposed its professionalism on all of us in the lower ranks. This was our troop. We were proud of her.

In some sort of overall holistic and maybe existentialistic way and for some strange and extremely fortunate reason we had all found ourselves in the troop at the same time. Double fortunate to be there just at the moment we were told we were going to war. Some guys missed out but they were 9 Troopers none the less. Unfortunately, they had found themselves drafted to other places in the Corps just before we went. Phil Marshall left the troop just before embarkation and was a key player in the troop and a bezzie oppo. Blue Young was sent on his para course and missed out, I believe, and was another bezzie oppo. Mac set sail with us but left us at Ascension Island and flew home. Lieutenant Dave Summerfield, our previous troop commander, left us for greener grass in the Corps. These were all big players in

9 Troop's reputation, and they were sadly missed. Too many more like JB and so many others who were true 9 Troopers but were 'unlucky' and on whose broad shoulders we stood. This book is for them also. If any of them had known this could happen they would have stayed in the troop; no one wanted to miss this party. My heart really does go out to those who 'missed the party'. It must have been unbearable. It must still be unbearable. But these guys are as much 9 Troop as those who went 'down south'. We make no distinction.

The company, Charlie Company,[4] was commanded by Captain Andy Pillar RM, who was a Special Boat Service (SBS) officer doing his career development as a company commander. The company 2IC was Captain Ken Hames, who was an army commando on loan to us from the Queen's Regiment; he later went on to the SAS. Our company sergeant major was WO2 Bill Howie a PTI by trade. Bill was and still is truly loved by all the company. In fact, all three were, but Bill was something else. He is 'one of us'. It is normal for a little water to leak from the eyes when Bill is mentioned, even today.

Is it a possibility for a man to love another man? I think so. The first man I loved was Kev Lock. We were in training together in 114 Troop, my first 'bezzie oppo'. He was a big bodybuilder before he joined, and he taught me how to breathe properly when running to clear the 'stitch'. He is sadly dead now, killed in Cyprus on a UN tour, and much missed by me, even to this day. Just to clarify when I say 'loved' I do not mean in the modern sense or the sense you may be thinking; this love is something else and is extremely ... manly. But it is love nonetheless. There is no other word for it.

This 'love' lingers in 9 Troop to this day. It lingers in Charlie Company.

The company was a strong company and 7 and 8 Troops made up the rest of the company and many of our closest oppos were in those troops. As Adrian Brown, a lance corporal from 7 Troop, and one of my bezzie oppos, says, 'There were some serious operators in the company, spread across all the troops.' He was correct, as usual. He went on to more special stuff and we remain best friends today. We are reciprocal godparents to our children.

---

4. A nominal roll of all of Charlie Company is at the back of this book. No ranks.

The unofficial anthem of the day was Monty Python's 'Always look on the bright side of life' taken from *The Life of Brian*. This could be heard being hummed or sung at most times. It was an anthem and an ethos. It had just enough metaphorical 'two fingers' and we loved it. Thanks Pythons, in an idle sort of way.

And so, this story starts with all its players. It does not end the same way. We start as if in the wings of the stage waiting for our call to do something significant and say those lines that no one has yet written. Many people are in the wings, many are waiting. No confusion, we know what to do, we just don't know our part yet.

However, more players are needed to complete the true depth of this story. These players are the members of the Marine Infantry of the Argentine Navy and specifically the 3rd section of the MAR Company of the BIM 5 Esc (Battalion de Infanteria Marina 5), who defended Sapper Hill for seventy-four days and fought until the last second of the war, on 14 June 1982, in a snowstorm. Their story will be told by researcher and biographer of the 3rd section of the company Mar del BIM 5 Esc, Marcos Antonio Basavilbaso. Marcos was not present in the Falklands conflict but has used his considerable historical expertise to bring their story to life for the purposes of this book. Their valuable contribution is noted. Marcos has been given latitude to write his own story and any amendments that may occur have been agreed by Marcos before publishing. These amendments are only made to ensure understanding by non-Spanish-speaking readers. His text remains unchanged and therefore retains the rough nature of the contributor. As an important note regarding methodology, no politics are discussed in this book. We agreed this at the start. Politics are irrelevant to soldiers on the ground and do not add to the story and are singularly the province of other more qualified but often less experienced writers on the subject.

Contributions by the Royal Marines have been altered to remove swearing. However, very little of it was written. This has been a difficult, constructive decision, but it is necessary. Royal Marines in 1982 communicated almost solely in swearwords and Royal Marine slang. Royal Marine slang has its base in Royal Navy slang, but with notable additions. Complete swear and slang sentences, with complex inflection, sarcasm and irony were always used. This language is unintelligible to outsiders and is meant to be so. If you could speak this language, then you were part of the family. If not, then you did not exist. Of course, this bad language will not be acceptable in any book so you must read into it your own reservoir of swearwords, if that is what you require. In that way alone does this telling not truly resemble true events. A swearword will only be used if and when it is absolutely vital to the telling and the strength of the moment cannot be told without it. Spanish swearwords will also be treated in a similar way. *Tonterías!* and mostly *Brills*.

Chapter 1

A Call to Arms

That men shall sing in battle and remember
When they are old and grey beside the fire:
Only a story gathered from the hills
And the wind crying of forgotten days,
A story that shall whisper, 'All things change'
Geoffrey Bache Smith. 1918.
Act 1, Scene 1
52 Degrees North to 52 Degrees South
A Preface for a Tale I Have Never Told

The stage is still set and now some players start arriving on stage. The 1st of April 1982 was notable by it being totally unremarkable. The Troop was at Altcar Ranges near Liverpool completing the APWT, Annual Personal Weapons Test, as was the whole unit. This required each Marine to fire his weapon at different ranges and move to different distances and set and adjust the sights of his personal weapon to suit *his* particular eye, and his eye alone. This is why it is called a 'personal weapon'. It *only* works for you. If someone else picks up your weapon, they will probably miss the target because it is not 'zeroed' to their eye. Your weapon belonged to you. Your weapon, your eye. You knew your rifle number and you protected your own weapon, like personal property and you guarded it very carefully. This was a strong bond relationship. This APWT process took the whole commando unit many days to get through. The ranges were very large and by the sea. Many are by the sea, due to 'overshoot', and they are therefore curiously interesting places. Often open, flat, windy and cold. Mostly windy.

Today, Thursday, 1 April 1982, was cool but sunny. Jono, a few others and I had successfully completed our tests and were sat in the Red Rose bar having a drink. It was midday 'ish'. It is very strange to have a bar on a military range, so we made use of it, and more importantly it was out of the westerly wind and we were quietly comfortable in our normal surroundings. The 'bar' wasn't open.

All Royal Marines are expert shots, which is claimed by many and is clearly not necessarily the truth. All Royal Marines are first and foremost riflemen and riflemen carried the Self-Loading Rifle (SLR). It is a 7.62mm rifle that automatically reloads a bullet (round) into the chamber so you can pull the trigger again, and repeat. It is semi-automatic. There is no automatic function on this weapon, so it cannot be used as a machine gun. Technically this is correct but using a judiciously, and illegally, placed matchstick, it will fire on auto. Matches are those small wooden things you can use to light fires and fags. However, this match adaption is professionally inadvisable if you want to survive the armourer's inspection but more to the point quite useless for hitting anything with any accuracy. 7.62mm is a large calibre, bigger than those used today; if you pulled the trigger on auto the barrel would 'climb' to the stars unless wrestled back into the horizontal plane. Again, inadvisable regarding accuracy, and accuracy was everything, at least to me. The SLR tended to make significant holes in people and would definitely upset your cup of tea and ruin your day if you were hit by one. Effective range of 800 metres with a muzzle velocity of 823 m/sec. One second for a round to travel nearly a kilometre. Quite hard to outrun … so they say. We called them 'gats', 'elephant guns', 'bullet pushers' among other things, but never my 'gun'; it's not a gun, it's a rifle. One round solved all problems and cleared up all ills. The correct term therefore is rifle and they fired 'rounds' not bullets. Rounds came in a small, neat, brown cardboard box and were decanted/loaded into a straight magazine of twenty. Sometimes a curved Bren gun magazine was used that increased the size of the mag to thirty. The problem with this was that the Bren is gravity fed with the magazine upside down on top of the weapon, so the spring is weak when turned the other way up to fit an SLR from underneath and therefore subsequently fighting Mr Newton's gravity principle. The spring could be made more powerful by putting a spacer/small block in the base of the Bren mag, thus crushing the spring. An alternative to this is to use black masking tape (HBM in Marine slang, which means 'Harry Black Maskers') to tape two magazines together, upside down to each other, side by side. This was the preferred method I used during the war and would make for faster loading in a tight space, maybe. I liked it anyway. It made me feel more secure.

As an admission, during the whole conflict I had one main fear and it haunted me day and night: I didn't want to run out of ammunition. This book could have been more accurately titled as such, frankly. I cannot emphasise how important this was for me. It consumed me, constantly. Death was initially quite low on my list but was an obvious consideration of the result of running out of 'bullets'. Taping two magazines together went some way to ameliorate this fear. It didn't solve it, but it did slightly help.

Sat in the Red Rose bar. Warm and comfortable. No alcohol, but a drink nonetheless. Ranges are either fiercely cold places or fiercely hot places. But always windy places, mostly fiercely windy. At the end of any day of shooting you may well exhibit a 'range head', meaning your head is full-on wind-blown, sun-blown and rain-blown, red and swollen and feels like it has been blowtorched. This is usually extremely funny to your friends and oppos who would be merciless in their admiration.

A day on the ranges is a day to be feared in Royal Marine commando basic training of the 1970s. Really, it should be a day of rifle work and perfecting the art of shooting, which is extremely precise as you would expect. Coaching would have been a good addition. In commando training these range days were torture and your heart sank if you saw it on the weekly programme. It seemed it was the excuse required by training teams to 'beast' recruits physically and mentally to exhaustion on Straight Point Ranges near Exmouth, overlooking the sea again. But conveniently out of sight of other CTCRM (Commando Training Centre Royal Marines) staff. How we ever hit anything I do not know. I could tell you some real horror stories, but it is irrelevant to this story so they will remain untold. But it does leave a lingering memory and a minor shudder. I am assured by excellent sources that these 'beastings' do not happen today, thank goodness. They are not required to make a better soldier; fact. Many of these 'beastings' forced extremely good recruits to leave training forever and therefore the Corps missed out on some very good, and probably highly intelligent soldiers, like my bezzie oppo Ian Hogg. Maybe that was their intention. At this stage I am tempted to name my nemesis section corporal in training, a true sadist of the highest order and for whom I have no liking and who inadvertently taught me *not* to be like him because clearly that is not real soldiering. I am tempted, but not that much. If given the chance he would claim that he made me the man I am today. This is incorrect as far as he is concerned but correct in its opposite effect. He did not make me. In his own words and sporting a wry smile, Nick Holloway says he made me who I am today. He is absolutely correct and I accept his conclusion and thank him for it.

We are lounging in the lounge. Officer of low rank comes into bar. 'Get your kit lads, we're off to war. The Argentines have invaded the Falklands.' No movement, just nodding and smiling. 'No seriously, get your kit ...' More nodding and knowing smiles are exchanged. 'Come on, sir, good try, April the first and all.' No movement, some more smiles, mostly out of pity for such an obvious bite. Officer leaves quite flustered and returns with a more senior officer. More senior officer encourages and convinces us that rapid movement is the best option and that the rumour is true. What a cool 'buzz'.

We look at each other and smile. 'Cool!' ... and we're off.

Let's go, this'll be fun. Lots of joking and laughing and absolutely no concern at all for the boys in NP8901 on the Islands. We're off on our holidays. NP8901 was a two-year posting in the Corps at the time. It was mostly seen as an easy draft. Not much to do and probably end up marrying one of the locals. These locals were called 'Bennys' by the Marines, not a clever or a positive word. Or even appropriate. This came from *Coronation Street*. It supposedly accurately described an archetypal Falkland Islander, but not in a positive way. It was used but only once or twice as I remember. Pictures of expansive Pancho-Villa-moustached and long-haired Marines dressed in anything but a uniform on patrol on horseback in the Falklands landscape were always in the *Globe and Laurel*, the RM magazine. The Pancho Villa reference is quite ironic in hindsight.

Leaving Altcar Ranges and the windy west sea behind, we travelled back to Plymouth in the usual Wallace Arnold civilian coaches. Plymouth was bustling with green military vehicles everywhere. Lots of rushing around. We were always being told to get ready to go somewhere to fight some unsuspecting native tribe and usually it was a 'bite'. A 'bite' is a lie and it does not happen, so we had no reason to believe it would happen this time. Like so many other times. Just another embarkation maybe. But we still needed to go through the motions. We accepted the inevitable and capitulated to the obvious. The normal rhythms of commando life were soon to be rearranged.

Back at Seaton Barracks just north of Crownhill on a cool morning and we were in our company lines, our buildings for Charlie Company. Loosely fallen in by troops. Andy Pillar came out with Bill and Ken.

'This is it lads … get your first line gear and be back here.' (I don't remember how long he gave us.)

Bomb burst of men. Lads who 'lived in' went to their barrack blocks. Married 'Fads' went home to their wives, and similar. Those of us who had flats went home. My flat was the other side of Mutley Plain in Plymouth. I lived there with Ben Gwillim, Viv Gwillim's brother. Ben and I had lived in flats together for a while. It was a big ground floor flat in a big Victorian terrace. Our first house was with Corporal Nellie Davies. One of the best soldiers I ever worked with, if not the best. He had moved on and had progressed in the military, leaving us to our own devices. We had a big living room in our ground floor flat in the big old three-storey house. A small TV, a large JVC music centre and a cassette machine that ate cassettes, vociferously. Blondie never stood a chance in that machine and pencils and pens could never mend the resultant cassette destruction. One way or another the hardest part is to picture this if you are not of that era.

Vince Comb, by his own admission, was our youngest member of 9 Troop and he remembers those days well and starts his story:

> Having completed my commando training in December 1981 and receiving my coveted Green Beret, I was posted to 40 Commando during the first week of January '82 (as the sprog). As a 17-year-old, it was very daunting at first, joining a brotherhood of far more experienced Marines but I settled in very quickly. As a reward for being so young as well as the newbie, I was given the privilege of the weighty GPMG! The heaviest machine gun always gets given to the sprog. I embraced it and never once complained about it. (Not that I can remember anyway.)

April 1982 came about very quickly, and we were to be given Easter leave for a couple of weeks. After Easter we were then due to visit Sardinia for a military exercise, which we were all hugely looking forward to. We had already been issued new uniforms that were much lighter than normal, ready for the expected warmer climate. Once we were given the news of the invasion of a hostile force in the Falklands, both the impending leave and our Sardinian trip were cancelled.

On our return to Seaton Barracks, we were stood to attention whilst further details were issued. It was at this point when our illustrious Sgt Nick Holloway said, 'All of those under the age of 18 take one pace forwards.' Nobody moved. Again, 'I repeat, those of you under the age of 18 take one pace forwards.' At this point I realised that I was the only Marine under the age of 18 in the whole of 9 Troop. I decided to keep quiet because I had a feeling that I was going to be left at camp and not sent to do my part. 'I will only say this one more time. Those of you under the age of 18 take one pace forward.' I remained still and then he boomed: 'COMB! Why the f****ng hell haven't you moved?' To my relief he was smiling though.

My response was short and to the point and along the lines of 'If you think you are leaving me behind you had better think again.' Fortunately, it was the kind of response he had been hoping for. Permission had to be granted by the Company Sergeant Major and I was 'invited' to go and have a chat with him. He ordered me to visit the NAAFI and buy some flowers to be delivered to my mum and give both my parents a call to let them know of my plans to travel far, far away. As it turned out there were a few lads under the age of 18 in the other troops.

My dad was really pleased when I telephoned him at first. His immediate response was I am so glad you haven't been sent to the Falklands. When I informed him that I was going very soon he was extremely shocked and kept saying that I was too young. He calmed down when I told him that it was my wish and that I had basically volunteered, plus I was surrounded by a great bunch of lads and we would all look out for each other. I, like so many, promised to write every day and keep my head down if and whenever the bullets were flying. I got that bit of the promise slightly wrong on the final day, June 14th.

Back at company lines and the drive from camp to my flat was in Si Poole's old Red Reliant Robin. We 'screamed' down through the red lights of Mutley Plain on the way to the flat, crashing all the red lights, laughing and shouting 'We're off to war, please get out of the way' and that sort of thing (read in swearing if you wish). Very exciting. Drop off, gear packed and wait. Si would come and get me later. I did not drive then so had to wait. Cup of tea. Watch one of my tapes get eaten. Wait.

Lock up, pick up and back up to camp. Company lines again, loosely fallen in, again ... exactly the same as Part 1. All green kit packed and ready to rock, everybody happy. Excited boys. Andy comes out of the offices. 'Postponed ... back here tomorrow morning ... no move before ...' So we had a last night in town to ourselves before we went. We were delighted.

Run Ashore!

A 'Run Ashore' is a peculiar Royal Navy thing. It is a thing of beauty and a thing of the times and something to be taken extremely seriously. This was 1982 and the Run Ashore was an art form, perfected over centuries of Royal Marines 'going ashore' around the globe. More of a skills-based exercise really. Skills are a practised thing and the more we practise the better we get. 9 Troop was very skilled at the art of the Run Ashore. Many man hours had been invested in perfecting the process. We could have been properly deemed Run Ashore professionals. I had come from elsewhere in the Corps and this was a new standard of Run Ashore to me. The intensity of the Run Ashore was intoxicating, a big learning curve. You had to take part; it was good form. Normally there are rules in life. This was truly a time when there were no rules, no limits and every opportunity was on the table, if it presented itself. Only the rules of the Run Ashore. One incident was the 'Battle of Castaways'. Castaways was a discotheque on Union Street (Onion Strasse) and was the biggest in town. A large fight broke out with all the bouncers of Union Street involved. The Troop were very seriously involved, as were the rest of the company. Two Marines 'turned to' on parade the following morning from a company of 100 men. Most were in jail or at A&E. This was normal behaviour and obviously nowadays self-appointed gurus would say it was teambuilding, or disgusting. I guess it was both. The team was built and well established. Long live 'The Lunatic Fringe', George!

'Shove off and come back tomorrow,' Andy P had said. The 'Run' was on. The last night before going to war and the inevitability of being killed. Surely this would go down well with the females of Plymouth. It happened like this in the films.

Long story short. The evening went as normal except locals were buying beer for us because we were going tomorrow, and death was imminent and acceptable to everyone. Tomorrow came and we fell in at company lines. Andy says again, 'Shove off and come back tomorrow.' Off we go again and round two Run Ashore starts. Much the same as round one. This goes on for several days and the intensity is killing us. How much longer can we keep this going? Forever is the answer. This could be infinite. Much beer was drunk, normal, normal, except women were not taking note of our new heroic status. Oh well. Can't win them all. In fact, can't win any. Plumbs is when you fail to go home with a girl. Plumbs all round. Failure was accepted and laughed about. It would be churlish to complain.

Finally we get the word and we're off. The buses arrive. Our normal civilian carrier. Long sunny drive along the south coast to Southampton where we are supposed to get a civilian cruise ship south and delivered into the arms of War. This is very abnormal; we never get civvie ships or more specifically civilian cruise liners. We are always crammed into the bowels of the Grey Funnel Line (Royal Navy ships). This liner's opulence was quite rightly internationally well known. This reputation ensured we were not to be disappointed.

Driving into Southampton docks, we all remember Gaz Pinches spying his wife waiting to see him. He asked to be given some time with her. Nick said yes. Pinch saw his wife for the last time. He had a strange smile on his face when he came back to us. We were pleased for him.

The ship we have been assigned to is the SS *Canberra*, a P&O ship. The Peninsular & Oriental Steam Navigation Company to give it the full, and grand title. A great big white thing radiating opulence at the dockside. Static, peaceful and just radiating. Not the expanses of grey we are used to. This is already starting to break new ground with new experiences and, quite pleasingly, much higher accommodation standards than our normal ride. This would definitely do.

I was not a newcomer to the cruise liner world. My grandmother who was a Royal Navy Wren in the Second World War subsequently became an employee of the Cunard Line and I had been on board the *Queen Mary* and the *QE2* in my younger days. I have to mention her. We called her Gommy because apparently my brother couldn't pronounce Grandmama, which she demanded. Gommy is long dead now, but I can't tell this story without mentioning her. Those who knew her would understand why I *have* to do this. This makes my mum laugh.

But this was not the expected grey Royal Navy ship and the *Canberra* sat majestically and serenely at berth in Southampton dock, just radiating that peculiar light that we were going to get so used to. A civil ship taken up for service[1] by the military because we didn't have enough of our own military ships to do the job. Apparently, this is normal practice. In her very civility I don't think she knew what was coming either.

New experiences are what we are made of as human beings. Our days in the Corps were full of new experiences. In one year in the Corps, you could probably live a full lifetime of 'normal' experiences. This also meant personal growth. This was a full-on rush to manhood and probably adulthood, and probably more. Maybe less. Edmund Burke (1729–97) wrote prolifically on the subject of extreme experiences and how these in turn produced a sublime effect, which in turn caused terror, therefore growth. We had no point of reference to work from. It was pretty much all going to be new and sublime, and a bit Burke-ish.

Nietzsche on the other hand coined the phrase used by many bullies, 'What doesn't kill you, makes you stronger'. This is a phrase of excuse and was probably at the heart of all military training in the 1970s. Nietzsche was a clever boy, but I don't think he saw how this would be sadistically abused. I am not a supporter of this thinking, especially in this misinterpreted context. But it may work well with Burke's thinking. In fact, nothing kills you until your final moment of sublimity and then it is all irrelevant, I think. I hope. Actually, I don't know.

---

1. STUFT – Ship Taken up from Trade

The ship still sat majestically beside the dock. Green military vehicles everywhere. Four tonners were the workhorse lorry for troops then. They carried everything. A bit like a C-130 aircraft nowadays. Multifunctional and rudimentary. Ammunition everywhere. Green had met White.

Unloaded from the buses. Find our personal kit that had been dumped on the dockside by some unseen department. Big brown seaman's kit bags, pusser's (from 'purser's) suitcases, Bergens, everything a Marine needed for a P&O cruise to the South Atlantic. All bags painted appropriate unit colours and named.

On arrival, Terry remembers

> moving through narrow corridors and smashing my Bergen against everything in the way, left/right/upwards/ downwards, against any inanimate and human obstacle. As I passed the purser's central office, I felt comforted at seeing civilian staff there. Observing them made me feel relaxed. Hearing their voices, the British accents, made me think that these people were here to help us, possibly having a more sympathetic ear rather than the sometimes-abrupt military manner. They will be a reminder of home, of England.

We were assigned our cabins. Each unit had its own deck. 42 had the top deck, we had the middle deck and poor old 3 Para had the steerage below. Each deck had its own unit entertainment room, but we all shared the main galley.

I was assigned a clean, bright and sparkling cabin with Alex. This was good. Whoever made that decision made a good move. I had top bunk and he was below. We even had a porthole, which let in even more luminescent light. A basin and civilised things like mirrors. Bewildering, but very welcome.

Movement everywhere, many people moving and doing. Not at speed, just with purpose. It was reassuringly normal in its comforting military beat. The rhythm of this adventure had just increased considerably. Kit stowed and directed to be back on the dockside to help with stores. No big heavy lifting machinery meant lines of men passing boxes hand to hand for hours on end. Normal navy practice for getting stores onto a ship. The boxes went up the line and disappeared below into the bowels of the ship. We had done thirty-two weeks of commando training at great expense to make us good box handlers. And we were good. At some stage it occurred to the Troop that some of the boxes contained liquids and solids that may benefit our personal diets. This meant that a box might be accidentally dropped so it was 'damaged' and could not be stowed below. This was poor handling on our part and we regretted our poor handling skills. In the navy this is called 'proffing'. Proffing is not theft. It is taking something with the express idea of using/reusing it, therefore it is not theft. Real theft is *not* tolerated in the Royal Marines and punishment is swift should you be caught doing this. The line between the two was slim, but discernible and perfectly obvious to the 'proffer'. The damaged box would swiftly disappear in a tangential direction and would accidentally find its way to our troop cabins. There seemed to be some limited senior management tolerance for this. Blind eye and all that. However, when a box of whisky went the wrong way, all hell broke loose, and searches were made of cabins until the box was found. This searching process went on for what seemed hours.

The sun slowly began to set westwards out towards the direction of Plymouth and life seemed to relax a bit. Some of the Troop were not with us at this time, as has been already established. Rick (confirms) remembers that Phil Marshall was drafted shortly before we went to Altar. However, he says:

> I remember him turning up at Southampton when we arrived there and I think Sponner smuggled him into his cabin. Nick Holloway somehow 'got the buzz' (as I think Phil was reported as AWOL from his unit) and so he fell the troop in and issued an ultimatum for Phil to hand himself in before the SIB[2] were called in. We all denied any knowledge of it of course, but Phil did the honourable thing before we sailed as he didn't want to get Spon or the rest of us in trouble.

The sun was setting and it occurred to me that Uncle Colin and Auntie Mary lived nearby. Colin had been a senior Royal Navy officer

---

2. Military Police Special Investigations Branch. Loved by all infantrymen.

on submarines for ever and had a suitable reputation for a gnarly professional submariner. I stood on the dock and wondered how they were. People I truly cared for, but too young and inexperienced to express it sufficiently or suitably. I knew where we were geographically and where they were geographically and looked in their general direction. Just in quiet acknowledgment.

The ship was clean, in a civilian kind of way. Royal Navy ships are spotlessly clean but they have pipes everywhere, bulkheads for bashing your shins/head on, ladders and the ever-present grey paint and the smell of fuel of some kind pervaded everything. *Canberra* was 'clean'. A proper cruise ship and proper clean. Spotless. Lots of space and colour and no bad smells. Big windows on some decks. Particularly in the William Fawcett room, our unit's collective home for the duration. Alex and I even had our porthole. It was just above sea level. I have already mentioned this but that may indicate how important it actually was to us. Portholes are peculiar things. Big enough for a head to poke through but definitely not big enough to climb out of. Maybe they are specifically designed to discourage those who wish to test the boundaries of evolution and try this. The light of the day slipped away.

The ship slipped its ropes and we moved slowly from the dock. I was on the port side rail looking at the Hampshire landscape. Just me, all alone at the rail, acknowledging. Not purposely alone, just by myself. George Porthouse was twenty feet away to my left also leaning on the rail, just watching. Cars were parked down the Solent facing seaward. They flashed their headlights and used their horns to say goodbye. This part of Hampshire is full of old retired matelots and bootnecks who probably knew more about what we were headed to than we did. Being old school, they were probably using Morse code to send goodwill messages, or alternatively knowing 'old hands' probably rude messages of goodwill. I didn't know Morse code and didn't even think of it at the time. I blithely watched as it all slipped past in the blackness. No feelings, none at all, void. Except maybe that passing thought that Colin and Mary were out there somewhere. This was building to a good adventure. This was exactly what I joined for, the thing I was promised. A fine adventure.

Retrospectively this was a true adventure. The outcome was truly unknown to us all. To every single man and woman on board, I presume. We had all arrived here at the same moment in our lives, by pure chance, and we were setting off on a Homerian adventure to sea. I didn't know Homer in those days, or how famous he would turn out to be even. In our own little way, we had all passed over our very own and very individual Rubicons, our points of no return. I'm almost mixing metaphors here, but it still works. At least no return to what we had previously called normal. The end point was a mysterious place, Mordorian, you could say. An adventure there and back. An adventure there and hopefully back. This would change our lives but we were not in charge of how this would play out, and we were blissfully unaware that it would even happen. Ignorance, and some arrogance, are such wonderful things.

In my limited 1982 mind, and experience, I thought of none of this; all I knew was that I was truly indestructible and invincible. This was an arrogant assurance. The overconfidence and arrogance were a heady mix, and I loved it. I spoke many years later to Malcolm Hunt, who was our unit commanding officer at the time, and we sat and chatted together quietly, like two old sailors in a quiet coastal pub, quietly reminiscing and explaining. We both recognised that in those days we were truly invincible and indestructible, as he said. He said the whole unit was totally indestructible. Not just me, and not just him, but all of us. Probably every single fighting man aboard this ship knew this same invincibility. This is both ignorant and absolutely brilliant at the same time. This ignorance is exhibited by many soldiers before war and has been documented thoroughly from Ancient Greece to modern Afghanistan. Unfortunately, it does not last. Quite the opposite, it is mere dust and mirrors. The mirrors shatter catastrophically leaving just dust in your throat. However, at the same time it is thoroughly brilliant, and I am sure that diligent military training such as commando or parachute (P Company) training gives this edge that makes us so good. Invincibility. Even our Royal Navy flagship was called HMS *Invincible*. We clearly all exhibited this team spirit and shared invincible attitude; it may not last. Maybe, unknowingly, this gave us the edge in what was to come. Of course, I knew none of this, I just knew we would win. This was a certainty, and now I feel privileged to have been there at that time in the world with the people who surrounded me. But just to clarify, I was completely assured in myself that we would win. It was just how this was going to happen. Invincible, implacable, and ultimately victorious. But again, mostly ignorant. Blissfully and brilliantly.

The ship pushed out into the Channel and down past France. Slicing through the water. Life on board relaxed into a normal daily 'on board' routine. A new rhythm of life. One we were all sure of and one we all recognised and slipped into with ease, it was a comfortable routine. Military training, first aid training, running, running, running, and did I mention … more running; fortunately I loved running and still do. 'Phys' was part of every day, just as normal back at camp. Phys took place on the top deck amidships where the swimming pool had been covered and was now a helicopter landing pad painted green. Bill Howie our Company Sergeant Major and a Royal Marines Physical Training Instructor (PTI) of some great renown recognised his opportunity to 'PTI' and would put us through our paces for hours of phys on this landing pad. It was always good humoured with lots of laughing and very hard work. Civilian workers had agreed to stay on board to do all the changes required to make it militarily compatible. They built the helipad; they would leave some days/weeks later.

Running round the promenade deck was the way to get running fit. The promenade deck went right round the outside of the ship. We ran 6 milers carrying full kit and weapons regularly. 42 did the same and of course so did 3 Para. We were fit when we went on board, and we became even fitter and stronger and probably even faster. Looking around the ship, body fat was at about 5 per cent max, collectively. Much less than that in the rifle companies. Possibly not like the normal P&O cruise clientele, maybe.

Companies and troops took turns pounding the green-painted promenade deck carrying heavy loads. A relentless, thumping pounding you could hear below decks, all day long. The deck was strong steel, but it soon gave up the ghost and started falling apart; we kept going regardless and careless of the damage we were doing. It was like having 2,000 international athletes on board eagerly pursuing the excellence required of our shared Commando and Para heritage. There was no distinction between the units. Just a socially agreed expectation of perfection. The phys was regular, just as it would have been in camp. This gave a stability to the days aboard. We all knew we were going somewhere and we knew that every push-up or every step on a run made you a better machine. The machinery moved onward, forever onward. Relentless and above all, fun. 'Royal Machines' as Uncle Colin called the Corps. I liked it.

Sunbathing was also a large part of the day. As we went south the sun got hotter and we would all go topside and lounge in our thin cotton Union Jack shorts made by Ron Hill and take the rays. Ron Hill made very short running shorts and he made them in Union Jack style. These unlined, very light cotton running shorts were de rigueur for Marines and Paras. We lived in them every day. Not just Union Jack but Australian green, purple, etc. Patriotism wasn't the main reason; they were just the best shorts available. They were *very* short; it was the early 1980s, and some of the men who were slightly larger, should we say, might find modesty being compromised with a visible peeping undercarriage. Needless to say, I did not suffer from this issue. Moose did. Fit, strong, positive, invincible, uncaring, ignorant and now suntanned and wearing short shorts. This was truly a tough, adventurous voyage and we were loving it. Maybe Homer sunbathed his way across the Med too.

We sailed south and slowly more ships joined the party. The convoy got bigger every day. It was most impressive and we seemed to be at the heart of the convoy. Ships of all sizes and all colours. Civilian ferries mixed with warships and Merchant Navy ships, all pushing headlong southwards to this unknown outcome. There was a feeling among the Troop that the landing would never take place. It couldn't. It was 1982, and who landed from landing craft and took on a fight these days? We were living in the world of Cold War possibilities. Clearly this would be cleared up long before we got close to the Islands. There was a surety about this that made the journey far more pleasant; just a holiday and another sighting of a ship over the horizon to show some nationalistic power. Surely our trusted politicians, and Maggie, would 'pull the iron out of the fire' and nothing would happen? Our trust was poorly misjudged. War is an extension of politics. Probably failed politics, but maybe not. This was obviously just very expensive flexing of national muscles. We were all wrong. Maybe someone, somewhere had already politically decided this was going to happen. We were just the tip of the spear and, you know, it was fun being the tip of the spear. In short shorts … and heavily tanned.

The Troop was strong, but with some weaknesses as always, and as is expected of any group of individuals. The company was not all perfect either. They never are. In any group of people there are those who you would rather not be there, and those who probably should not be there. Normally these individuals are inexperienced Marines, but not exclusively. New to the job but learning fast and therefore given some slack to come up to the required standards, which most do. Sometimes these 'lacking' individuals are more 'time served' and sometimes are those who have been promoted to corporal or sergeant. This then is unforgiveable and is barely tolerated. Unfortunately, this is on permanent view and is for all to witness. Military discipline allows these people to exist, and the discipline keeps bad things from happening to them. They are truly tolerated. I was a perfectionist, and still am, and this meant I did not tolerate these people too well on a personal level, but on a military discipline level I allowed them to exist, just not near me, thank you. I am better at this now, really. But I still struggle with those who do not try to attain perfection. I recognise this is my issue and my personal fault, but I have learnt to never allow it to appear in public. I can keep it inside now. In that way I am a happier person. I expect less of others and always more from myself. It works.

The company is made up of approximately 100 Marines and 9 Troop had thirty-two of these. The 'non perfect' percentage for the company was replicated within the Troop. This made for an eclectic mix of individuals from many backgrounds. These individuals made up the collective 9 Troop. Believe me, there are faults aplenty within this group of people, but this is a normal steady state. I include myself in this, of course. It's 'what else' that happens in the group which makes the difference and brings up overall standards. The 'what else' is almost untouchable, unknowable. But this 'what else' resided in the men of 9 Troop. We were okay. We were invincibly okay.

The bright blue, radiant sea passed by the great whiteness of the ship. At least from our point of view. The ship had gained the nickname of 'The Great White Whale'. The convoy bashed forward against all weather through the Bay of Biscay and onward to North Africa. The sea became brighter, almost luminous and this luminosity spread throughout the ship. It was everywhere, it was comforting. I'm not even sure why it was comforting. The ship seemed to glide through the still water on good days. It was almost perfection. On not so perfect days when she would roll slightly, our porthole would repeatedly go under the water. Peculiar sensation watching this happen. We were very close to the waterline.

I was born in northern Nigeria and lived my first years there in Maiduguri and Gombe on the very edge of the luminous Sahara Desert. The Arab/Berber merchants passed the bottom of our dust garden on their way north or south. Camels and blowing loose-fitting cotton clothes, colours you wouldn't believe and immediate smiles radiating at me and my brother as we all waved at each other. I spent many days in the bush with Wapada, who would take me for trips in the desert, maybe for days on end. I think this is where I get my deep love of open spaces, and other cultures. Those seven years were an influential time.

Africa hove into view over the horizon. My Africa. The great glittering expanse of open ocean to our right and the greatest continent to our left. Merchant ships on the horizon reminded me of my youth in Southwold where my top-floor bedroom in Marlborough Road pointed east over the beach and out from a similar luminous coast, and similar ships slowly going somewhere. We came back from Nigeria because of the civil war. Returning to Dad's hometown of Southwold in Suffolk. From a perfect place in sand and dust to another perfect place on a luminous seashore. I still live nearby.

The merchant ships did what merchant ships do. Passed slowly, going places far away, sometimes only the superstructure visible on the horizon looking like distant castles. Memories are strong and I felt them here; they rushed in on me. I could swear I smelt Africa. Rich smells, embedded smells from a childhood. Of course, I couldn't smell it, but memory is strong. Memory can conjure all sorts of things and apparently smells can prompt and stimulate memory. Maybe even imagined smells.

We pushed on, the sea flat and perfect, like oil but clear and bright. We were heading for Freetown in Sierra Leone said the man on the Tannoy. We were kept informed of what was happening by senior naval officers, Commander Yarker RN being one of them. We never met him; he lived in a small speaker above our heads. Requests could be made by those on board, and they would be read out by another Tannoy man. One day Alex Hepburn wrote a request to the onboard DJ Tannoy man. It was read out. It read, 'Commander Yarker, Commander Yarker, your beans are ready in the wardroom.' This caused much merriment below decks. Alex had a habit, maybe a skill, at doing this sort of thing at opportune moments. He retains it to this day. The British 1970s counterculture was alive and kicking. A very funny man, and still is. Never had it confirmed whether Yarker got his beans. I hope he did.

The Tannoy also played music. A Marine from our B Company took on the role of DJ and played requests and ran a radio show. I always wondered why he wasn't doing phys with the rest of his troop. He was tolerable on the air. More to my personal pleasure was the BBC World Service. This service may have been what we listened to in Nigeria by default, but I felt very at home with it. The weather forecast/shipping bulletin is still broadcast in the same way with its splendidly soporific introduction music ... Tyne, Dogger, Viking, North Utsire, South Utsire, Trafalgar, German Bight ... emotive words of imagined places in our known world. It was a very imperialistic and colonial broadcast and fitted perfectly with our imperial adventure. It seemed to significantly contribute to my comfort levels.

The ship pushed on. The soldiers on board trained their hearts out and all the rest of the ships did what they were doing. We were part of something very big. This very big was soon to become even bigger.

This bright, direct sunlight every day and the reflected light from the sea was the feeling of home and lent to that all-pervading feeling of cleanliness and perfection on board. I felt very at home on board. I guess this is where relativity comes into its own. I was unaware that others may not have felt as comfortable as me, relatively speaking. Because I was young, I also did not care and the only appropriate word to describe me was, as has already been said, arrogant. Probably most of us on board were arrogant and young and relatively they were experiencing the same thing, but probably in a very different way. Who cares. I have always found it interesting that we can experience the same thing but see something quite differently. This difference becomes our own truth and that is what we believe. It is our own personal reality, a mellifluous reality. Relativity is based on our perspective and is called multiperspectivity (sometimes polyperspectivity). We both see ships on the horizon. I see Southwold and Andy sees ... well, ships maybe. He came from Walsall. I would think all experiences are a matter of perspective and maybe the perspective is based on the point of reference from which we start. Points of reference are sadly lacking at this early age. But these limited points of reference may be challenged in our futures.

Freetown, Sierra Leone, is a West African port. We slid into the port on a hot West African day. I stood on the deck with Jono and Andy and watched the process. No uniforms, just PT rig, as always. Not much said, just watching and absorbing. Africa has an aura, and I must have unconsciously recognised this and was instantly home, and comfortable. Terry felt the same with his lineage from India.

Babar and Celeste is a children's book by Jean de Brunhoff and is about elephants in Africa. It is a whole series with Matisse-like illustrations. We read these books as young boys in Africa, avidly, absorbing every picture and story. In the books, Celesteville is a colourful coastal African town set on a small hill, next to the sea. It has white houses with colourful roofs. There is green between the order of the white houses. Palm trees and exotica. Sierra Leone looked just like this. More transportation by memory, but more appropriately it just emphasised how normal this whole process of going to war was … to me.

I have to say that these were quick internal thoughts. Not discussed with Jono and Andy. No need to, they seemed such ordinary thoughts to me. You only *need* to talk about the extraordinary. Don't you?

Celesteville had a long industrial pier. Pipes and business. On this pier was a family. A white European family, come to see the might of England going to war maybe. Terry says it was the governor and his family. Dressed in loose tropical clothing, a father, a mother, a son and a daughter. Not the wisest decision by those parents and quite unfortunate. The pent-up energies of 2,000 elite soldiers were released on them. I felt slightly ashamed and of course could do nothing to alleviate the avalanche that engulfed them. To that family I am collectively sorry and I hope you have recovered, and that you will forgive the youthful arrogance of the passengers. Maybe I do not have the right to be collectively sorry, but I will leave this here in case it is relevant and in case it helps.

Bumboats came alongside trying to sell their wares to what they thought was a standard cruise ship full of rich Americans, not broke British soldiers. The word 'bumboat' has a Dutch lineage. We were ordered not to buy anything from them. The item may have infection, they said. These boats had to be kept away from the ship; they were obviously lethal. Fire hoses were deployed and many boats were sunk. Some enterprising individuals lowered ropes with loops, as if to allow items to be drawn up for inspection before purchase. They fished the loop over the long, elegant prow of the boats. Once caught, the rope was hauled by many men and the boat would tip up on end and soar into the air, Apollo like, Astronauts and their infectious goods flying everywhere. I'm not sure why this was tolerated but it was. The flotilla of small boats went away, never to be seen again. The same applies to this incident as to the previous incident with the family.

The ship lay alongside, the sun was beating down and the ship urgently required diesel if this adventure was to continue. That's what I was told. The ship could not work without some barrels of diesel. I'm not an engineer and was not experienced enough to actually ask what this meant. I was very bad at questioning then.

Day turned to evening and then a sultry African night. I was on duty as 'Corporal of the Gang Plank'. In charge of a … plank. This was a proud moment in my military career. The plank went from industrious pier to a hole in the side of the ship. The hole about 10 feet by 10 feet and slightly lower than the pier. My plank sloped down to the hole. I say 'my' plank, but it was mine. On the pier were 50-gallon drums of diesel. Maybe ten of them, maybe more. The plank was a plank. Like you would see on any building site. Long and about 10 inches wide. The problem I was told by a young Royal Navy officer, who was also on duty, was to get the barrels on board via this rickety plank. I arrived on scene, briefed by the officer who was somewhat flapping by now as he had no militarily acceptable and safe answer to this challenge. Youth, ignorance and invincibility arrive with me. Local workmen stand around on the pier awaiting instructions. I know Africa. I am comfortable and at ease and we joke and laugh together. The order is that no man is allowed ashore. I went ashore and made friends. One, who was a really good lad, instant friendships made. Big grins all round.

'Sir, to solve this problem, would you go to the Tannoy man and tell him to send 9 Troop to the gangplank, please.' Officer trots off into the gloom. Tannoy man tells 9 Troop to muster on forward gangplank. I thought they'd be fed up with me, and I felt some minor guilt turning them to so late. The boys turn to in the dark. The officer is not far behind, still a bit flappy. He is nothing to do with my Troop, so I ignore him.

I brief: 'Lads, these need to be on board asap or we'll be late for the war.'

Instant action and a plan agreed by all. Barrels are flipped onto their sides on the top end of the plank teetering over the sea (*ogin*, in naval slang). A judiciously sharp boot applied by one of the lads and it bounces and hurries its way into the dark hole in the side of the ship.

Banging and clanging and whooping by all of us and by the local lads on the pier. One, two, three they follow each other at great speed and much noise and much merriment and the job is done in double-quick time. Now can we please sail to war? The boys returned to their beds. I remained on duty. I was proud of my plank. We all grinned at each other in the hot night.

I breached orders again and went ashore to finalise details with the local lads. I was a Royal Marine and I was Corporal of the Gang Plank and could rightfully do anything I wanted. I talked to the local lads on the pier for some time and we laughed and enjoyed each other's company. I felt at home. All was well in the empire. My empire. My very little empire. Time to go. We shook hands and said our fond farewells, smiles all round, down the gangplank and I ducked into the hole and disappeared into the dark inside of the ship. My job was finished. My gangplank was gone so I had no other responsibility to fulfil, obviously.

We slipped our moorings and set sail for the South Atlantic. Diesel safely on board. Friends made and time for a cup of tea. The darkness enveloped us. Due south to Ascension Island, we are told. No idea what it was. No maps and no Google. We'll find out when we get there. Out of Celesteville, turn left and over the equator; do not pass go. No thumping through great seas here, just gliding through the clear blue sea and the clear azure sky. Or maybe it is the other way round. Reflected and refracted light everywhere. Apparently, Ascension is a volcanic island. We haven't been to one of those before. This really is the best adventure. Phys is now at full-high intensity. So is sunbathing.

The sea has become crystal clear and the bluest reflective light blue you have ever seen. Turquoise, transparent, sparkling and to use Jules's word 'luminous'. Flying fish by their thousands, shoals of them jumping out of the water and skimming the waves in total control, just to plop back in after hundreds of yards. They don't fly, they glide. No flapping involved, just gliding and skimming. Cool as you like. Now a favourite of mine. The reflecting re-entry splashes came back to us and we languidly watched from our promenade deck. Turtles slowly moving past the ship in no hurry to be anywhere, seemingly to barely acknowledge our great existence. We mirrored their slowness and sureness. The sun beat down on deck and we continued the relentless running and circuit training. The days were long and languorous, or they seemed that way. Sunbathing became a daily routine, snatched at every opportunity. Surely, we were the fittest, brownest and healthiest soldiers in the world at that moment. Body fat was steadily reducing on the ship. A calm certainty pervaded. There was never any 'rush' in our journey. That rhythm, well it had slowed to a peaceful beat. It was a journey by itself and may have lasted forever for all we knew, or even cared.

Sharing the cabin with Alex was a pure pleasure. Thankfully he was a very 'clean Marine'; I appreciated this. It was a friendly existence. I had pictures on my wall above my bed. They were small black and white photos of my brother Jules and his friends at York University. I knew them all and liked them. Their 1970s student counterculture was refreshing and a little bit dangerous. When with them there was a healthy air of antidisestablishmentarianism that I particularly appreciated. The pictures meant everything to me about home.

News came to us by post and sometimes by telegram. A small piece of pinkish paper with a short and curt formally typed message on it. Rick remembers that while we were on our way 'down South' aboard SS *Canberra*:

> Matt Maloney (who was the 7 Troop 'Daddy'), received a letter from a couple of his old schoolmates giving their support to him and the rest of the troops heading for war. Accompanied with this letter was a small package. It was a 7-inch single of their first record, which they said would be a massive hit. Matt was hard as nails, but luckily he possessed a great sense of humour, and therefore took the many jibes from the lads in good spirit, as the lads referred to his schoolmates as being 'zeros' and 'nobodies', although he said they were good mates and that they were real rebels, etc. However, it turned out that Matt's schoolmates were in fact George Michael & Andrew Ridgeley, and the record they sent him was 'Bad Boys'! Matt had the last laugh in the years to come, as his old schoolmates ended up being one of the most successful pop groups in British history!

Our ship life echoed Club Tropicana, in a calm, measured, tropically peaceful way.

One bright day I was called to Andy's office. Bill was there and they told me about a telegram received from the police back in Plymouth addressed to me. They said that the flat I shared with Ben had been burgled and that items had been taken. There was great concern and some seriousness by Andy and Bill. Great seriousness. I was unmoved and quite ambivalent. Like I have said, there wasn't much in the flat anyway. The list was meaningless until they came to our stereo/cassette machine. That great big thing. I was very proud of it and they had taken it. However, I was ambivalently unmoved but also slightly amused. The cassette-eating stereo was gone. Inside I giggled. They were welcome to it. I was a bit miffed that they had waited until we had gone and then done the burglary. But it was probably well known locally that we were Marines in the flat. I remain indifferent to this day, but still smile a little inside.

We crossed the equator. Over the equator or 'Crossing the Line' is a naval tradition that requires an appropriate 'ceremony'. Accompanied by a volunteer dressed up as Neptune and others dressed up as his helpers. Mostly men dressed as women. Dressing up is a Royal Navy tradition, wholeheartedly adopted, and perfected, by the Royal Marines. This ceremony definitely came into the saying 'If it's worth doing, it's worth overdoing', a motto we all lived by. If you were new over the line, you were unceremoniously, in a militarily ceremonious kind of way, dunked into water or some such ritual of public humiliation. A kind of Neptunic baptism. All on board would watch this event with much laughter and jollity. A colourful certificate could be issued proving this had happened in your life. This ceremony happened on board *Canberra* apparently, but I didn't attend. Just no interest really and there was valuable sunbathing to do anyway. How could you possibly attend a war looking pasty white … not good form at all.

One bright day Jono, Andy and I were stood on the promenade deck looking blankly out to sea. Probably no thoughts between us, collectively nothing. It was just standing and looking at the sea. A bit of a thump and the ship wobbled almost indiscernibly. This was odd. Like hitting a pheasant in your car, maybe less. We looked over the side of the ship and into the clear water. Now red water. Chunks of flesh in the red water, that's odd, even curious. Are they throwing old meat out of the galley into the sea, we pondered. The sea was very red and we slipped through it and passed it, leaving it behind in the white, churning wake. Hundreds of yards in the wake of the ship whales came from all sides and converged on one point. Blowing water into the air and all heading for that same location, tailfins and big black backs curling in the water. We had hit a whale and its friends had come to see what had happened. They had taken a casualty. Clearly extremely dead. Did this mean anything? How does a whale get run over in the South Atlantic by an enormous and noisy ship? Some people took this as a bad omen, I am led to believe. Personally, I thought it was a whale playing 'chicken' with the ship and coming off worse. Quite sad really and I didn't know whales exhibited this kind of boisterous behaviour. The Great White Whale had hit a smaller, greyish whale. We shrugged at this impossibility and moved on.

The routines of the day solidified again. New rhythms again. Running and circuits. Military training and sunbathing. Running and circuits. More time spent on first aid than normal. This threw up a red warning flag that most of us didn't miss, and it wasn't wasted on us all either. The heat intensified.

Inter-Unit Competition. It had to happen. 'Competition' had to rear its ugly head. An inter-unit competition was announced. A healthy competition between arch-rivals, it had to be a good idea. There would be running, tug of war and all the normal associated ways to measure physical ability. We had Ricky Miller, who was picked to run the 6 miler for 40 Commando. This was run round the promenade deck and was a real test of our collective fitness; it had an inordinate meaning and would reflect 'reflected glory' on the units aboard. 3 Para won. They had a guy who went like the wind. Very impressive. Rick did a fantastic job and we were all proud of him; he came in the top five. I didn't take part; I had very personal 'losing issues' that were not healthy for a human being. Maybe I still do. I can't remember who won the overall competition, I wasn't that bothered. Or maybe I was too bothered. It was fun to watch. It had the carefree air of a public-school sports day with an undercurrent of menace and quite probably a dash of malevolence. It was deadly serious fun. It finished in good spirits between units and we all settled back into our daily routines. Personally, I never felt competitive towards other units. I had served in 42 and knew her well. I professionally respected our Para brothers who seemed to take to aquatic life perfectly well. I always thought we were a collective whole. A team of experts. Working towards an obvious collective end. I knew we were good, but I also knew the Paras were good. That made us all 'gooder', collectively. I also knew we would have our own jobs to do if we ever did actually get onto the Islands. But, much more important than that, I just had my specific job to do in 9 Troop. Specifically, with 33C, and specifically with the gun team. This was my world, my very small world. No one else had this job, just me. If I took care of my bit, then I presume everyone else would take care of their respective bits. Sweat the small stuff and the big stuff will take care of itself. In the novice-to-expert model we were clearly all at the top end of expert, I knew that. Again, a quiet, possibly arrogant, certainty.

HMS *Ardent* was a small ship, a small grey frigate, with a 4.5-inch gun in its small, sleek forward turret. She looked fast, grey and fast, like a greyhound. One blustery day when the sea was up a bit, she came alongside at full speed, her crew manning the ship's sides and cheering. We cheered back. In the middle of the South Atlantic we cheered each other. It was almost absurd. But absurdly cool. She sped past and came again and fired her big gun to impress us. We were impressed. This was useful knowledge to know for the future, probably. She sped off and we all cheered. Her resting place is at the bottom of Falkland Sound. This would happen weeks later on a dark Friday night in May. We witnessed her death that night. However, that was the future, and for now she heroically sped through the churning seas. All spray and Royal Navy stoicism, and their very hearts made of dense English oak. Nelson would have waved his arms in appreciation. Arm. We reflected their stoicism back to them as best we could. Good lads. My admiration for Jolly Jack grew during this adventure; they are truly experts and truly heroic at what they do. Hearts of Oak.

The seas continued to give as we ambled our way south. We were definitely not going at full speed. Somebody knew something we clearly did not know. Hot tropical routines continued. We gave blood. It was not voluntary. Apparently, the medical teams required more blood in their banks and we were the perfect captive donors. Nobody really complained. Maybe we'd get it back one day. Traditionally many Royal Marines had their blood group tattooed on their right shoulder in training. Not compulsory but it was a recognised badge of being part of the gang, the family. Apparently, and according to the buzz, while donating blood some men were told they had the wrong blood group tattoo, which could have been a bit lethal in the future. This may not have been true but it's a good buzz and a good buzz is a good buzz, and we all appreciated a good buzz. Technically your blood group is officially on your dog tags; no one will look at your right shoulder to identify your BG, surely. At around this time we learnt that there was a huge morgue on board to cater for the normal aged cruise clientele. This would come in handy in the future, we were told. We didn't smile. Military medics have a propensity to humorously scare their patients. Like morticians. We did not smile, and we may have been a little scared. They had done their job.

RAS, replenishment at sea, is a Royal Navy thing. Ships would run out of fuel, perishables and consumables and therefore required replenishment while at sea. The *Canberra* galley had particularly good white bread rolls; they were excellent and came with every meal. A big grey replenishing stores ship would draw up beside our ship. We wouldn't stop; this was done on the go and at great speed. We would be 200 feet apart maybe and lines would be shot between the ships. The lines would be pulled, and pipes would then be pulled, in turn, across and attached. The pipes were maybe 8 inches in diameter, maybe more. We would dispassionately watch this process from the promenade deck. A well-practised process by all. I always wondered how they pumped our bread rolls across. This quietly amused me.

Days turned to hot nights and after one hot night we woke to a very new scene. The ship was static. No gentle hum of the engines. No gentle roll of the sea. Looking out of our cabin porthole we could see the massive convoy that had accumulated and anchored off Ascension Island. Sun beating down, Ascension Island looked like something out of the original TV series in black and white about a blond-haired Robinson Crusoe from my childhood. It was uniformly brown around the edges with one triangular mountain right in the centre, which reached up to heights where green vegetation replaced the brown. A proper volcano. A Pacific island in the South Atlantic Ocean. The mountain was green and was therefore uncreatively called Green Mountain. All around this island the grey ships and the coloured civilian ships sat at peace, waiting. Helicopters buzzed from ship to ship like wasps. Landing craft dodged in and out. The common saying for this kind of gathering is, 'You could have walked from one side to the other across the decks without getting wet'. Of course, this was untrue, but it definitely gave that impression. It was vastly and magnificently impressive. Our adventure was becoming slightly more interesting. We were adventuring with intensity.

Static in the sun, heat beating down. Time for landing craft training. Just in case we had forgotten how to do it. We were briefed that an LCT (Landing Craft Tank, which unsurprisingly was the biggest one we had) would come alongside the *Canberra* and we would cross-deck or get aboard it, have a sail around and return to the ship. This to be done at night with full kit and heavy Bergens. A Bergen is Marine speak for a *very* large rucksack. I believe the name has Norwegian lineage but this is contentious and mostly irrelevant. We used civilian green Berghaus Cyclops Roc Bergens. 70 litres. BIG. It was simple, green, hard to break and tough, a bit like most of us.

Well, this was a bit different from our normal routine. We had done this many times on the Grey Funnel Line, Royal Navy ships, and we were quite used to it. We returned to our 10 feet by 10 feet hole in the side of the ship last seen in Freetown. The ship had many holes, of course, with watertight doors, and we were going to use one of these. This hole was slightly higher up the side of the ship and maybe slightly smaller. Line up in the corridors one behind the other fully kitted with heavy war-scale kit. Slowly shuffle to the door in the dark, step out of the door and onto the side of the landing craft. Sounds easy. They said. Fighting orders/belt orders were full and Bergens were full … of blankets and pillows. They weighed nothing. We giggled. It was expected. The night was still and the stars were clear above our heads; the world was very quiet, too quiet. This is another fine mess you've got me into. I sensed some Charlie Company silliness coming on. Very serious amphibious officers whispering responsible orders and being sufficiently serious for their specific roles. It didn't take long. In a moment all seriousness just fell away. One hundred men on a large landing craft at night, in the all-consuming, inconspicuous hot darkness. The officers were desperate this all went well. It would mark their careers maybe. Out of the dark came the gentle sound of a sheep 'baaa-ing', which spread throughout the company. More giggling and more farmyard noises. Officers were becoming apoplectic with their military amphibious seriousness …

which made it all the worse and encouraged more farmyard sounds. Open laughter and school silliness in the dark. Big toothy grins on everybody's blackened and 'cammed out' faces. No one could be identified by the non-Charlie Company officers, but I am sure it was a *very* large and very muscular ginger corporal in 7 Troop who started it, of course. What is it about Royal Marines that they will not take *anything* seriously, ever? I love it, and always have.

I am not sure how this came to an end, but it did. My memory stops at the open laughter and silliness, which was a normal state for a commando in those days. I am sure we were harangued in the debrief. What disgraceful behaviour in the middle of the South Atlantic. None of us cared, our shared ambivalence probably perfectly obvious and probably infuriating. It had been a successful exercise and all was well with the world. We shrugged and moved on, skills updated.

It was here that one of the Troop guys left us. Ricky remembers that

> one of the lads in the Troop received tragic news while on board SS *Canberra*. One of his parents (can't remember which one) had suddenly passed away. This resulted in him being flown back to UK on compassionate grounds from Ascension Island. The next time we saw him was at Southampton, as he was there to greet us on our return from the Falklands. Incidentally, shortly afterwards, his other parent also died. This was very sad indeed for him and for us in his 9 Troop 'family'.

He missed the fun but is still at all our reunions as if he had been there. Nobody makes the distinction. I was in my own microscopic world and didn't realise he wasn't with us for the whole time until years later. Many years later. I'm not sure what this means about me. I just always assumed he was there with us. A very good bootneck.

Days rolled by on board the hot ship in the full blast of the sun. The convoy got even bigger as more and more ships arrived. Then our day arrived. We were going ashore! It was *very* hot, really, really very hot. We boarded an LCT again. Now we were experts, this went very well. Only humans this time, no farmyard animals, embarked. We were dumped on a bright white sandy beach with volcanic rocks surrounding the small bay. Not big, but nice. Again, very Pacific islandish. We were told we were going to do some long marches in the heat and fire our weapons on some ranges on the island. We were not surprised. The Americans were here. They had a very big runway in the volcanic dust, one of the longest in the world, they said. We were suitably but ambivalently impressed. They had big satellite dishes and serious military stuff. They were Americans, they had everything.

33 Charlie gun team. As we have established Brian was my number one and fired and carried the 24lb gun, and Ged was the number two who loaded the gun and maintained it. He also carried the 30lb tripod. Plus spare barrels and big bag. The gun was the General-Purpose Machine Gun (GPMG, or 'jimpy'). It was a powerful weapon. In the army manual it says, 'The 7.62mm machine gun is designed for general purposes.'[3] Its calibre is 7.62mm and it can destroy things at big distances. The rounds are exactly the same as our SLR's, so bullets can be exchanged if required. Very accurate, although it was designed as a 'beaten zone' area weapon. This meant it distributes the rounds in a pattern across a large piece of ground, rather than putting every round through the same hole. Unlike the Bren. This means 'everyone gets a bit'. I liked this weapon; I loved this weapon. Jock T and I had previously won a shooting competition with the weapon. It is accurate in very small bursts, or single taps. Ammunition comes in belts of 'link', 200 rounds per belt. A belt weighs 12lb. The belt may come in a thick green nylon sleeve with a shoulder strap. As a team we must carry all that we require. This can be a heavy business, but always worth it. Riflemen in the section will also reluctantly carry belts for the gun team.

All 'the guns' (GPMGs) from the company went to one dusty range on the far side of the island. I have no idea where the riflemen went. Nine GPMGs all lined up together on their tripods in the SF (sustained fire) role in the volcanic dust. We patiently sat behind our guns, sweltering. Three men per gun. Me with binoculars. We knew what was coming; we had done this so many times before. I needed to see the fall of shot at such long ranges, to adjust accordingly. Hence

---

3. *Infantry Training Volume 1*. Infantry Platoon Weapons. Pamphlet No. 6A. The General Purpose Machine Gun. 1966. Point 8(a). Page 4.

the binos. We were to spend the day using the weapon and getting the sights sorted. The sights are an attachable set of metal drums (very basic description). Each drum has graticules a bit like the degrees on a compass. These can be set and recorded for known points of interest out to our front. If the enemy came from that point, maybe randomly known as 'lone bushy toptree', then I could look at my notebook and programme the sights with the pre-programmed location numbers, which meant the gun would be set and locked so that all the rounds would impact that lone bushy toptree, and around it. This process takes some time and some serious application. But it is precision, and I like precision. We were precise.

The sergeant from 7 Troop is in charge of the range. Taff shouts, 'RAPID FIRE!' Everything as it should be and absolutely normal. Taff was a corporal when I first met him and he took me through commando training; he always held my respect for his professionalism. One of the truly good guys. I bring my binos up to me eyes … *poof* and *whoosh!* The world decides to instantly rearrange Newton's gravity. The microscopic volcanic dust leaps into the air and swallows everything in a brown choking cloud. This is different. The guns roar with furious anger, spitting red hot metal for thousands of yards. The noise is deafening but exhilarating. Parachuting and diving are exhilarating but nothing comes near to the deep-rooted base feelings of a big roaring gun. You can't help but smile, one of those ridiculous huge face-splitting smiles … some say it was almost sexual. Not me.

It is the expectation that at all times your weapon should be spotless. That is not a euphemism. Your weapon should be absolutely spotless whatever you are doing. Dirt, rust, grease, stones, elephant toenails have no place in a professional soldier's weapon. This is the LAW and must be adhered to. The endurance course in commando training establishes this in a commando. Lessons are learnt hard. The dust is everywhere. Swirling and moving with the power of the guns. I am concerned the dust might foul the working parts in the weapon and therefore jam, or worse. Never mind not being able to breathe. But, in a Royal Marines world being able to breathe is second to having a spotless weapon. I worried about the weapon. No need to worry. The dust is so fine and the weapon deals with it magnificently. We carry a cut-down, one-inch DIY paint brush in our personal kit for such moments. It's quick to clean a weapon when the dust is so dry, and oil is applied at a minimum. Over-oiling only attracts dust and turns to paste. Not sure if this is going to be a problem on the islands.

We spent a hot day perfecting our employment skills base. My Uncle Pete was an officer in the RAF. Peter Wilkes came up from the ranks. Flew. He would say that it was 'circuits and bumps, Chris, circuits and bumps'. This is when an aircraft continuously circles an airfield and does a wheel-tip landing and takes off immediately again for another circuit. A circuit followed by a bump. This improves the pilot's landing skill. Repetitive perfection. I appreciate that. Repeat, repeat, repeat.

The intense heat intensifies. The brigadier comes for a visit. No idea who he is and never met him. We know his name and his reputation as an excellent soldier and a soldier's soldier. We are told to remove our bush hats. It may offend. Bush hats off and on with our berets in the growing heat. Not particularly practical but it makes superior officers happy, and it is an order and we comply, with a little bit of whining, and much jollity of course. He comes and goes. We replace berets with floppy hats and we keep on going.

Guns running perfectly. Gun teams are now fully up to speed and we have achieved our relative perfection. It is generally agreed that we have shot a year's allocation of ammunition, easily. Guns are hot, men are hot. Loads are heavy, water is minimal. Distances significant. We march back miles across the lunar landscape to the beach where we landed. It is a hot yomp. It is preparing us for an Antarctic winter. The beach sits serenely just as we left it. Bright white sand, azure clear water peacefully lapping the beach. We arrive and incrementally the noise level significantly increases. More of the company have finished their evolutions and are turning up to 'our' beach. More noise than this beach has probably ever experienced. We had the beach to ourselves; there are no local people here. They all live at the cooler base of the green mountain.

Bill Howie, using his Captain Common Sense and his shrewd PTI thinking and seeing the beckoning possibilities of water, shouts to the company. It is what PTIs need to do. 'I want to see the last man in the ogin.' Off kit and sprint for the sea. Two disgruntled guys have to set up a GPMG on a volcanic spit of rock for shark watch; no sharks come. I don't blame them; it would have been a very bad idea to attack

100 Royal Marines in the water, especially when they are enjoying themselves. The rest of us play like children in the sea. This is perfect fun. And obviously perfect training for the Falkland Islands.

The landing craft returns and runs up the beach, ramp down. We get dressed and get our gear and leave this shore for our ship. All beaming smiles and joking. My last visit to Ascension. Predictably the US airbase had a shop. The PX. Some of 9 Troop were given the chance to go. They bought T-shirts for us all and other trinkets. Elvis bought a blue T-shirt for me. I was grateful.

The convoy is static for what seems a long time. Helicopters are permanently shuttling between ships. It's a busy scene, but remarkably still quite peaceful. Busy but peaceful. Our ship is still in its established normal comforting routine. We are all static and awaiting the start gun. The day arrives, somebody decides it's time to go and situational gravity pulls us away from Ascension Island and down further into the Southern Ocean. The adventure continues and morphs.

We are heading south into the realms of raging seas. Life continues as normal but the sea becomes a bit more angry and has a bit more vertical energy. I remember doing circuit training on board with the Troop. This includes 'star jumps'. Bend fully at the knees into a squat and leap into the air, flailing arms out wide above your head. Normally this is an unremarkable exercise but in rough weather with the ship going up and down it meant that if you jumped when the ship was going up you would find yourself 12+ feet in the air as the ship fell away beneath you. The return to the deck meant you were coming down as the ship was coming back up to meet you. Initially a bit worrying but inevitably this became a game to time it correctly to be left hanging in mid-air, weightless. Fun had to be found where we could find it and we could always find it. Much jollity.

The sea progressively became more fuming and threatening. The ship rolled and pitched. This was a new state of affairs. Apparently, we are told that the ship has stabilizers, which are deployed like wings beneath the water on each side and this stabilises the ship from excessive rolling. The sea started to turn from the azure-blue clear water to a darker and more forbidding black froth. We continued running and exercising but it was getting colder, and darker, almost by the day. We leave the equatorial world of warmth. Most of us will be back.

It all becomes slightly more serious. A new focus overcomes us all. We spend time painting our equipment in browns and blacks and reds. This is normal and is a professional requirement. We camouflage our SLRs with scrim and netting. Time is spent getting this perfect. Just enough for camouflage but not too much to interfere with any working parts of the rifle. Helmets need covering and painting and scrim attaching to break up the outline of the head. Scrim is a torn-up sandbag (hessian). You can't cut it because it gives a straight edge, so tearing the scrim gives an edge that is quite natural. The same theory applies regarding quantity of scrim attached to helmets as to rifles. Equipment is reworked to a state of perfection. Time is spent in a 'rock of eye' kind of way. We have been issued Hawkins Cairngorm mountain boots. They are a predictably thick leather and with a tough Commando Vibram mountain sole with red laces that turn black with polish applied. They are exactly what you expect of a mountain boot. They are hard and unyielding when new and need to be worn in. Soaked in hot water and then used to run in, they soon comply to the feet. Some people soak their boots in boiling water and put red hot boots on their feet and suffer for the mistake, but at least it is funny. In the end the outcome is the same. The process of wearing in is accelerated by more pounding miles around the deck carrying increasingly heavy loads. Big boots, lots of kit and Ron Hill shorts.

More first aid and learning how to inject morphine into your oppo's leg. Morphine is given to us in small ampules, like a small tube of toothpaste or a small tube of superglue with a similar screw-off head but with an inch-long needle within it. We are told these are to be attached to our dog tags around our necks and that you only use the casualty's morphine on them; never use your morphine on someone else. This makes sense but leaves an obvious screaming question. Have I got enough for me? War pain is going to be a new experience and we presume it is not an acceptable pain. It is a similar question about how deep is a trench. How many morphines do you think you would like? That is your answer. We decide that we need to surreptitiously proff more morphine ampules. Our surreptitiousness works and we manage it. At least two each. We also learned how to bring down naval gunfire support (NGS) – that 4.5-inch gun on the speedy frigate that we had never used before, now we are experts, or at least competent. We spent much time learning the procedure. This is all new stuff to us and it all seems to be getting a bit more serious. Of course, we don't pay any attention to such silliness. It'll be good to get ashore and get on with this thing. Invincibility and as Spandau Ballet would say, 'indestructible'.

Days pass and the seas get *much* bigger. We are in the deepest South Atlantic. It is black. The *Canberra* is now blacked out with blankets over all the windows. We are scared of submarines. I am not scared of submarines, I am very scared of torpedoes. Jono, Andy and I decide to go onto the promenade deck one night when the ship is violently rolling. Will this thing actually stay afloat? The scene that greets us as we push through the blankets to get outside is total blackness, and totally horrifying. The ship is big but it is rolling badly, wings out hopefully and working hard. The terrifying South Atlantic seas. Well, I don't really have words for it. Huge, scary black waves crashing at the tops, coming from every angle, bigger than the ship. Is this possible? It is quite clear that the Antarctic Circumpolar Current is in full energy now. This is bad. We look at each other in momentary shock, communication that takes seconds. We hurriedly agree it would be preferable to die inside the ship than outside it, so we push back through the blankets, keeping our cool. Hiding our scared. That was scary. Leave it to the experts, I'm sure they know what to do. If we sink, at least it might be quick, our ignorance saving us. Maybe our suntanning, halcyon days are very, very far behind us.

Somewhere in the south and at about this time we are told over the Tannoy that the Argentine cruiser *Belgrano* has been sunk by one of our submarines. Tannoy man says she was torpedoed. This is mostly good news, but we don't cheer. That sea is not where we would want anyone to be. Poor lads. We are glad the menace of a big fighting ship is gone, but not a nice way to go. This is all getting a bit more serious and we respond by becoming even more lethargic in our worry. No need to worry. It's just what we do. We can't affect any outcome so just go along for the ride. We lose ships from our fleet too. *Atlantic Conveyor*, HMS *Sheffield* and more to come. Things are now becoming less normal. Ships do not sink, but they do now. This is becoming a proper war.

Running has stopped, it's too harsh outside and the deck is being destroyed by thousands of feet repeatedly smashing it. The preparation is becoming more task focused. We learn some Spanish phrases. We are not taught the words for 'I surrender'. I never thought of it at the time. Why would we need it anyway? We are taught flora and fauna of the Islands too. Leopard seals incongruously seem to be the fauna to steer clear of, apparently. They are particularly vicious and particularly large and when approached from behind will rear up and flip over and take you by the throat, they say. I had no previous intention of approaching a Leopard seal from behind anyway. Why on earth would I need to do that? The practicalities of what we were taught were somewhat questionable.

We are issued another Marine into our section. Paddy was at Grytviken, South Georgia, when the Argentines invaded and when they had their massive punch-up. All those Grytviken lads voluntarily came back to the units to fight again, and to finish their own story. Paddy had no fighting gear. We had to beg, borrow, proff or steal kit for him. Mostly steal or proff. We got most of it but not a smock or a helmet with the supportive liner/spider in it. We would have to make do. He would have to make do. He would overcome the lack of items by cutting a hole in the middle of a pusser's grey blanket and wearing it like a poncho would balance the helmet on his head with the metal securing pin/stud pointing into the top of his skull. Genius.

The day came when being on the Great White Whale was no longer strategically or tactically sound, apparently. We could not land from this monster. We would have to move to another more appropriate ship we were told. HMS *Fearless* and HMS *Intrepid* were Landing Platform Docks (LPDs). They were specifically designed for commando forces and amphibious landings. The great back door, like a landing craft ramp could be lowered, a bit like a Channel ferry. But unlike a landing craft or a ferry, this let the water into the back of the ship and the sea would flood in, allowing egress of landing craft from inside the hull of the ship. Clever stuff. It was like the ship was having many babies when the landing craft emerged.

We were to move to HMS *Fearless* and land from her. We all knew her and had been on her before. We had all done this type of thing before. All we needed to do was get from *Canberra* to *Fearless*. This cross-decking would have to happen in the middle of the great South Atlantic swell. Cross-decking is, as we have established, the action of moving from one deck to another. Sounds simple, often isn't. The South Atlantic may not have been the best place to do this. On the day the weather was just grey and unremarkable, flat grey like a North Sea day in mid-February. Thankfully, the sea was calmer than we have seen her for a while; she was being kind. We would use the same Ascension door as before on *Canberra* and then get onto an LCT, just as we had done at Ascension. We would leave our warm, comfortable, clean home of nearly six weeks and move to the cramped conditions of an embarked force on the Grey Funnel Line. We were told to leave unwanted kit on board *Canberra* and only take war gear.

Loaded up in the gangways, we shuffle to the door. A very slow process, almost imperceptible movement. The sea is in a long swell and the landing craft is miles below the door or equally miles above as the waves take her up and down the side of the white ship in a rhythmically slow swell movement. The skill was to wait until she was rising towards the door. As she came up, step out with all your kit and be taken up further to the limit of the swell. You were then safe on the landing craft. Each man had to do this; 600 or so men had to do this today. Mostly it worked.

We watched in horror as a lad from B Company – Ged remembers it was a Marine chef attached to our company called Steve G – lost his footing and went down between the boats and hit the grey swirling sea, no sound. Just swallowed. Confusion regarding the identity of the individual is quite normal. The sea continued crashing; it has swallowed him whole. He's gone. He must be gone. He's got 150+ pounds of gear strapped to him. The ships remain apart by some minor aquatic Neptunic miracle as he disappeared into the black. Looking away was impossible. I presume there must have been air in his kit because he bobbed back up like a cork. A Marine Landing Craftsman with great urgency snatched him from the water with a billhook. No one cheered. Just a collective silent sigh of relief for the skill and strength of the billhook man. Nothing really unusual. We lost interest, shrugged and moved on; we don't need to see the rest. I presume the sopping wet Marine was dragged on board, and we continued the process. One at a time.

A short journey on a very small and insignificant boat in the great vastness of the South Atlantic seemed absurd. Nothing to worry about here. Into the flooded rear of *Fearless*. This is our new home. Does this mean we are actually going to do this thing? We agree that we may have reached the stage of no return. We still didn't really believe this was going to happen, but that assertion was being slowly rocked by events. Events seemed to be moving faster.

The ever-expanding stage was beginning to be reset. People were arriving. But only half of the players were on the stage.

Many, many miles away on the Islas Malvinas the Argentine Marines are digging into their defences on their mountaintops and preparing for the coming storm. Alejandro was still on Sapper Hill and remembers this time quite well:

> On May 1st at approximately 22:30 there is a strong British naval bombardment carried out with 105 mm cannons to our area, which constitutes the baptism of fire of BIM 5 and that unfortunately takes the life of the Conscript Marine Hugo Daniel Caviglioli, this being the first suffered by the Unit.
>
> Sapper Hill in the vicinity had been installed with several antennas as well as the Anti-Aircraft Radar of the Argentine Air Force.
>
> These naval bombardments would take place uninterruptedly during the totality of the days until the end of the conflict, always at night, with center [targets] both at the airport with the aim of destroying the runway, as well as a large flow of them directed to the positions occupied by the Battalion, particularly as those corresponding to "Sapper Hill".
>
> Also during these first days of May, from our position we were privileged witnesses of the enemy naval deployment of several of their ships as they moved in front of our sights first in a south–north direction without firing and then in the reverse direction, already firing their cannons.
>
> We watched with incredulous emotion as the pilots of their own aviation attacked the fleet at very low altitude and absolute proximity to their targets. These aircraft were literally launched on their targets in order to successfully accomplish their mission, in a show of admirable courage. These images were definitely taxed on my retinas, by the degree of absolute recklessness demonstrated.

I had in my position a small radio that allowed me to listen in a defective way radio Colonia, that is why by that means comes to my knowledge the sinking of the cruiser *General A.R.A. Belgrano*, occurred on May 2.

We have all come very far. Distance travelled is measured in the thousands of miles travelled mirrored by the distance we may have all travelled in an internal sense. New experiences come at us all thick and fast. Absorbing and dealing with them and placing them in an internal safety box somewhere and then moving swiftly to the next one. Unthinking. This is a true Homerian adventure. The difference being Homer did his adventuring in warm waters. Lightweight. We have been at sea for a long while and now we look forward to some time back on land doing our primary role. Soldiering.

Chapter 2

Blue Beach and Blue Sky

*In the midst of the dark sea is a land called Crete,[1] fair and
fertile, surrounded by the waves.*

The Odyssey of Homer, Book XIX

Diary Entry
On *Fearless* in Stokers' Mess deck, good lads, had air raids – very
nervous about landings, no one knows if San Carlos is occupied
or not.

On board our new cramped grey home. We were back on a ship of the line.
We had been on her before many times but this was markedly different.
It was dark and cramped. Just … dark. Marines lie in gangways with all
their gear. Urgent movement of sailors all the time. People are urgently
busy. This is new. Quite exciting really. Quite urgent.

New experiences tend to give new knowledge. We were learning
fast how to interpret and adapt to our fast-developing surroundings.
Circumstances were very definitely not in our hands. The Troop is split
up into small groups and I am sent below decks to a small mess deck
with a few of the lads including Si and Paddy and Pusser. Starboard
side of the ship. We are used to being on mess decks with their cramped
conditions and cramped three high and slim bunk beds and pipes
everywhere. Not one inch is spare in these places. It's a warship. At
least there seems to be some room for us in here. The sailors don't use
it, they must be permanently busy. Busier and more urgent than normal.

---

1. Replace 'Crete' with 'Falkland Islands'.

The whole ship was busy and urgent. We had joined her very much as passengers and as passive observers.

A Marine has the ability to find comfort wherever he finds himself. This is the skill of being a good soldier. Get comfortable, above all else just get comfortable. 'Any fool can be uncomfortable' is the well-used phrase. The hours roll by and nothing urgent happens. In fact, nothing happens. Just in a small grey room on a large grey ship sitting or sailing around the South Atlantic. No idea where the other lads are. We are stuck there, nowhere else to go. No idea of anything. We are obviously very small cogs in what seems to be a very, very big wheel. The wheel is moving. Normally on ship you can slip away and see some sunlight somewhere; not now. We are very much 'in' this ship. Enveloped in its greyness. New colours and new smells compared to *Canberra*, not new to us who have done this many times. Again, the smells are strangely comforting.

We have a new Tannoy man. This is not his first rodeo either. He calmly tells us that we are at 'Air Raid Warning RED'. This means we are in dire straits, and as brothers in arms we are definitely down to the waterline. Actually, we are just above the waterline. This took some figuring out. So, we logically worked out that we are starboard side, amidships and just above the waterline. Seems to be a good place to be. Why worry.

This took some minutes to calculate. Logic takes some time to process when being a Marine. And more time to realise the danger. Risk tolerance is trained into us, but some risk is just not advisable or necessary, or even clever. Tannoy man says an Argentine plane has released an Exocet missile at us. At us … what a nerve. We have heard that these things skim the water from a great distance away and home in on the middle of a ship. Very powerful weapons and very fast too. The Tannoy man calmly informs us that we are turning starboard beam to the missile so all defences can be brought to bear on the missile. Logical. Hang on a minute! We've turned starboard side on. But we're starboard side! The missile will hit the middle of the ship. We're amidships. Panic rises slightly but is managed and quashed immediately. The missile skims the water and we are just above the waterline. We calculate the missile would come through the wall about … there; we point at the grey bulkhead about 10 feet from us. Looks of logical unhappiness. Some grins of fatalism. We all agree this is not good. We suddenly feel so far away from safety and home. We have no control over this situation. We need to get out. We can't get out, we are locked in. Panic is no good, focus is good. Focus on a solution, not the missile. We find a semi-circular, screw-on plate on the bulkhead behind us. Dimensions of about 1 foot by 2 foot. Maybe this is our alternative way out. They have locked us in. No point in having Marines running around the decks with their hair on fire when the sailors are trying to work. We successfully get the plate off. Inside is a long, dark, vertical tube disappearing into the depths and heights of the ship. It goes up and it goes down. About 2 feet across and very, very dark. Up or down lads? We discuss options and the more we discuss the less any sensible option becomes obvious. Logic is sometimes silly. We decide that the absurdity of six Marines being found dead and charred in a vertical tube in the depths of the ship is just too embarrassing. We opt to stay. Logic is disappearing fast and being replaced with fatalism. Dying on the mess deck sounds much better. Being neat, I replace the metal cover. No need for a messy explosion. Tannoy man is giving us the countdown ... options are limited. 'One mile, half a mile ...' Something like desperation takes over and we arrive at our last possible option. We put pusser's heavy wool grey blankets over our heads and sit individually like mushrooms waiting for the impact. Our reasoning is simple. The blankets will stop the blast. A bit like the film *The Battle of the River Plate* (1956). The irony. Anthony Quayle would have been proud of us. We did not know the similarity at the time but I am glad to see it used by others, so it wasn't so silly, maybe. We sit in silence for what seems like an eternity waiting for the big bang. Time slips by and holds its breath. Joking and giggling continue and the funny side is always found. Always look on the bright side of life, some soft singing of Monty Python fatalism. Of course, we would never hear the bang, we'd just be vapourised, hopefully. We wait. It never comes, Tannoy man calmly informs us that it has all been resolved and we should return to normal procedure. Blankets come off and some shrugging of shoulders and beaming smiles. Maybe embarrassed smiles. Blankets folded neatly and stowed away. We continue as if nothing has happened. We didn't speak about it. It is unspeakable.

The world has just got a little bit darker. Our world is recognisably physically darker than being on our bright *Canberra* but this darkness is not something you see. But it is real. Rubicon again, maybe. A very dark and forbidding Rubicon. It may be an internal time dilation. Time is beginning to be like stepping onto a wet floor. The slip is going to come; you're just not sure which direction it will take you. It is not a linear journey. Time is doing silly things already.

We need feeding and we are told it is our turn to go to the galley for some scran. 'Scran' means food in Marine/Royal Navy slang. The ship is locked down tight as we make our way through busily stuffed gangways to the galley. We get there and the galley is dark. Soldiers everywhere, some SAS in a corner; maybe John is there. Not SBS, I don't recognise anyone. Not our business, just getting food. We are on war rations and that means a sandwich and a cup of tea. We have our own metal mugs. Not much food but the tea is welcome. Maybe spam or corned beef sandwiches. We're not there for long; other people need to come here too. No hanging around so back to the mess deck. Life is becoming 'efficient'.

We wait again. Our confidence is good. This is a blind waiting game, and we can influence absolutely none of it. So, we didn't worry. Fatalism. Somehow we are told what is happening. We're landing. We are briefed and we take notes. We are given a hand-drawn map of San Carlos. Apparently drawn by the SBS. Their drawing skills were probably absent that day. We don't know if the landing will be opposed. We don't know! Someone must know. Good grief. There's no north pointer or scale on this map. Good grief, Charlie Brown! It could be anywhere. The confidence slips and some raised eyebrows and nervous looks between us about an opposed landing. We know what that means. We had been extensively trained, watching black and white war films when young. 'The Fear' wheedles its way in and its tentacles take a firm grip somewhere inside. It has an initial grip but we laugh it off, shrug our shoulders and move on. Indifferent to it.

We are encouraged to write a 'Death Note'. This is encouraging. This should be addressed to the person you want to receive it in the event of your slipping off this mortal coil and joining the choir invisible. It is written and then handed to Bill. He will care for them and should we be killed, they will be posted to the address on the envelope. Apparently, this is a time-honoured British military tradition, but new to us. I pained about what to write. I pained a lot, but good words eluded me. I had no skill in this literary department. None whatsoever. I hadn't quite got to grips with any of my personal feelings, so I found this a very, very hard thing to do. What could you possibly say to the best people in your life? The brevity of my note may say everything about my own shortcomings.

I still have the note.

Small blue scruffy envelope with the address handwritten to Dad:

Mr J. R. Pretty
1 Barkis Meadow
Blundeston
Lowestoft
Suffolk
NR32 5AL

Notepad paper 4 inches x 6 inches. Two bits of blue paper.

Paper 1
IF KILLED PLEASE FORWARD TO ADDRESS BELOW
My Signature

Paper 2
Dear Family
If you receive this little lot you will also know what has happened to me.

Do not take it hard, please. It was a risk and I lost. There is nothing I can really say. Except I loved you all very dearly. My love.

Chris

I always was a big talker. It is a woeful letter. We were also given some very official papers to carry in our smocks. This would ensure that the war would adhere to prearranged and accepted international rules and regulations.

PAPER 1

W.O. Code No 13662 Geneva Prisoner of War Convention 1949.
Point 1 of the paper says. *'This Convention sets out the rules, internationally agreed, regarding the rights and treatment of prisoners of war during captivity.'* We didn't read it. Capture was not a possibility and was irrelevant.

PAPER 2

F/IDENT/189 (Rev. 11/78) BRITISH FORCES IDENTITY CARD.
This has my Royal Marines number, rank, date of birth and full name.

PAPER 3

A Green A4 Casualty Sheet. Battle Injury etc.
I presume this was for someone else. If I was wounded paperwork may not have been at the top of my priority list for completion and submission.

PAPER 4

Peculiarly I carried the 'TUBUNIC' morphine instructions. For ampule/syringe, instructions for use.

I didn't really need this as we had practised injecting each other on the *Canberra*. It turns out that when injecting someone in the upper outside quadrant of the thigh, it's best not to wiggle the needle. Apparently. Why I took the instructions I will never know. I wasn't exactly going to read them under fire or when wounded. Or maybe I was. Maybe I was too concerned to leave the instructions.

Returning to dog tags. Dog tags are your personal identification and they hang around your neck on very slim para cord. There are two of them. One green and rectangular with the corners cut off and the other is red and round. Heavily pressed cardboard. They have your basic details on. Name, number and blood group. If killed the red one is taken and the green one is left on your body. A simple body identification process.

Before leaving Blundeston I was given a small sixpence by the old woman down the road. Emily liked me and Jules and she was lovely. We liked her too. She lived alone. She would wave at us as we sped by on our bikes being very busy and being very young. She never seemed to be too busy and was always in her sunny front garden full of colour and flowers. We sped and she waved her hand, waving from the wrist loosely in a way we have never forgotten. I liked her. The sixpence was for luck, she said. I was not superstitious, or even religious at all but would it harm if I taped it to one of my dog tags? Maybe she knew something I do not. So that is what I did. It was attached to the green one and that is where it is right now forty years later. And here I am forty years later.

There is an obvious observation, and there may be many answers. I have none. Maybe the irrelevant sixpence worked.

We are off! Quick decisions are made, as Carl remembers. Due to the BBC World Service releasing the news that a large task force was just off the Falklands, we needed to move fast. Even the Argentines listened to the World Service. We moved fast. Urgency was everywhere. Calmed, metered urgency, no flapping. We all knew this procedure, so the skillsets engaged and we moved slowly, but fast.

We are given timings and orders and I return to the mess deck. Gear on and everything secured. White lights are switched off and we are universally on red lights now. Is there anything in here we can proff and make use of before we go? No. The atmosphere shifts a bit and becomes even darker. Into the gangways and bumping through the bulkhead restrictions with sailors patting us on our backs and helping where possible. Lots of 'Good luck, Royal' followed by 'Good luck to you too, Jack'. They would need it too. We all grinned at each other. Jack and Royal always get on. There is an unwritten loyalty.

Through the rabbit warren of darkness and red lights. The Tannoy played music and the song I remember was Hazel O'Connor singing 'Would you just politely say goodnight', which I thought was strangely ironic and hopefully not an omen. I also remember 'Strangers in the Night'. Other guys remember other songs. Maybe 'Strangers in the Night' didn't even play, but only played in my head. Through our last bulkhead door and into the tank deck, the well deck. This is a large, open space inside the ship and darker again. Some more red lights, but still dark. It's dark outside but you can see the outside world from inside the tank deck. People everywhere moving with purpose. All as normal really. Nothing unusual here. However, there is just a slight perceptible difference.

I probably incorrectly recollect Bill Howie sat a collapsible table handing out ammunition with a big smile on his face as usual. He loved this. He lived for this. Bombs and bullets. The LAW 66mm anti-tank weapons, flares, grenades, bullets, etc. It was like a buffet of all things that go bang. Take all that you want, an 'all that you can carry' buffet. Bill is merrily giving away hand grenades. Fragmentation, smoke or white phosphorus? Can I have all please? Of course ... how many? As many as I can stuff in my kit. Ammunition in every pouch and pocket. We weigh a ton each. A good ton. A comfortable ton. A reassuring ton.

Our final leaving presents are two mortar bombs in their hard green plastic carrying case. Another 10lb of weight. We were to carry these ashore and dump them in a prearranged pile for the Mortar Troop teams who would follow. This is all good fun and quite new. It was great fun, but I started to realise a strange, recurring irritation that would turn into my main fear and all-consuming obsession during the war: I really didn't want to run out of bullets. We call them 'rounds'. I *really* didn't want to run out of ROUNDS. I cannot express how this elevated itself in importance. It was all consuming and became much larger than it probably should. This seemed primal. Admittedly, deep down it kind of scared me. I hated the thought of running out of rounds. I hated the thought of the thought of running out of rounds. Totally illogical. But equally, totally logical. I instantly became a secret ammunition hoarder.

We file onto the LCT. We have two small tanks at the back of the craft and we are stacked up in front of them. (Jono remembers that the tanks were at the front and we were behind them.) It takes time to get everyone on board. It's not a free for all. This is the Royal Marines at their organisational best. So, everyone has their allocated position and everyone needs to be in the correct position. There is clear order to this amorphous, amphibious mass of green human beings.

The ship is half sunk with the dark ocean sloshing around inside her. The landing craft starts up and we move to the rear exit of the ship, the engine quietly throbbing. There is a point where the deck above stops and the great expanse of the cosmos comes into view. There is no light pollution so the serried ranks of stars are clearer than I have probably ever seen them before. It may have been the same in Africa, I cannot be too sure. But I was comforted. It was mind-blowing in its immensity. All of us remember the sky, that night. It is a collective memory. The LCT edges out of the back of the ship. We have to get in a holding pattern of landing craft going round in circles until all the landing craft are present, then we can start moving to the shore together. This takes time. We have time, lots of time. It isn't a bad place to be. We have infinite time.

My assigned place is at the front of the landing craft on the right-hand side looking from inside the landing craft. I am first man out in our 'stick'. Ged is immediately behind me. To my right and a few feet forward is a 2-foot hole in the side of the landing craft, to let water out. It does the reverse too. Water sloshes in and then out. Fortunately, there is a slight drop in the deck at this point so I don't get wet feet. Someone was thinking when they designed this thing. Clever design. Intelligent design. Thank you.

We are to land on Blue Beach.

We stand and wait. To my left somewhere Adrian remembers that they were sat down on their Bergens. It seemed warm enough, I didn't seem to feel the cold, the sky was clear. But it was cold. I felt good. I felt great. This was all good stuff. We were masters of the universe. Invincible.

The sky is vast and black. The stars are bright and the night seems to be going quite well, from my point of view, of course. The Troop are happy and standing, or sitting in their lines. The *whoosh* of NGS (naval gunfire support) shells going over our heads is an interesting addition. Not something we have experienced before. An addition maybe indicating the seriousness of our position, which I did not necessarily recognise. It is when the Royal Navy ships sit offshore and fire their hardware/shells onshore. Naval artillery. It was a weird noise, just like on TV but again strangely comforting. At least someone was paying attention. The Japanese have a word and might call this '*Yugen*'. I would call it cool … but yugen'ish.

This sky is vast. It is something we are going to get used to over the next few weeks. I use the word vast and I really mean it. It was vastly bigger than I expected. My brain at this stage of my life was only marginally developed and this probably contributed to the size complexity. Small brain, big universe. We are very small compared to all of that. I could get philosophical, but I was not quite sure how to do that. I can do it now, but I couldn't do it then, so I just looked up and enjoyed the scene. Vast. Vastly vast. In an American book back in Africa when I was a boy the vastness of the sky was illustrated by children standing in water and looking down and all they saw was 'stars between their toesies'. Memories are weird and pop up everywhere quite unexpected.

It is about 0200. We chug around for a normal amount of time, soft engine noises. Formed up and heading for the beach. We had been given that SBS hand-drawn map of San Carlos settlement. It was not very good. I was trained as a map-maker, and I should know. Not even a legend, not a scale and no north/south pointer. Strangely unhelpful, but also strangely just enough, so maybe they did get it correct, and I was wrong. I accept that. It was exactly enough. We had a good briefing on what we were expecting and what we were expected to do. NATO Sequence of Orders was a very thorough process. Nothing was ever missed.

Looking around, everyone in the company was very heavily burdened. More than normal. Our stay was supposed to be a long one so we had lots of extras. Totalling up the weight is quite complex but it was well over 120lb ++. Well north of that figure. Actually, probably well south of that figure down here. Everyone is cammed out with camouflage cream on. Dark faces. It would be good to say we all looked grim and toughened but the bright white grins in the black faces made it obvious we were still not taking this adequately seriously enough. The small 'commando' magazines would have drawn it very differently. Cheerfulness in the face of adversity as the commando ethos puts it. Cheerfulness in the face of impeccable ignorance more like.

Two small tanks at the rear of the landing craft. The company on foot in front. This seemed slightly illogical, but not enough to mention at the time, and impossible to change while on the move. Hours passed, it seemed. Time started slipping again. Hours, minutes and seconds are strangely interchangeable. Just don't question it too much.

At one 'lightbulb' stage I had a troubling thought. I had seen lots of Second World War films ('Broadsword calling Danny Boy'), as had we all. I knew from popular myth and from *The Longest Day* what would happen when the ramp went down and if we were going into an opposed landing. They told us they were 'quite' sure it was not going to be opposed. QUITE! That was questionable and left a large messy residue of doubt. My limited logic told me that standing at the front when the ramp went down would probably mean I would be first to get zapped. I pondered this and found this to be an unsatisfactory situation. Ged is a *big* man. Wide in all directions. Left to right and front to back. Front to back was my calculated key consideration and the one I was completely focused on. Bullets travel very fast, and with much destructive force. 7.62 bullets go through thick things.

I turned round to Ged and looked up. Ged's big shoulders, huge moustache and Bergen were outlined against the stars of the huge galaxy that obviously didn't know, and ultimately didn't care, that I was in immediate mortal peril. My plan was good … my calculations were good … my trap was good.

'Ged, do you fancy being the first person to land on the Falklands?'

'F****** right, Chris,' rumbled the voice from deep within that deep chest. The chest at my head height. The chest that was quite probably big enough to stop a 7.62mm round, according to my calculations.

We smiled appreciatively at each other, my obvious altruism evident to us both. I was cheerful and unselfish. My plan had worked. We changed places and I immediately felt safer. I informed him about this years later and he thought it funny. Funny enough to swear a lot at me. It still makes us chuckle. Altruism is a wonderful thing, but so is the alternative, sometimes.

Adrian 'Buster' Brown was a lance corporal in 7 Troop, doing the same job as me, and was somewhere over to my left in the dark landing craft sat on his Bergen. In fact nearly everybody was over to my left. This part of our journey did not affect me. I found it fascinating. However, Adrian had his first major scare on the landing craft. Nothing happened to him that didn't happen to me, or many others. It's the brain you know. Too much reasoning. It does horrible things, and he started his journey down the rabbit hole … in a relative way.

The metaphor of the 'rabbit hole' is used many times in our culture. However, this particular one is different in many ways. *This* RABBIT HOLE is like being in a minefield. You don't know where the hole is, there is no obvious indicator. No warning. One of the main differences is that in our social culture people talk of the rabbit hole but in a way that the rabbit hole is just a hole, with no consequence. It is just a hole. The 3D depth of the hole is never discussed. What is at the end of the rabbit hole is never discussed. This particular rabbit hole has something particular at the end of it. Like Alice we trot along quite happily doing normal things on a normal day in our normal lives. Life and experiences are normal. Nothing new. In this particular metaphor we step into the rabbit hole, and down we go … it is our hole, our own very personal hole. No one else comes with you. You are alone, very alone. You fall down the hole and into the dark/or light. At the end of the hole everything is different. Time slips and is not normal. An hour can be a minute and a minute an hour, a second can be an hour or a lifetime. Colours and smells are exaggerated, emphasised or muted but definitely distorted. There is *slippage*. People can become caricatures like the Mad Hatter, the frantic White Rabbit. There would be lots of these caricatures to be seen in the next few weeks. The hole is clearly a mad place to be. Curiously … mad.

Adrian had gone …

One of the best soldiers I have ever met, and one of my lifelong friends. He recounts this better than I can write it. It doesn't paralyse you, it mostly focuses the mind, just in a different space/dimension. Adrian is one of the most level-headed, intelligent people I know, so this didn't seem to affect him. We can bury this deep so it's not visible at all. If you've been there, you know what this means. If you haven't been there, then you now know what happens. The rabbit hole exists. It kind of eats people. At the end of our war, should it come, there may be options. Is it possible that after falling down the hole we climb back out again, little affected and continue on our way. Maybe actually stronger for our experience. Or is it possible that maybe we climb back out and are badly affected, maybe irretrievably leaving something of ourselves in the hole, and continue as 'half men'. Maybe we don't *ever* come out of the hole and unknowingly continue to live there for the rest of our days. Forever caught in the moment. It is actually mad.

I recently explained this to Rory, a climbing friend, much younger than me. He thought it quite 'Matrix' like. John Lennon apparently once coined the phrase 'sitting below myself'. A curious phrase of significance and it may be relevant here. Sitting outside of yourself.

The stage changes and new players arrive. Across the Island at Port Stanley/Puerto Argentino and approximately 70 miles due east from our landings … people/players have been preparing.

Alejandro writes:

MARINE MIDSHIPMAN – CHIEF OF THE THIRD SECTION – SEA COMPANY – INFANTRY BATTALION OF IM NO. 5. My name is Alejandro KOCH and I belong to the 110th Class of the Naval Military School. I graduated at the end of 1981 after the instructional trip on the Frigate ARA *Libertad.* Along with four other comrades I was assigned to the Marine Infantry Battalion No. 5 School, with seat in Rio Grande province of Tierra del Fuego to which we moved in early 1982.

Bim 5 based its operational configuration like most battalions of the time and in our case as midshipmen we were appointed as Section Chiefs of the Marksman Companies and me from the Third Section of Company M (Sea).

Prior to April 2, 1982, the first Unity campaign was carried out, in the vicinity of Cabo Peña, Tierra del Fuego, this was the first contact I had with the soldiers in my charge; and it is on that date that we are informed of what has happened in relation to the development of Operation Rosario and the consequent recovery of our Malvinas Islands. From that moment on, rumours began to circulate related to the possible reaction that the United Kingdom would have and ultimately also the still unconfirmed possibility that the Battalion would be assigned the mission of deploying in the territory of the islands.

It was not until April 8 that such a possibility was effectively confirmed.

From that moment on, we were told of the urgent and urgent enlistment, in view of the imminent transfer of our unit, through the use of Navy transport aircraft, and our arrival on 9 April was finally effective.

My callsign as Section Chief was YELLOW was made up of a total of 37 men. Two groups of shooters a machine gun platoon, composed of two MAG heavy machine guns, with their corresponding complement, that is, with their pointer and server. Also as a reinforcement, we were assigned and two rocket launchers were incorporated, with the corresponding personnel. As far as the troops were concerned, it was composed of conscript soldiers class of 1962, who were close to obtaining their discharge, by virtue of having completed at that time their period of compulsory military training, according to the regime in force at that time.

Our combat equipment was complete and adequate to the performance of combat operations in the Austral zone, whose characteristics are very similar to those corresponding to the seat of the Battalion.

Our combat clothing proved adequate, as well as the footwear that is so important in the Infantry, armament and ammunition, according to standards assimilated by various armed forces of the world. In particular, the fraction had the following weaponry: FAL PARA 7.62 Light Automatic Rifle, 9 mm pistol, MKII hand grenades, FAP rifle Heavy Automatic Rifle, MAG heavy machine gun, anti-personnel and anti-tank rifle grenades whose acronyms are PDF and PAF. I was personally assigned a FAL rifle of Belgian origin with infrared sight, plus a night vision device, with a very high degree of efficiency that allowed to visualize the surrounding terrain during the long night guards, with extreme clarity.

The plane that took us and that had been stripped of its seats to increase the cargo capacity of the staff with their equipment, after a brief history [flight] landed at the airport of Puerto Argentino.

We immediately began our march in the direction of the town first, then immediately crossed it and continued south.

That first night found us spending the night in a shearing shed, near Puerto Argentino. Immediately the next day, with the first lights we restarted the march and in the direction of the position that would constitute our defensive line and shelter until the end of the conflict, this is the Hill of the Sapper (Sapper Hill), distant about four kilometers southwest of Puerto Argentino.

The remaining components of BIM 5, as far as the shooter companies are concerned, did the same in the William and Tumbledown Mountains, located to the west of their own position. Particularly my Section, was deployed in front of Puerto Enriqueta (PORT HARRIET) i.e. facing the sea, and in the foothills of SAPPER HILL.

That first day together with the Section, we began to define the places where the positions for each of the shooters and the support weapons that we had would be located. I personally stood in the center, sharing the fox hole with whom I performed and fulfilled the function of radio operator. The company command post was located near the top of Sapper Hill and the remaining two Sections surrounded it. By the very location of my section, quite far from the company command post we enjoyed a relatively important autonomy. Wireless communications were absolutely forbidden, that is, radio silence was governed for obvious enemy location reasons, with a relevant telephone communication line, although extremely labile, in that after the intense bombardments to which we were subjected, both by naval and air fire and ultimately by ground artillery, this was subject to frequent and successive cuts in its lines.

During the remaining days of April, we dedicated it to strengthening our positions, as far as possible because the characteristics of the terrain itself, similar to those existing in Tierra del Fuego, made that task extremely difficult. It was tried to maximize the use of the rocky headlands, as protection and always having as main objective the planning of crossfires.[2]

As Alejandro was preparing, Jono remembers his experience of the landings:

John Travolta and Olivia Newton John were bashing out 'You're the one that I want' from the film *Grease* on the mess deck TV. Watching from the bunks throughout the mess deck sat the marines of 9 Troop Charlie Company, 40 Commando.

Faces darkened with black and green camouflage cream, fighting orders and weapons at the ready, Bergens close to hand, helmets on.

The lighting throughout HMS *Fearless* had changed to a dim red to preserve night vision. Some crewmembers were sat on the mess deck in full anti-flash; there wasn't enough

---

2. Please note it would be very easy to succumb to editing all of Alejandro's words to make it easier for you as the reader. But I have let them remain unchanged. All I have done is close up some text into paragraphs.

to go around for the embarked force so we were told in case of hostile action to use the blankets and mattresses, for what I wasn't sure. We were creeping through Falkland Sound between East and West Falklands towards our jump-off point for the landings. The ship's internal Tannoy crackled into life; it was the call to assault stations. The lads grabbed their kit, then the skipper, Captain Larkin, started to announce the cricket scores from the latest match in England; everyone relaxed and it broke the tense atmosphere.

Thirty minutes later the call came, 'Embarked forces to assault stations', followed by mess deck and stick numbers. Our turn came and we made our way through the narrow passageways, through hatches, down and up short stairs, heavily laden with weapons, fighting order and Bergens; some, like me, carried a small patrol pack strapped to the outside of my main Bergen, full of essentials like extra ammunition. Eventually we arrived in the docking area at the rear of the ship. Here we were issued our grenades, I was given two H.E. grenades, two white phosphorus and two smoke. We screwed the detonators into the base of the H.E grenades and stowed them for easy access. Then as we walked down the ramp onto our landing craft, we were also given two 81mm mortar bombs, as if we didn't have enough to carry ashore. My thoughts of storming up the beach vanished – it would be at best a stagger. We filed onto the craft past a Scorpion armoured fighting vehicle that was positioned at the front of the landing craft, presumably to give us some cover while we staggered off the ramp at the other end. The docking area was full of fumes from the landing craft engines as they fired up; our ramp came up just enough to allow the gun barrel of the Scorpion to protrude over the top. The walkways above the docking area was full of *Fearless*'s crew and as we backed out they shouted down, 'Go get 'em, Royal' and 'Good luck.'

At about 0230 we left the red-lit dock and emerged into a dark icy night; above, the sky was clear and full of a myriad of stars, the sea was calm and somewhere in the distance we could hear gunfire and could see flashes out toward Fanning Head. We circled and waited for the other craft to take station, then we waited some more; rumour had it someone from 2 Para had fallen in while disembarking from a side door of the ferry *Norland*. Eventually we got word from the coxswain we were going in and the craft began to throb as we headed toward our landing area, designated Blue Beach, which was just below our objective, San Carlos settlement.

The run-in was over some distance and gave us plenty of time, crammed as we were, albeit behind an armoured vehicle, to contemplate what awaited us. We began to discuss contingency plans if it turned out to be an opposed landing. The general consensus was to ditch our Bergens and go over the side with weapons and fighting order, then take it from there. The run-in continued and the chatter quietened down, each lost in their own thoughts. I was thinking what a great way to spend my birthday!

The order came, 'Five minutes to beach', and we strained to see the prearranged signal from the Special Forces guys hopefully to signal the beach was clear. If it came, we didn't see it; the Scorpion's engine burst into life, then suddenly we felt the landing craft shudder as it beached. The order came, 'Down ramp, out troops', but the ramp didn't move; a crewman ran forward with a sledgehammer and gave it a tremendous whack, and down it went. The Scorpion[3] moved off and we staggered after it through ankle-deep water, spreading out and moving up the pebbled beach.

We quickly dumped our mortar bombs at a predetermined point, shook out into formation and advanced off the beach, heading in to clear the settlement. All quiet so far.

We advanced quietly toward the small settlement and I caught site of our embedded reporter, Max Hastings, striding ahead in a long, brown waterproof coat and walking stick. I thought: Off you go then mate, you're our Argie

---

3. Jono and I really do disagree where the tanks were. Who knows, but equally, who cares?

detector. Suddenly a shot rang out and we went to ground; after a few minutes we set off again, Mr. Hastings was a little further back this time.

Our troop commander was given the task of locating the settlement manager's house and making contact to ascertain if there were any enemy troops nearby. We quickly located the house and a small party of us approached the building that was in darkness. The boss moved up to the door and we gave him cover from nearby. He knocked quietly on the front door. No answer, he knocked again, a little louder, nothing. He tried again a bit louder and eventually the door cracked open. The conversation went something like this.

Manager: 'Who's there?'
Boss: 'Royal Marines from the British task force; we've just landed. Are there any Argentinian troops nearby?'
Manager: 'Who?'
The Boss repeats himself.
Manager: 'You've taken your time.'
Boss, without missing a beat: 'We've had a bit of a voyage.'

The manager eventually informed us there had been some Argie troops in the settlement over by two big barns. We moved across and cleared them; no enemy to be found. Satisfied the settlement was clear of enemy troops, we pushed on a little further beyond the settlement, spread out and began digging our defensive positions.

We had arrived and we were staying.

Friday 21 May
Day 1
Ashore at 0700 dug in in defensive position, expected to be bombed, nothing. Saw first aircraft. Mirage, no attack.

The advance through San Carlos was very easy. No casualties. Paras had casualties at Port San Carlos where Company plus was dug in, 42 helped them.

During the war I carried a thin blue Smith's memo book and used it as a diary for the whole time. Writing was in blue ballpoint pen with some drawings to help. I am a visual person. I think it cost 15p. I still have it. I have no idea why I kept a diary; it just seemed logical. I had never done it before or since.

I remember it was still dark. We creep into the shore. No one speaks. Eyes narrow and grins become bigger. The LC Rating (Landing Craft Rating who is also a Royal Marine) says, 'Down ramp.' He doesn't shout but it is enough to hear. The big grey ramp goes down and open space is revealed in front of us. I peer round Ged. Nothing. We might be in luck. Looking into the dark we see many figures already ashore. 'Out troops,' says the LC Rating guy. Expected words and sounds we are accustomed to. Out we go into the water. As Marines we are taught not to step off the front of the ramp. If the landing craft gets picked up by a wave and moves forward, the ramp may lift and trap you under it. This would be unsatisfactory and slightly unsavoury and probably a little embarrassing. We are supposed to go off the edges of the ramp. It's a big ramp so we go off the front. Into the water and we wade ashore. It's dark and it's quiet, too quiet!

Alpha Company also lands in exactly the same manner. Lance Corporal Phil Moch accidentally drops his two mortar rounds and they sink out of sight. He instantly dives under water to recover them. He is soaking now. Good man. Always a good man. Leggy is with him and recounts the story much better than I can.

We keep going. We are okay. The water gives way to a small pebble beach and then a step up as the peat starts. Up the peat bank step onto the short grass. The step is about two feet high. People everywhere. The word in my unforgiving head is 'clusterf***' and it seemed appropriate. However, I could have been totally wrong and it was probably working perfectly, like a well-oiled machine. Nothing went wrong so I guess I was wrong. We drop our mortar bombs in a big pile and move off. We have a very clear task to undertake. Our Troop will clear all the houses on the right-hand side of the track. Not bothered what anyone else is doing, it's not our business. We shake out and creep into the settlement. Each house is cleared. We reach a noticeably large, lone house. We go down in all-round defence lying on the damp peat and expecting an Argentine response.

Bang.

Are we being shot at? Are we in it already? No response; discipline. Can't see any enemy, scanning ahead. That shot was very close.

No enemy. One of the lads in 7 Troop has accidentally fired his weapon. It's called an 'ND', negligent discharge, which is a very big and nasty offence in professional soldiering circles and extremely embarrassing. Normally he would be 'charged' for this misdemeanour. We giggle when we find out who it is. We still do. Relief it wasn't you. The peat here is very damp and dewy; there are no rocky bits anywhere, just grass, acres of perfect, sheep-clipped grass. Lying there on the peat grass with the damp seeping into your body all senses working at their maximum, I still couldn't believe there was nobody here. Still smirking from the ND incident.

Who knocked? Captain Pillar, Andy, but others remember it as Carl. Even Carl remembers it as being Carl. It is also confirmed by Andy that it was Carl. Jono says it was Carl. I am convinced to this day that it was Andy, but I am clearly wrong. Which is slightly troubling. Carl strides to the door of the house and knocks, peculiarly politely. In my peculiar mind Andy does this. I am a few feet away. I look over my right shoulder. The house is in darkness. No response. He knocks again. Eventually a dim light comes on upstairs and someone peers round a curtain. Many minutes pass. The door opens a bit, a small light behind the occupant. Scrooge comes to mind.

Carl (Andy) says, 'We are the British task force and we have come to liberate you.' Sounded good to me.

The man says, 'About time too.' How rude.

Stories may vary and directly oppose each other. I now believe this to be normal and acceptable. I accept that I am probably incorrect about who knocked. Response wise I'm not sure what we were expecting, but I wasn't expecting that apathy. The curious situation is finalised and we move off again, doing our normal job in the dark. Clearing houses and barns and outbuildings. A process we are thoroughly used to. Subsequently Carl remembers that Max Hastings gave the owner of the house a small bottle of whisky, thus securing a warm bed for the night. Good move, Max. He had different priorities.

We shake out into formation and keep moving swiftly forwards. At the edge of the settlement the ground becomes the 'camp'. Not camp in a Charles Hawtrey sort of way, but more of a landscape way. Any rough land not in a settlement is called a camp. Clear, open, grassy ground rolling down to the sea to our right and then the camp leading to the mountains to our left. Great expanses of that same clipped grass. The sheep obviously work very hard here.

Once through, we stop some distance from the settlement, still in the dark. Trench digging begins. Quiet determination. We are given our 'arcs' (of fire) and we start construction immediately. The peat moves quite easily not like the rocky ground of Woodbury Common on the tortuous exercise in commando training called *Holdfast*. We have spades and pickaxes and take turns between the three of us to construct a suitable shelter from the many expected possibilities. Each man carries either a spade or a pickaxe. Our trench needs to be big enough for three of us, and Ged. Others in the Troop only need to dig for two, except the gun teams. We were obviously digging for four.

We dig and dig and dig. A very good question exists in trench digging. How deep should it be? There are, of course, regulations for this, and Military Regulations must be adhered to, most of the time. I will ask you the question. You need to dig a hole that will protect you from God only knows what is coming at you in the morning; all possibilities are possible. Some possibilities are impossible but in your riotous mind, they are still possible. The mind runs riot with possibilities. That is how deep you dig a trench.

The top turf is planed off and placed grass to grass in a neat pile. This means it can be replaced clean when you fill in the trench and move somewhere else. There is always a somewhere else, but we had no idea where our 'somewhere else' would be and leaving a clean landscape is tactically sound and very neat, and I approve. Collectively we are pleased with the trench. It is big enough for our big gun on its big tripod, and our Big Ged.

Not so long ago we were a commando unit of 600-plus men. On *Canberra* we became less of a unit and became a company of 100 men, not really noticing the other companies. Definitely not noticing other units. On the landing craft we became a troop of thirty-two. Clearing through the settlement, we became a section of nine. Now we are three. And three we shall be for a long time. In fact we have no idea how long the three shall be. Outside of the three is not important. Martin 'Jonah' Jones, a Royal Marine commando from the much later Afghanistan War era, agrees that the world shrinks to the micro size when you're right in it. Only the guys right next to you become all of your world. Outside of that you still have your best oppos but they are not part of 'your' immediate group. It was me, Ged and Bri. Thank goodness they were really good guys. I had spent six weeks with Alex and now I didn't really know where he was. Slippage and maybe creepage.

The dark of the night slips and dawn creeps over the mountains. I have checked all the trenches with Dee and made sure we all knew our arcs of fire. Arcs of fire are given to each man. His arc intersects the next man's arcs and so on. Therefore, all the ground ahead of you is covered and no one is shooting randomly. You only fire at those things in your arc. This ensures total coverage of your frontage. Weapons are cleaned and prepared. Immaculate. GPMGs are sited on their tripods and ammunition belts fed in and readied. Rounds are cleaned before inserting into the GPMG. You really don't want mud getting fed into your working parts. And that is also not a euphemism. Grenades are got ready. 66mm rocket launchers are prepared and tea is put on, ready for a wet. This is a ritual. This is how we will meet the enemy. Tea, bombs and bullets.

A cup of tea is called a 'wet' in the Marines. Of course, it is called other things in other regiments. The wet is the way forward, it heals all ills. Always be prepared to get a wet on, any chance you get. It is never selfishly made for just yourself; it is made for all your small group, your little group of oppos. Metal mugs and a wooden spoon. The mug was metal and had a piece of masking tape on the rim to stop yourself burning your lips and it was usually a 1944 '44-pattern mug and metal water bottle. The wooden spoon meant there was no clatter of metal on metal. It's a tactical thing, a good-soldier thing. Wets are shared and passed round. Etiquette is everything. It is almost a religious ritual. The Royal Marine sharing instructions were 'sippers not gulpers', which meant you couldn't have too much, just sip it and don't gulp at it and then pass it on. 'Sandy bottoms' meant you could drink the whole thing. 'Sandy Bs' were for your best oppos and indicated a closeness of relationship, either existing or invited. Drinking from the same mug was normal. If you passed your mug to your oppo and he wiped the edge before drinking it, then it was an insult that could negatively affect your friendship. No wiping. There are rules to this ritual. Etiquette is everything.

I would like to say the day came up like thunder and we were attacked by thousands, but that is not true. The day slowly crept in, almost painfully slow. I thought they must come now, surely. We are at our weakest. We stand to. Stand to is when everyone gets up and gets kit on and lies on the ground awaiting an imminent attack, weapons ready. This happens from just before dawn and then ends just after the sun has risen. It also happens at sundown. Same procedure, reversed. This is because it is presumed that all enemies attack at either dawn or dusk. This is not true of course, but we still persist with tradition. There are other more sensible tactical controlling practicalities for such a ritual to happen two times a day.

'Stand to,' whispers a voice before dawn.

We wait and wait. Watch the light come over us. Watch your arcs. Where are they? Come on. It's fully light.

'STAND DOWN,' shouts a voice, very similar to the last voice, but louder.

A bit disappointed, but also privately a little relieved. Back to tea and breakfast. Comfortable routines perfected from years of practice. In modern times we know dawn and sunset by times set on a clock. I learnt later in life that Arabs and Mongols would attack at dawn. How would they all know the exact same time to attack without watches. Maybe a very pertinent question. They had sewn a black thread and a white thread onto their sleeves, side by side. When you can distinguish between the two, that is the exact moment of dawn. Try it, it's brilliant. Why didn't we know this?

The blue Smith's diary says that the Paras had been in a fight in Port San Carlos. This just shows how the 'buzz' system works. The buzz goes round about anything. We were not sure if this was true, probably not. Shrug and move on. Not our business.

Rations are as they have always been for our generation. A twenty-four-hour ration pack is given to you in a brown prepacked and sealed cardboard box (approx. 6 x 6 x 7 inches). There are varying menus available. Some more desirable than others. There is a main meal, a breakfast and lots of other bits. Tins and tins of processed things. These were made in the 1970s, probably earlier. Designed to bung you up so you don't have to poop too much. This may have been a myth, but in practical experience it is believable. Tea, coffee and hot chocolate. Spangles, Mars Bars, Rolos, cheese processed (possessed). Many strange and wonderful things to eat. Biscuits AB. Biscuits ''ard bastards'. Biscuits fruit. These are Biscuits AB but with a few rock-hard sultanas in them, but much nicer. The oak cake. What can I say. A prime individual in a crowd of inconsequence. A bargaining chip of great value and never to be squandered. This was worth much more than its 'coaster' size in its thick green packaging. This was worth something and it had real bargaining power. Also matches and a pusser's can opener. A brilliantly simple metal piece of kit. Just brilliant. Robust and simple, like quite a few people I know. The cardboard box was emptied and thrown away, or burnt, and the food distributed throughout your kit. Some in your fighting order/belt order and some in your Bergen. You had choice. We were experts.

To cook on we had hexamine blocks on a small collapsible, foldable, metal-frame stove. It all came packed together and was about 4 x 4 x 1 inches. Metal on the outside and hexamine blocks on the inside. Wax sealed. We usually used camping gas stoves (Blueys) but there was no resource for gas stoves down there, so we reverted to hexamine. Hexamine is just like the fire lighters you can buy in your shop, but a bit more solid. Same principle. Looked like Kendal Mint Cake. Solid and dependable, also like a few people I know. Issued one per twenty-four hours. Hoarded by many.

Cooking is quick and efficient, and mugs and utensils are rigorously cleaned afterwards. Never, never, never left dirty. This is rigorously bashed into us during training. Stowed away into belt kits, ready for the next time. Rations are stowed away and rubbish is stowed and never left. There are very good tactical and hygiene reasons for this. *Never* leave rubbish behind. It is a good soldier's sin.

No attack by the enemy yet. By my notes indicate that a Mirage jet came over, but I do not remember that now. Life was settling back into a normal routine. Nothing too abnormal yet. The bay is full of ships. *Canberra* is visible. White and big, almost throbbingly white in the subdued South Atlantic scenery. Radiant and not in a good tactical way. A really good target. Selfishly though, it may keep them away from us if they attack her. We are worried for her.

9 Troop was one-third of Charlie Company, which was spread out over a considerable area and all dug into trenches. We faced south

towards Sussex Mountain. The Troop were comfortable and easy with the surroundings and all was well with our little world. People say war is hell. Fighting is hell. War is getting yourself comfortable in difficult and demanding situations. War is admin. This required resupply of water, food, mail, all the things that Abraham Maslow would place at the bottom level of his often mis-maligned Hierarchy of Needs. One certainty is that you will not put on weight while on operations, not in the front line serving as a Grav in a fighting troop. As an average we were probably between 11 and 12.5 stone each before we landed. This would have reduced while on the Islands over the next few weeks.

Jono remembers these days and that

with the settlement secured, Charlie Company pushed out forward of the settlement to take up positions about 500 metres outside of the outer buildings; each troop was designated a defensive area and within that each section was positioned. We broke down into pairs and began digging our own trenches. By now dawn was breaking and we could see we had good fields of fire to our front, over open moorland, no hedges, no trees, no fences, wide open space. Part of San Carlos Water was visible behind us and to our right, and we could just make out the grey superstructure of an LSL nestled in the bay.

Marines are not keen on digging trenches and not really used to static defensive positions, being more used to mobility and movement; the digging was grudgingly done, it became even more of a chore when we discovered that after digging only a few feet down we came across water, due to the water table being so high. The only thing to do was to build up, and so small round mounds appeared on the landscape, each mound housing two men, with a fighting and sleeping area.

Suddenly a scream came from one of the positions; it turned out that over-zealous use of the pick on one part and slow reactions by the trench partner had resulted in the pick penetrating a hand; the medic was summoned and first aid applied. The next call came for someone from the troop to go to the rear into the settlement and pose for the raising of the Union flag on the settlement's flagpole. We drew lots and the hand-injured Marine somehow won, so 'Sponner' picked up his rifle and walked back into fame, his picture featuring on a few books, and knelt looking 'rugsy' as the flag was raised.

Everything was quiet, and we got ourselves dug in and organised by mid-morning. We occupied San Carlos, and over the inlet 45 Commando had landed at Red Beach and taken over the refrigeration plant that would become the now famous 'Red and Green life machine' or the regimental aid post, and also our logistics area.

At about midday an Argentinian Aermacchi MB-339A naval reconnaissance aircraft, who clearly had no idea we were there, suddenly popped up over the mountain ridge above 45 Commando's position on Red Beach. Suddenly all hell broke loose, every weapon simultaneously opened fire, small arms from the troops and Bofors guns from the shipping; the pilot suddenly finding himself over what must have looked like a replay of the D-Day landings and being the main attraction of a lot of flak, did the only thing he could do and popped back over the ridge very quickly. He disappeared but we now knew he would have reported what he had seen and very soon we could expect more visitors.

Later that afternoon the first of many air raids came in. The procedure was: the ships out at sea using their radar would pick up the incoming raid and notify the ships in San Carlos Water who would sound their foghorns and sirens to warn everyone a raid was inbound. Air raid warning Red would be declared, helmets would be donned and all ground troops would disappear into their trenches.

As the first raid swept in down 'Bomb Alley' toward the inlet, they had to fly between 40 Commando's position and 45 Commando's position and onto the ships in the bay. Every weapon was brought to bear and a cacophony of sound was generated as they flew low and fast through the gap. GPMGs let loose from both sides, Marines fired their personal weapons, mainly the 7.62 SLR and the ships engaged with Second World War-vintage 40mm Bofors guns and the outdated Seacat missiles. The Rapier anti-aircraft units had not had a chance to get ashore and set up yet.

It was a very impressive display of firepower, but it quickly became apparent after that first raid that 40 Commando's rounds were landing among 45 Commando's positions and vice versa, and the ships' Bofors were landing everywhere. Also apparent was the skill and bravery of the Argentine pilots to press home their attacks, so the shovels reappeared and trenches went down another couple of feet, and overhead cover was suitably reinforced!

After a couple of days, it was decided we were dug in too close to the settlement, so the decision was made for us to push out another 500 metres, which called for more trench digging. We would go forward to our new positions with digging tools and weapons only, then when the ships' horns sounded for an air attack, we would sprint back and take cover in our old positions. Once established in our new positions, we had a Blowpipe team (shoulder-launched anti-aircraft missile with a crew of two) come and join us; they positioned themselves in a trench in front of our positions and told us they would give us warning when they were about to engage. Blowpipe was designed to engage aircraft head on or going away, not crossing left to right.

The next raid materialised; a mix of Daggers [Israeli-made Mirages] and A4 Skyhawks, they came thundering down the valley and we all looked to the Blowpipe team. They began to track the target, 'STAND BY FIRING.' We in rear ducked down to avoid the back blast and *whoosh* off it went; we all resurfaced to watch the result as the missile flew out very impressively toward its target for a few seconds, then began a left turn, and we watched as it completed a 180° turn and flew back towards our positions. 'Rogue!' came the shout, 'Take cover', and heads bobbed down below ground again. The missile flew overhead and impacted in some open ground behind us. Despite the various derogatory shouts toward the Blowpipe team, they remained in position.

The next raid arrived about an hour later, the same pattern played out. 'STAND BY FIRING!' The missile tracked out and we all watched expectantly, then to everyone's horror it began to turn again and came back towards our positions, this time just missing the company commander's trench. After it all quietened down the company commander climbed out of his position and went and spoke to the Blowpipe team. A short time after, they packed up and departed towards a small peninsula of land jutting out into the inlet, well away from any of our positions.

It was decided to push out a listening post/night OP some distance forward of our position; it was only to be occupied at night, two men, staggered watch. The route to and from the position would be out and in through one of our machine-gun posts. This post was manned by some very keen Marines and I always began whistling 'Rule Britannia' whenever I was approaching it or coming back in at night.

Each morning just before dawn we always stood to in our positions. One morning as we stood to, I could hear a bit of a commotion coming from one of the trenches nearby, and a raised voice or two. Then I saw one of the team roll out of the trench and go into the prone position. I climbed out of my trench and went over to tell them to keep the noise down and find out what was happening. As I peered down into the trench, I could see Marine Pusser Hill, still in his sleeping bag but lying very still, eyes wide open. By now a couple more of the section had crept over to see what the problem was. Pusser in a rather shaky voice explained that his sleeping bag zip was stuck, and worse still, his white phosphorus grenade on his webbing – which he was wearing on his return from the forward position and which he'd kept on as he'd climbed into his bag – had somehow come apart or unscrewed itself inside his bag. He wasn't sure where the bits were and was concerned in case the pin had pulled loose on the material. The first thing that happened was everyone took a very smart step backwards away from the lip of his trench, and then began offering advice as to how to extricate himself from the situation; in the meantime, Pusser's voice had raised itself to a controlled panic. Eventually he was able to release the zip and open the bag, then carefully located the parts of the grenade and all was well, apart from the stick he received for days to come.

Two days later we watched a Royal Navy frigate come limping into the bay, smoke and steam leaking from her superstructure as she dropped anchor not far offshore. Apparently, she had been bombed earlier by a concerted air attack and she had two 1,000lb unexploded bombs aboard. Later that night the bay was lit up with an almighty flash followed by an explosion, and the frigate HMS *Antelope* could be seen burning in the bay. Unsure of what had happened, all positions stood to, and a rumour went round of Argentinian divers having got into San Carlos, but it was an attempt to defuse the second unexploded bomb that had ended in disaster; we watched as helicopters hovered around the ship, searching the water with their lights. She burned all night and the following day broke in two and sank, but her bow and stern remained visible above the water, creating the impression of a V sign.

After about a week of constant air attacks on the positions, it was decided to break out of the beachhead. 2 Para set off for Goose Green and 45 Commando prepared to leave the area of Red Beach. The Rapier anti-aircraft systems were now established on the hills overlooking the bay and we were tasked with moving over and providing security for the Rapier units and the commando logistics area. I can recall cramming myself and Bergen into a Gazelle, and with my feet outward on the skids, rifle in hand, we set off during an air raid warning for Red Beach across the water, flying at zero feet across the waves, hoping not to attract the attention of any Argie[4] pilots who were inbound.

---

4. This word has been retained in the text. It was the term of the day. Not derogatory.

On Red Beach there was the refrigeration plant, which housed the regimental aid post that became famous as the 'Red and Green life machine'. Behind that was a POW cage and it was here we saw our first Argentinian prisoners, dressed in green parkas and caps, looking very dejected. They were mostly stood staring at us staring at them. We quickly deployed up onto the surrounding hills to our allocated Rapier units manned by the Royal Artillery.

One evening it was just getting dark and from our position we looked over the refrigeration plant across the bay to Blue Beach, our old positions. I watched one of the Rapier crew walk over to the generator that powered the missile unit; at night these were switched off as the Rapier had no night capability. He was about halfway back after turning the generator off when four A4 Argentinian Skyhawks suddenly swept around the end of our hill contour flying below us, heading for the logistics area. He immediately turned and sprinted back to the generator, but it was too late: two Skyhawks turned right and headed over the bay toward San Carlos settlement and the small unloading pier, and the other two pressed home their attack on the refrigeration plant. We watched as black objects detached from the aircraft, then small parachutes appeared from them, followed by the inevitable flash and explosion as they impacted in the logistics area. The Skyhawks streaked out across the bay followed by streams of tracer, and below us we watched as secondary explosions indicated they had hit their target as ammunition stored in that area blew up. We watched it burn well into the night.

Sometime later we went down to the logistics area to dry out a little and were shown one of the bombs that had hit the building but had not exploded; it was suspended over the medical area, a dark green cylindrical shape with a yellow band around it.

While there, I attended the burial of the members of 2 Para killed at Goose Green; they were laid to rest in a temporary grave dug by one of the engineer's vehicles. Each body in a green body bag was carried in by members of the battalion and their names read out, a quick salute then the next one was carried in. A very sobering experience.

I was having a wet inside one of the many rooms in the refrigeration plant when a medic came in and asked us to get ready to move out; they had a possible mass casualty situation developing. We got our gear together; then the medic came back and asked for volunteers to help as stretcher bearers – a ship had been hit, one of the LSLs. As we got outside, the first Wessex helicopter was just arriving and men with stretchers ran out to help those onboard off and into the RAP. This was quickly followed by more helicopters, Sea Kings and Wessexes coming in every few minutes; we ran out with a stretcher and as the cargo door of the Sea King slid open, an overpowering smell of burnt flesh greeted us; we helped the casualties out onto the stretchers, all of them badly burned, some covered in flamazine, with their hands in bags, wild eyes darting around from heavily bandaged faces; it was gut wrenching. A Wessex landed not far from us and as we went across to help, the crewman jumped out, ripped his helmet off, walked a short distance away, fell to his knees and began being sick. Several lads turned away from the sight that greeted us inside the cab, but we did what we could and got the injured into the aid post as quickly as possible. As we came out of the main entrance, I will always remember seeing about eight of the Chinese crew from one of the LSLs, still dressed in their orange 'once only' suits, some with skin hanging from their hands and arms, looking totally bewildered at the hell going on around them, but waiting patiently to be taken inside for treatment.

There are still certain sounds and smells even to this day that instantly take me back to that awful afternoon. Unknown to us at the time, the air strikes on the LSLs *Galahad* and *Tristram* would alter Charlie Company's war completely.

Graham (Pusser) Hill remembers that in the early hours of 21 May

we were given our final briefing. 9 Troop gathered its kit together, carried out final equipment checks, and we applied camouflage to our hands and faces. We were then called down to the ship loading bay where landing craft were waiting to take us to San Carlos beach. The whole of the ship's interior was bathed in a red light to help us quickly obtain our night vison when we left the ship. In the eerie, hazy red light, we were led to a vast number of boxes and resisting the temptation to take more than we could carry, we drew our ammunition, high-explosive and white phosphorus grenades and light antitank weapons (LAWs). We were then loaded onto a landing craft and waited as suddenly its diesel engine spluttered into life, and we slipped away from HMS *Fearless* into the darkness of San Carlos Water. The weather was cold and dry, the only sound the low hum of the craft's engine and the sound of the bow waves breaking as it moved through the water. I remember looking up at the inky, black sky and thinking that there was no going back now; my thoughts turned to home, a home that was over 8,000 miles away on the other side of the world. Suddenly someone opened a bulkhead door on the side of *Fearless* and a beam of red light shone out over the water in front of the landing craft and in the background Freddie Mercury of Queen was singing 'Don't stop me now, I'm having such a good time'. Almost immediately the door slammed shut and it was quiet again. It was a surreal moment and to this day whenever I hear that song it transports me back and memories of that moment come flooding back.

As we approached the beach, I found myself nervously checking my kit one final time, making sure my safety catch was on my weapon, my ammo pouches were fastened, and the pins were tight in my grenades. To this day I still have the habit of continuously checking where things are in my pockets and my luggage when I travel. Suddenly the landing craft came to an abrupt stop; as it grounded on the beach the ramp at the front dropped down revealing the moonlit beach; we quickly and silently moved out and into the darkness.

Saturday 22 May
Day 2
Good weather. Duty in forward trench. Sgt Pete B***** and Tom M**** + 2 came through our position. Were stood to.

I saw them coming in and we stood to. I recognised them as a four-man team from the SBS (Special Boat Squadron[5]). The sergeant had been my training sergeant on my SBS course. Tom had been there too, a superbly impressive guy. I was busy so I didn't go over and say hello. Andy Pillar was SBS and he would take them for a wet and a debrief. They came through our position and headed straight for the HQ element. Not our business. The training sergeant was called 'Harpic' by our SC course. Why? Because he was clean round the bend! They looked like they had been out for some time. Rough and tough and very well weathered. Shrug of shoulders and back to a wet with Ged and Bri. They had been away doing their job and we were doing our job. As Nigel Devenish, a Royal Marine Mountain Leader ML1, says about the war, 'It was a team game.' This is exactly how we all saw it. Just do your own little job and do it perfectly. Somebody else will do the other bits.

The routines you so easily fall into are comforting and calm and well-practised. We did one duty in a forward trench, quite a distance in front of the main trenches. If it makes it easier it's like sitting in no-man's land of Great War popular myth. The idea was that you saw the enemy first and alerted the main group, then you died. This seemed a bit flawed to me and very dangerous. But duty done and back to your big trench. Our big wet trench. For a big wet.

---

5. At this time it was still the 'Squadron'. It has increased in size and become the 'Service' it is today. At the time it was known to us as 'Shaky Boats', 'SB' and 'SC' (Swimmer Canoeist).

As Jono says, the water table was very close to the surface and the trench started filling up almost immediately. My sleeping position was on the right of the trench at the bottom. My perception was that this was filling fastest. As night came on and sentry duties continued, I tried to sleep in the bottom of the trench; rookie mistake, and unforgivable. I totally deserved what I got. I got wet, thought better of it and slept outside the trench, behind it, in full view but dry at least. This needed to be fixed the next day. The Argentines may come, but the water will definitely come. Priorities driven by practicalities. We adapted and built a shell scrape behind the trench. Looked like a shallow shell hole. Not deep but deep enough to sleep in with just enough lateral cover and away from the water table.

Clearance patrols were sent out at night. The tactical thinking is that you start at a gun position and walk out a certain distance on a bearing. Turn left and walk another distance. Turn left and walk in towards the next gun team position. This seemed like a bad idea knowing that Adrian, Matt Maloney and Dodger Humberstone were that gun team. They were far more dangerous than any enemy we might meet. This was done with some delicacy and safety was reached but with a bit of a squeaky bottom moment. It would've been better to have been in contact with the Argentines than Adrian, Matt and Dodge. Great oppos but inordinately searching for a scrap.

'Contact' is a peculiar military word. Exclusive in its meaning and relevant military importance. It means just one thing. It means that you are now fighting the enemy and are directly in shooting contact with him. The word should not be used for anything else, especially if using the radio. It is a powerful military word. If you contact the enemy then the radio operator shouts, 'Contact, wait out' over the radio. Everyone else on the radio net goes quiet waiting for the next call from those in contact to allow them space without other callsigns cluttering up the net. I still struggle using the word out of military context.

We started digging a forward OP trench about 800 metres ahead of the main trenches. We were called to 'Air Raid Warning Red'. We all stood to including the SB boys. The day went by and we became more comfortable in our surroundings. Unremarkable but all admin achieved and comfort created out of the earth. A new shell scrape was ours too. Sleeping would be better. Life was good.

Sunday 23 May
Day 3
Beautiful day, attacked by nine aircraft, eight shot down. Three we saw go down. LSL attacked and hit. Days are from 11.00 to 20.00 at night. LSL exploded and Frigate, had no sleep.[6]

Today the Argentine Air Force came to play. If the weather was good, then they came. We were on the eastern shore of the Sound. 45 Commando were on the western shore. 2 Para were to our south on Sussex Mountain and the Sound was full of ships. Some of these ships were stores ships and some were fighting ships. The fighting ships were bristling with weapons and the matelots manning the weapons were bristling with anticipation. Everyone was armed to the teeth and very happy to let off their share of ammunition. The aircraft flipped over 2 Para on their hill/saddle and raced northwards up the Sound, bombed, gunned and strafed, got shot at and turned at the far northern end and came racing south again. We spent the whole day standing to and standing down. Those lazy halcyon days on the *Canberra* were long gone now, by golly. Replaced by air and sea warfare of a past age. We were all very deep in this thing now.

I grew up in Suffolk. North Suffolk to be specific. It does make a difference to a Suffolk boy, I assure you. Every day as a schoolboy on the Norfolk border we would witness American jets overhead making afterburner noise all day long. Training. It was the Cold War and any sunny day brought out the deafening sounds of US Phantoms climbing and wheeling. The Argentine aircraft were just what I was used to and they came out on sunny days too. All was relatively normal. Noise, speed, afterburners and away …

Until suddenly, on one bright sunny day just like at home … life changed. One of them was rushing over us and charging up the Sound at low level. It was hit and crashed; this was definitely not normal, this turned everything upside down. Another … then another. Good grief, Charlie Brown! This was definitely new territory for me. At first,

_____

6. Some arrows drawn in my diary might indicate that some of this text was the next day. Fog of war, I guess.

I was quite shocked and it took a few moments to compute this new experience and deal with it. But like all new things we got used to it very quickly, probably a bit too quickly, maybe even disturbingly too quickly. This is a common thread of this war. You learn fast. You adapt your behaviour to your learning and move forward to the next new and unexpected event, and then quickly adapt again. These rapid, small changes coalesce and require you to make significant changes over a short space of time. A progressive desensitising process where feelings are buried every time you see more … just 'see more'. The more you 'see' the quicker you become at packing it away somewhere. Mostly it is great fun.

Air Raid Warning Reds were all the rage. We would get a warning shouted round the defensive area. 'AIR RAID WARNING RED,' a qualified voice would shout and this would be picked up by many other voices as it was repeated and sped its way around the trenches. Your correct and expected trained response was to get into your trench, and fast, being diligent and professional. Initially we all did this, and fast. After a very short while this became the new norm and response times were extended and often not even believed or heeded. Much laughing and joking at our new danger. We adapted and laughed in the face of danger.

A sunny moment and we are sat in the trench system of the Troop, idly looking down to the calm seashore. Work details complete and now with tea in hand. In the distance Bill Howie is walking down to the shoreline with a spade. Business to be done. We watch. He disappears out of sight. 'Air raid warning red,' comes the shout; we repeat it. We continue sitting waiting for something to happen. Bill appears again with trousers round the ankles and spade in hand. Hurrying to his trench. Business obviously not done yet but the need to get to the trench has overcome the initial evacuation process. We laughed and shouted. We laughed so much we nearly spilt our tea. Funny how these inconsequential incidents are seared onto the memory. Planes came and went among much shooting from the Sound. The planes forgotten but Bill remembered.

The wet and flooding trench situation was amended. Everything here was wet. We had dug our shell scrape behind the main trench. About 6 feet behind it. A shell scrape is as you would imagine it to be. It's a shallow dish-shaped hole. Just deep enough to be above the water table and enough to be out of the wind, and whatever else the future had for us. This became the sleeping position. Much happier. So much happier it gets mentioned again.

Life has steadied into a comfortable routine of tea and tiffin and planes and ships and us all shooting at each other. This happens remarkably frequently but is assigned to the 'normal' pile of experiences and we look forward to the next few days. Life is good. Our lives are still very good. Routines have been established in all sorts of areas. Fast jets now fall out of the sky.

Monday 24 May
Day 4
Spent day standing to – but no one came. Paras vittled each other up on Patrols. LSL has an unexploded bomb in her aft. Expected attack at night. No one came.

What a beautiful clear and blue sky, bright day. The clarity of the air here is amazing. Have I said that enough? It is still astonishing. Here we sit on the eastern shore of the bay. Sat in our trenches, as normal, waiting. More accurately, sat on the edge of our trenches with legs dangling into the trench making wets of tea in the sunshine and passing them round. If you are feeling particularly in need, then a hot chocolate will do. The mood is still very good. What could go wrong when you're with all your best mates on an adventure across the world. The war was almost irrelevant. Almost.

A well-used military saying is 'Hurry up and wait'. In the military waiting is everything; you learn patience and you learn to wait your turn. We were waiting our turn, whatever that 'turn' would be. Patience, waiting, queuing were all specialities of the Marines. We were expert 'waiters'. I am still an expert waiter, in fact we all are. It's a good skill, much underrated by the frantic and frenetic.

Inactivity can be debilitating though, and we knew that this was all getting a bit more serious even though we were static. The presumption was that someone was moving somewhere. But this didn't stop the Troop having fun. Some Royal Navy ships have been sunk in the past weeks and that hasn't happened since the Second World War, I believe. This is serious war stuff. Top-end war stuff. Aircraft are being shot down daily

75

too. This is also serious stuff. Maybe it's our turn on the ground next. However, we are left alone and no one comes to visit, thank goodness. My life has changed a bit in the last few days and I have learnt some new personal things. One very important aspect is that we have no idea how long this will go on for. In the films they always glibly say 'It'll be over by Christmas' and this seemed logical to repeat, and we repeated it and laughed. Christmas was a long way off. We could be here a very long time. The laughter was not jolly laughter; it was the acknowledgement that it may actually be Christmas, or beyond. It definitely could become a worry if we allowed it to be. Worry is a decision. We decide not to worry; it's just our lot and actually it's quite good fun. So far, our lot has been okay. Some people's lot has clearly not been okay but that's not our business.

The bay was bathed in sunshine, cool but not cold. The sun makes all the difference down here at the end of the world. The bay was full of ships as usual disgorging their stores and logistics for the push forward. Landing craft slowly moving around distributing stores and people. No rush. Benign, even. Helicopters buzzing above doing similar. It was all movement on the water. The bay at San Carlos got its new name. Bomb Alley. Newly baptised. This seemed totally appropriate. We lived in 'Bomb Alley'. Apartment 9. 40, Bomb Alley. San Carlos. The End of the World.

Obviously, if it was a sunny day, we would have some visitors. We did. Nine aircraft. Eight were brought down. We all opened fire on them with our personal weapons as well as Blowpipe, Rapier and Seacat and much, much more. LSL, a Landing Ship Logistics, was attacked and exploded. This also happened to a frigate. They brought her into the bay to die. We were told it was *Antelope*. It was pitiful. If helicopters are airborne when the Argentine jets come over, they rush to a fold in the ground and temporarily land, rotors still spinning. Waiting for all clear. Taking some cover probably as much from friendly fire as from possible fire from the enemy. Had no sleep tonight with the continuous rain and duties.

Doing duties or sentry duty was a 'space' of time in which you are designated a specific time and specific location and a specific arc of ground out to your front. Your job is to observe the ground at all times. Never deviating. They say time always passes really quickly when you're by yourself staring into black nothing and looking for advancing enemy. This is clearly not the case. Time passes sluggishly, it stretches into the blackness and with no small internal panic from the sentry fearing if he were to go to sleep. Going to sleep is not an option. It is professionally committing suicide. Like having an ND. The reputation of going to sleep while on duty will follow you, and no one will be happy with you. You are untrustworthy and therefore a poor soldier. *Never* go to sleep on sentry duty. You put your oppos at risk. To find out if you can do this sentry duty then dig a hole in your garden and get in it. Fill it with water. Starve yourself. Freeze yourself. Try to stay awake from 0200 to 0400. Occasionally get your partner to come out and throw a bucket of cold water over you. These are the worst hours. In fact, 0300 seems the worst time. 0230 to 0300 is the truly sluggish time. A second feels like an hour. It's not night and it's not day, it's not today and it's not really tomorrow; it's a limbo time and belongs to no one. No wonder the SS would visit you at 0300 in the morning in the Second World War – it is truly a dead time. I have heard this said. You learn every trick you can to stay awake and stay silent and motionless. Most often it is an hour on duty, lying on the ground, feeling your body heat seep into the cold earth beneath you. Or alternatively feeling the wet seep up from a cold Mother Earth into your small, pink body. Just before your hour is up, your replacement should arrive. Sometimes this does not happen. This is very unsatisfactory. Mostly you can't leave your post to find him, so you lay there on the ground or in the trench and seethe with mounting hatred knowing he is warm and stealing your sleep. He arrives at just the right moment when getting back into your sleeping bag is mostly useless because you have no residual body heat left to heat the bag again. Being cold is part of a soldier's life. You can train your body to accept this, but it is a truly painful process.

You also see things at night that you never see as a civilian. Being immobile and silent, the animals appear and disappear unaware that you are silently watching them. The stars rotate on their axis slowly and predictably and shooting stars streak across the sky. Planets do what planets do and wander around. The moon does its thing, sometimes hiding behind clouds and making the world disappear in enveloping blackness. Weirder things happen too. You are just a silent individual witness to it all. Mostly you are on your belly and the cold of the earth seeps into your bones very slowly. At some stage the cold becomes painful, but you can't move ... not a muscle. Accept the cold. Movement attracts the eye and is a soldiering skill you must master. It's one of those things that is simple to say and very hard to do. Stillness equals survival. Move and you're dead. If you don't want to be seen in a crowd, just stand still.

Curiously at night, if you look directly at an object, you can't see it. You need to look off slightly to one side. It's something inside your eye, and it's a real physiological thing. In the night sky there is the Pleiades, I believe. A small cluster of stars, quite faint and if you look directly at this cluster it disappears. You need to look off very slightly and then they appear again. Also, looking directly at an object can make it appear to move. This means that inanimate objects can seem to move in the dark. You need to master all of this. Being cold on duty is a good thing and quite often the more uncomfortable you are, the less likely you are to go to sleep. Sometimes preferable. Cold can be your friend. So lying in cotton trousers and a cotton smock for an hour by yourself with a rock-hard, iron discipline is a difficult thing. This is a silent and very individual thing, and it is pounded into you during basic training by your lovable training team corporal. Pounding is probably actually the correct word. Lying on the ground, not moving, staying alert and absolutely silent. It's an iron discipline and can be very hard to do. Not totally unpleasant though.

The cyclical turn of a day is accepted by us all but the full turn of a dark, lonely night is very different. The nights on the Island were very long; fourteen- to fifteen-hour nights at this time of year that unluckily meant that with nine members in the section, two duties could be your normal lot for the night. This meant leaving your warm sleeping bag twice. Your 'gonk' bag was the last bastion of comfort and normality and was guarded and protected very, very carefully. If it got wet, then all was lost. Our issued bags were feather bags and when wet were useless. Wet feathers have no 'loft' and therefore no thermal qualities; ask any bird. Manmade 'Holofil' had not really come onto the civilian market yet; it was in its infancy. It did arrive just after the war and changed everything. Feather and down had to be protected and kept dry at all costs. Holofil is still warm when wet. Well, warmer.

Sleeping was done with clean socks on and the wet ones stuffed under the arms to dry, and your wet boots put at the bottom of your bag. Feet cleaned and foo foo dust applied (military talcum powder that stops rot), not to dry your boots because they wouldn't dry completely but conversely they wouldn't freeze either, so they were good to wear the next day. Sometimes they would be kept on if you thought the tactical situation demanded it. Many things were kept inside your bag when sleeping just to keep the items warm and dry, some personal and some military, but all were ultimately personal and required protection. Sleeping in smock and trousers ready to go. Also in your bag was your rifle. Dry, cleaned, lightly oiled and warm, your only spotless friend (obviously not loaded, i.e. with bullets in it, that would be very silly). Head resting on your fighting order/belt order where all the rounds were stored and ready to go for immediate use.

We had our 'Chairman Mao' suits with us. Quilted dark green jacket and trousers. Very rudimentary but they did help when combined with our wool jerseys and Norge shirts. Some Marines loved them. I took my jacket to war but not the trousers. Personal preference was always allowed.

Paddy Porter and Pusser Hill had a disagreement today. My understanding of this was that Paddy decided to sleep with grenades in his smock pockets. He had already seen combat so he was probably slightly more aware at this stage and probably more blasé than us. Pusser was not keen on this idea. This escalated fast. Pusser was horrified. Paddy was uncaring. This rocked backwards and forwards and like most disagreements, a suitable compromise was found by them. The grenades would sit just in front of the parapet of the trench, in safely and mutually agreed ground. As a Troop we all watched and laughed; it was a good show. I privately thought Pusser's argument to be well reasoned but didn't get involved. Just not my business and I had not seen combat yet like Paddy.[7]

9 Troop was functioning very well, as we would have expected. Nothing out of the ordinary and only small adaptions to the new 'scenery' of war. Some people called this a 'conflict', and politically and technically it was. But practically, for any other reason it was 'war', and needed to be treated as such. Maybe not total war yet but getting

---

7. Jono's recollection differs to mine again. Don't let it worry you; it just indicates that we all saw things differently.

quite close. Limited war. Tactical routines had been established in basic training and in all the exercises we had done together in the unit. The routines were easy and comforting in their normality. The Troop was its usual self. Days were spent laughing and joking and generally mucking around as we worked. Laughing was our staple diet and finding the joke in everything was the pastime of all.

A buzz came round the Troop that the Paras had accidentally shot themselves up. The rifle company term was 'vittled up'. It's probably a way of making the issue casually acceptable, I guess. This was innocuously termed as a 'blue on blue'. Apparently not unusual in times of war. Getting shot by the enemy is quite unacceptable, but by your own side probably worse. Not good and faintly embarrassing. But the 'blue on blue' term makes it strangely acceptable. The buzz often came round and could have arrived in the form Chinese whispers and only started for fun, so no one really took any notice. Just hoping it had not actually happened. Unfortunately, it would happen several times throughout the war. This seemed to have a great effect on those who had shot their own side. This is a lot to live with and to process, I have been told.

Overall, the day was not so busy for us. A day of consolidation and building. Construction and perfecting. However, it was busy for those on the ships. Very busy. I'm not sure how Jack did his job on ship just getting bombed again and again and again. Good lads, Hearts of Oak. Sitting in a grey metal box waiting for it to explode. Well, we had some limited experience of that feeling of expectation already. But already that seemed like a lifetime ago, and totally irrelevant. Jolly Jack Tar was doing his job in sterling fashion. It's what we expected and it's what England expected.

Tuesday 25 May
Day 5
3 Aircraft came over, one shot down Pilot ejected plane went up in a ball of flame over *Fearless*. LSL also hit. Good day of sunshine, but some rain, had good shave etc. Lots of explosions all around us. Nearly got shot by Bofors, landed at feet. LSL caught another unexploded bomb up.

Another day dawned and the usual routines were undertaken. This was easy. I had no idea at this stage that today would be a small landmark for me and my 'personal war development'. And probably a slight extension to my desensitising process. Today we had another attack by the Argentine Air Force. This was expected. The weather was clear, cool and sunny. Not warm, but at least sunny. Three aircraft came over the mountain that 2 Para were occupying. They were travelling fast and low and they got through their defences as you would expect, although the buzz claimed that 2 Para did apparently shoot one down from that position later on. The aircraft dropped in height and sped north up the Sound towards the peaceful scene of waiting ships. The metallic clatter, clatter, clatter of small-arms fire reverberated around the Sound. This was all as normal and became our new norm. Occasionally you would hear the *whump* of a surface-to-air missile as it was released towards these crazily brave people in their flying machines. I secretly admired their lunacy, and bravery.

Unfortunately for them, but not for us, most of their bombs did not explode on impact. Apparently, the groundcrews back in Argentina were setting their fuses for a higher drop. This meant that because they came in so low to drop their bombs, by the time the bomb hit the ship or other target, the bomb hadn't actually fused itself to explode so they just sat there at the end of their flight like great useless lumps of metal. Big lumps of possibly inert metal. In my ignorance I presumed they could have exploded at any time but most of them didn't, so I believe. It must have been very disappointing for the pilots to have flown all the way here across the sea, through our outer and inner defences, run the gauntlet, only to drop a 500lb or 1,000lb lump of inert metal on a ship that should have blown into little tiny bits but now only had a neat hole in the side of it, just like a keyhole.

One of the LSLs was hit again today; somebody seemed to have it in for these small ships during the war – they were always being hit. Thankfully, we seemed to be largely ignored. Once the planes had flown away or been shot down as one of them had in spectacular fashion, life went back to normal. The plane that was shot down was blown to bits; it went up in a huge ball of flame just over HMS *Fearless*. Very pleasing for the boys and more jumping around and back-slapping. Poor chap. The pilots came in on the exact same route each time. This was wrong. Brave but wrong.

A round of trench modifying, patrolling and drinking cups of tea or hot chocolate, laughing, joking and trying to get people on bites ensued. A 'bite' is telling an untruth at the listener's expense. It is a favourite in the military. I had a shave today. Even mentioning this probably means it was a big deal and was worth a mention.

Pusser and I had decided to go and have a cup of tea with Andy and Sponner in their trench, which, as I have said, was off to our right about 100 yards away and further down the slope towards the water over the perfectly open, grass-covered peat. It was a pleasant day and the sun was shining although it still wasn't particularly warm.

We had strolled over and started chatting with them when the 'Air Raid Warning Red' was sounded. A blasé and nonchalant response had been developed towards incoming aircraft. So we just stood around and continued talking for the now socially agreed and acceptable time lapse between the alert and the appearance. Previously, we had hit the deck at the first sound or warning of aircraft. We were turning into old sweats already and didn't even know it. It was a visible process. Maybe we should take note of these indicators. They could indicate us getting closer to our rabbit hole.

Unfortunately, we had got this calculation dramatically wrong this time. As I was talking to the boys, I happened to look over Pusser's shoulder and up towards Sussex Mountain and saw the planes pop over and come in very low and very fast, as normal. Andy and Sponner were looking up at me as they were stood in their trench, their backs to the planes, blissfully unaware that the adrenalin had exploded and was beginning to pump around my body. Igniting every system. I had a metal mug of tea in hand and my eyes must have popped out on stalks. Pusser happened to look around at about the same time and he saw the planes too. I stood still, Pusser took off like a gazelle towards his trench, big, long athletic legs taking huge pumping strides away from me. He always was faster in a sprint than me. A quick calculation in my head and I thought my shorter legs wouldn't get me across the distance to my trench in time so I jumped up in the air with the aim of landing in Andy's trench between him and Sponner and ultimately in a place of safety at the bottom of their trench and between them. Tea in hand. I remember the feeling of jumping and it still feels as though I had jumped up 10 feet in the air and hung there weightless. Very odd and obviously incorrect, but everything seems exaggerated at these times. I hung there for what felt like ages.

They hadn't seen the planes and thought I was messing about so they blocked me and pushed me out with flailing arms and big grins. I tried to get back in. They started pushing me out again, laughing and joking. I was ejected back onto the grass squirming with a little bit of panic and probably with twenty-five pints of adrenalin pumping around my system and with them continuing to grin from under their steel helmets. They still hadn't seen the planes. 'Shiiiiiiiit!' I was gone and running as fast as I could towards my trench. A similar route to Pusser. Maybe slower. I zigzagged as much as I could. I was convinced that these planes were after me, personally. As I sprinted I could feel clods of earth hitting me as I ran and I heard great cracks pass right next to me. I was nearly flying by this time. When I got to what I thought was about 20 feet from the trench, I jumped and did a wonderful swan dive into the bottom of my trench. Home and safety at the bottom of my hole.

I lay there and caught my breath, letting my soul catch me up and come back to my body as the adrenalin subsided, I hadn't disgraced myself, to myself at least. The planes went and I had no idea what had just happened. Seconds had passed but it felt a much longer time. I checked my body for holes; I was okay. This was an excellent new experience. I stood up and decided to go and see what had happened. As I was walking back, I found huge divets taken out of the earth along the route I had just taken. The divets were about 10 feet long and about a foot wide, and there were loads of them right along my route of flight. By the time I got to Andy's trench, I had mellowed a bit and the fight had gone out of me. Very thankful for not getting any of that metal in my back. Andy said later that he watched me go and was certain I was dead. Thanks, and he was my best oppo. Knowing him, he'd laughed himself silly. Little did I know but I had probably moved on slightly in myself and was maybe now coming in sight of my own personal 'rabbit hole'. I think this is where Lennon's 'sitting below myself' is appropriate. I definitely felt as though I was 'separate' somehow. Maybe I was beside myself. Curious.

My soul had caught me up again and resettled where it should be. Maybe a bit bruised and stretched. Seamus Heaney, the Irish poet, says the weight of a soul is the same weight as a snipe. A small bird of about 80–100 grammes. MacDougall says it is 21 grams. Apparently, a soul weighs something. Mine had caught me up and I now weighed the correct amount.

We reckoned that the divets had been made by 30mm/40mm cannons from the ships and these were their fall of shot after they had aimed at the planes coming over. Of course, we were experts on the divets of cannons by now, but this was the only explanation and it was sufficient for me. I felt I was lucky. Not too much of a visible drama, but slightly shaken in a very private kind of way. Later we found this whole episode rib-ticklingly funny and we laughed heaps about it. But it did dawn on me that I would definitely have been dead right then, on that spot if I wasn't so lucky. But, to focus the brain, I wasn't dead, fatalism … where's my wet of tea? Smile, shrug and move on.

From now on we were far more carefully aware regarding friendly fire than we had been. We did figure out though that our small-arms fire must have fallen on 45 Commando, while theirs fell on us and how 2 Para's must have fallen on everybody. With the ships contributing and blasting all the surrounding shores and giving everybody something to think about

Steel helmets and trenches started to look more attractive all the time. We are told in basic training that we are invincible when we wear our green berets. If we wore them, we could not be killed; this was starting to make less sense as new proof and new experiences were revealed to us. Steel helmets became more attractive. You must remember that Marines didn't wear helmets in those days. Berets or a black/green woollen hat were the norm. Never a helmet. It was beneath us, but not in a Lennon kind of way.

The fifth day passed, and we had survived it, just. To add insult to injury we were still here. Who was fighting the enemy, if anybody? It certainly wasn't us, that's for sure. The irritation at being here was beginning to mount as the days passed. How long could we sit and do nothing? The Troop was intact and doing well. The days are passing and life is settling into a rhythm that seems to work for everyone. Night approaches and all the nightly routines are completed. Stand to, stand down, stand up, sit down, supper, tea, sentries and lots of laughing.

> **Wednesday 26 May**
> *Day 6*
> On duty at night on SF. Stood to and advanced 200m and begun digging again. Several times were on 'warning red' but no enemy aircraft came. Several were destroyed by Harriers. One exploded close to position. Mail came today from Granny and Dad, burnt them. Position move to Ajax Bay as 45 Cdo are bombed and have casualties.

Last night I was on duty with Bri on the SF[8] GPMG (machine gun on tripod). We nearly had a blue-on-blue incident with Jono and his guys on patrol. I couldn't believe we'd nearly vittled up our own guys. Just goes to show how easy it is to do. Pay more attention next time; lesson learnt. (Jono may have been whistling.) Blue on blue.

This morning we stood to, as normal, waiting for the inevitable infantry attack to come. Needless to say, they didn't come. Maybe they were unsure of the rules of this game. Maybe they hadn't been told that this was currently the way we were set up to fight them. Should we have sent them a memo to make sure they came? We are British so maybe a very polite letter would have sufficed. The morning stand to was always cold. Getting out of a warm sleeping bag and lying on the ground is never comfortable. The Earth is a very big thing. I am a very little thing. The big thing had a lot of cold to transfer to the little thing. The inevitable happened.

It was about this time that Gommy started sending knitted 'comforts'. She was part of the generation that always smelt of mothballs. These items arrived in a brown paper parcel wrapped up with string. Knitted hats, gloves, mittens, fingerless gloves, the list goes on. These comforts arrived regularly. I used them to keep warm. Apparently, this was what they did in the First and Second World Wars and she was just doing what she knew to be correct. My mum recently said she didn't allow anyone else to send any. Peculiar. When too many of them arrived for my private use, I distributed them to the lads in the Troop. It was like looking at one of those oddly camp old knitting patterns of the 1960s

---

8. SF = sustained fire role. This means it is on its tripod.

when you looked at the Troop, only in greens and browns. But we were warm, and thankful for her efforts.[9] Her peculiarly selfish efforts maybe.

Rick had a similar experience and in his words, he says that from the time we left for the Falklands to the time we returned,

> my mum sent me regular parcels containing letters from her and the family, my boxing & karate magazines, and even packets of custard cream biscuits and chocolate tea cakes for me to share with the lads in the section. Even when the Troop were split up to act as protection parties for the Rapier missile sites, I still received her parcels. From start to finish my mum's parcels always got through. Therefore, a massive 'well done' and 'thank you' to the British Forces Post Office [BFPO]!

After breakfast, which usually consisted of porridge made out of biscuits AB and the rolled oats biscuit from the ration packs with some apple flakes and raisins in it, we just got on with the routines of the day. The compo packs were good and you could quite happily live off one for twenty-four hours of moderate effort. More time if the situation required. It would be required often. Arctic ration packs are the best and we were normally issued them in the Corps. Double calories, but dehydrated. Understandably, we didn't really get them here. The biscuits that you get are in a pack of five, which are about 6mm thick and two and a half inches by one and a half inches. They are solid to say the least. If you were to put some down the main sewer in London, they would have swollen and blocked the whole thing. They had a similar effect on the human intestines. The dehydrated Arctic rat packs needed water, and quite a lot of it. This is not really a problem in northern Norway in winter, but down here where it rained all the time and the water collected in stagnant puddles, it was a problem. Chlorine tablets were issued in the ration packs: small, round, flat white tablets. These could work sufficiently with boiling. I never threw these tablets away and continued to hoard them.

---

9. Note to self: whenever you read this, and we may well be in another war when you do read it, just send knitted hats and gloves to the troops. They will appreciate it. Green and brown only please.

Breakfast done with and all cleared up we were tasked to move 200 metres forward and to start digging our trenches again. We'd just got ours looking like a palace and now we had to change. But we were advancing. This wouldn't be the last time we would do this. The bosses had a great sense of humour and we really appreciated it. Maybe they had attended a conference and decided that if 40 Commando weren't going anywhere, maybe just to make them feel better they'd advance us 200 metres forward. I suppose we got what we wanted and we did get to advance but I seriously doubted if it was going to pressure the enemy sufficiently. We went forward and dug the new trenches, the water seeped in and we felt at home again and the Argentines obviously felt just a little bit more pressured by this aggressive advance. Second trenches were a much better design than version-one trenches. We had learnt to live like First World War soldiers and find comfort in anything. Trenches had expanded and included small kitchen areas and proper sleeping areas. We were only limited by our imaginations. Our imaginations were limited by our youth.

Good news! The mail came today. In war the little things in life suddenly become very important. They begin to become vastly over-exaggerated regarding their individual relative importance. One of these things is the mail. In fact, probably the main one is mail. As a corporal, you could see the guys' morale pick up with a letter arriving from home. No letter and they were unhappy. Once personal letters were read by the owner they would be passed around to the guys who hadn't received anything, especially if they were from girlfriends and had the smell of perfume on them.

'Mail call!' the shout goes up. We gather.

'Wilson!'

'Yes,' excitedly.

'Nothing for you.' (Old soldier joke.)

Today I got a letter from Granny Pretty and from Dad. No perfume. Granny Pretty always wrote very supportive letters and I always thought well of her; she always wrote how the family was and what everybody was doing. Dad's were good too and I really appreciated them, so I burnt them all. Dad's writing was always so neat and precise. I had no idea how this was all affecting the family at home. No empathy whatsoever. Quite disappointing in hindsight.

It is the accepted rules that during a war you burn all your mail as soon as you have read it, not before you'd read it, that's silly. Once caught, the enemy would use this information from your letters to prise more information from you … presumably about your granny. If the MOD didn't want me to give the Argentine military my secret information about Granny and her small granny flat in Reydon, and her subversive OAP friends, well then, I wouldn't. At this stage if they'd given me so much as a cup of tea, they could have had all my information in my head. I had nothing of interest for them. Nothing. All we had done so far was emulate Hobbits. There is a part of me that regrets burning them now.

Part of Royal Marine Commando culture is the 'drip sesh'. This is when Royal Marines will moan about everything and anything from politicians to the state of the biscuits, or the odd white colouring of the Mars Bars we were issued in our rations but which we still ate regardless. Everything could be 'dripped' about. All subjects were acceptable and nothing was off-limits. The depth of dripping was a true skill developed over years of being a commando. The strange aspect was that this was all allowable and was tolerated and no one contested the 'drip sesh' or even questioned it. It was a right of all Marines to drip. It nearly always ended in laughter between the protagonists, but it was an acceptable process. The saying goes, 'every Marine is entitled to drip'. It never goes further than a drip either; that would be poor form. It was both harmless and essential. Dripping was the Falklands War.

We heard today that 45 had been severely bombed at Ajax Bay on the opposite side of the Sound almost directly due west from us. They had taken quite a few casualties and had had quite a few killed. Poor sods. I had loads of good oppos in 45 and wondered if any of them had been hit. Ajax Bay had been turned into the field hospital led by the greatly esteemed Rick Jolly RN. It was also where the brigade stores and ammunition were stored. All in all, quite a tactically sensitive area. The Argentine pilots were not slow in identifying this and then giving it a good bomb run, even though it was a hospital. But apparently if you have stores near a hospital, then you can't put a huge red cross on your building to protect it. So how would they have known? I was on the other side of the Sound and was blissfully unaware that today was the day when Mac McAndrews was killed at

Ajax Bay.[10] He was the unit sailmaker and we had shared a grot when we were younger in 40 with Steve and Taff. We'd had many a good night ashore together down in Guz and in foreign ports. Mac was a bezzie oppo of mine and a good run-ashore oppo. In hindsight it went something like this. The jet flew in very low with Mac in his trench firing his GPMG at the belly of the plane from his bunker. The pilot released the bomb and the bomb hit the bunker. He didn't die straight away, says Rick Jolly, but apparently, he was a real hero; that sounds like Mac. Rick told the story well. Sapper 'Goosey' Ghandi from the Commando Royal Engineers also died today. He was a friend and together with Sponner we had rock-climbed together quite a bit down in Cornwall in earlier years. A nice lad. Two good guys gone in the twinkling of an eye. It was costing us as a task force and it was costing me personally now. But as I said, I didn't know that at the time. I had lost two mates and I was blissfully unaware that they had gone.

However, 9 Troop's normality was still intact and the day was gone. We'd moved position albeit not very far, but we had moved. We were sat in our holes blissfully ignorant, and static, as to what was happening. People everywhere were on the move. Just not us. Hobbits. Static Hobbits.

Note in hindsight: today Private Dave Parr from 2 Para was on his way south from Sussex Mountain with his battalion to attack Goose Green. He was killed later at Wireless Ridge even though he had been wounded previously at Goose Green. Good bloke. He was from Lowestoft and was known by all of us 'Lowestoft Boys' and he was a mate. I knew nothing of this at the time. Three good friends in a day. Plus many more.

We had reinvaded the Falkland Islands to recapture them for our country. We were vastly outnumbered by the Argentine Army. This was not the preferred tactical or strategic situation. It should be that the attacker has many more troops than the defender. However, we were extremely well trained, so Voltaire (1694–1778) may have been correct when he said, 'God is on the side not of the heavy battalions but of the best shots.' I hoped we were the best shots.

---

10. Mac was killed on 27 May 1982 according to Official Records. Clearly, I have become confused over the years.

Chapter 3

Move to Wreck Point – Backwards

It takes all the running you can do, to keep in the same place. If you want to get somewhere else, you must run at least twice as fast as that!

Lewis Carrol, 1865

Thursday 27 May
Day 7
Moved North to Wreck Point

Got woken up at 9.30 – still dark – after having a brills nights sleep. Still got two hours till sun up. Helis were late so we waited and proffed all of 8 and 7 Troops left kit. i.e. L2 hand grenade. Picked up by choppers, flown to north to set up OP/defence with Rapier. Arrived did recce of area, after relieving 45. A good day of weather, no rain but much wind. Am on duty tonight. Found whalebones on beach. After scran me Dee and Bri went and put out an L2 pull system booby trap in a re-entrant. We were attacked by aircraft. Our Rapier brought one down in the 'Straits'. Another went down over the hill. It was fantastic.

New orders. We have been told we are definitely going to move to a new location. It looked as though there was a slim possibility that we were going to take part in this war. This was good news and was appreciated by the whole Troop. We are going forward. Our orders were to go by separate sections to Ajax Bay where we would split up to different locations. Jono and his section would stay on the high mountain behind Ajax Bay, George and Alex and their section would be near Ajax Bay. Our section would go north by helicopter some 5 to 6 miles and up to the most northerly point of Wreck Point. This promontory formed the bottom jaw of the pincers where Fanning Head made the upper jaw guarding San Carlos Bay. It was to be a lonely place and even though we thought we were going to take part in this war we were going backwards, away from the front line! Not good news and the boys were not too happy with this. Still, it was a move away from Blue Beach and the rear echelons, so we should consider ourselves lucky. But it still was not forward. Others had gone forward; what was wrong with us we asked ourselves. However, it would give us the feeling of autonomy, and we liked that. It would be the last time we saw the rest of the lads from the Troop for quite some time.

Our orders were that once at the site we had been allocated, we were to guard an artillery Rapier ground-to-air missile firing post and its crew. We were also to be the westward early warning OP for our area; we would certainly be that – we couldn't be any further west or any further away from the war. Not our preferred option. However, it was our position and it was our job to do our job and let others do the their jobs.

Nick had woken us in the dark before the move, so we sorted ourselves out and had breakfast in our soon-to-be-vacated trench positions. Now all we had to do was wait for the helicopters to come and pick us up. The round of 'hurry up and wait' started again. The helicopters eventually came and started to lift the company away in groups to their various areas of responsibility. The whole company was being split up and distributed around the island. The weather was clear and sunny, so we said cheerio to the lads we knew from other troops as they went. We didn't know when we'd see them again. The company was being dismantled. For some reason it didn't seem that important to us at the time. The world is extremely small in war and ours just got very much smaller.

It looked like we were to be the last to leave the area at Blue Beach. We made more wets as the time passed slowly and the choppers lifted the company away, section by section. The weather had become changeable, but it was still generally sunny and reasonable, with only passing rain. The ground was still waterlogged. Its steady state. Us in our steady state.

7 and 8 Troops had now vacated their trenches to our left and rear. They had been lifted away by the choppers to our shouts of encouragement; there is some glory in being the last to leave the scene. This left us

to do some proffing and scrounging. We wandered off to their empty trench positions and started to search through the stuff that had been left behind; there wasn't that much really. There was a general feeling that we would be returning here sometime in the future. I found an empty bandolier, a pair of gloves, a sling, about 800 rounds of link and an L2 hand grenade which, had obviously mistakenly been left behind. I was pleased and my principal fear demon was satiated for a short while. I was pleased. I really liked grenades and the more I could get hold of the better. I loved my SLR but I loved my grenades just as much; you could do heaps of damage with one of those little beauties. Whereas a rifle is selective in its destruction, a grenade is definitely gregarious in its nature. I stuck the spare rounds in my Bergen along with the other finds. They would all come in handy at some stage of this little adventure.

We had been issued three types of hand grenade. The first was the L2, which is a high-explosive grenade made up of an explosive charge encased in a metal sheath that has sectioned 'piano wire' wrapped around the explosive inside. This means that 'everyone gets a bit' is generally the rule of thumb. It blasts the ripped and jagged piano wire for some distance depending on the ground surface onto which you throw it. Quite a piece of ordnance and one to be cherished. The second grenade is the white phosphorus grenade or WP. Willie Peter as Alex called them. This has less explosive and, instead of wire, it has a filling of white phosphorus. As all chemists know, and I'm sure you remember your chemistry from school, phosphorus when exposed to oxygen spontaneously combusts and continues to burn unless the oxygen is prevented from coming into contact with it. Water is the obvious answer when trying to extinguish it. Should you get a small particle of this on you, it will burn until you cover it. It is particularly nasty and is very good for enclosed spaces. It can be used for starting brushfires or as a smoke screen to cover your movements when attacking, so long as you throw it in the right direction considering the prevailing winds. The third grenade is the trusty smoke grenade. For generating smoke to indicate your position or to conceal your position. This came in different colours. Not lethal, but extremely effective in concealing any move you might make. Again, wind dependent. The winds at the end of the world are mostly always extremely strong. Diligence would be required.

Back to the day. The company had gone. The Troop had also now all gone and we were the last nine to be picked up. The Wessex helicopter finally came for us and we were taken north; we were not going to see the bay from that location again for a long while now. In fact, it would be a lifetime till we next saw it from this piece of land. We would fly north and we would be on our own. Perfect.

The helicopter came in to land and we deplaned onto the diddle-dee, the local name given to the soft heathery vegetation about two feet deep. The neat sheep-clipped grass was gone, a memory now. This was more of our accustomed environment. The weather was still reasonable although it had got darker and more forbidding. It always felt like it was about to rain here. Everyone deplaned and we went to ground, a soldier always goes to ground when exiting a chopper. This is lying down in a defensive circle while the Bergens are taken off the chopper and piled. Once safely off, the chopper leapt into the air and disappeared south. Quiet fell on us. We went over and met the guys we were to take over from, a section from 45 Commando. I went with Dee and introduced ourselves to who we presumed was the section corporal. He was a big guy with a massive fearsome moustache. Typical 45 rate. We discussed the area and the tactical implications, a quick show-round and some ground appreciation and he got his men together and they went out on the next chopper. The handover didn't take long but it was quite sufficient for someone taking over a barren piece of land in the middle of the South Atlantic. The chopper flew away and peace descended again on our new location.

Once they had gone the area quickly quietened down and we took stock of what we had just inherited. 'One day lad, all this will be yours …' 'But I don't want it.' The land was very open, no trees. As normal in such a windswept landscape. Like being on a headland on one of the small Hebridean islands of Scotland. The Falkland Islands do not possess any trees in the camp. It is too windy for them to exist. It was much windier here than in the bay. Much stronger and more constant. Standing on a small hillock it was possible to look north and see Fanning Head. Out to the west was Falkland Sound, which is the strip of water approximately 8 miles wide between East and West Islands, named after Viscount Falkland in 1690. West Falkland was easy to see, in normal conditions. Consequently, we hardly ever saw it. This was a wild and windy place. We were about 250 feet above sea level and the wind howled.

Southwards the land rolled slightly uphill but almost imperceptibly. Our position was on the grassy knoll. East, we could see the higher mountains of East Falkland. Everywhere was desolate. Not a bush, nothing, just great swathes of heather and diddle-dee. The only thing this place would be useful for was fields of fire; there is no real cover anywhere. It is bare and windy. However, it is utterly beautiful in its wildness. It is also an environment that is quite easy to live in. We were used to this.

Areas were allocated where we were going to build our bivvies. An obvious location on the knoll was discussed for a sanger. We couldn't dig down so we would need to build up. It became more obvious that if we were attacked by a raiding party, it would only be us and them. We had no back-up, no one was coming. The isolation factor was obvious to us all. The sanger we built was about 12 feet across and made of rock and turfs of peat.[1] It was about 5 feet high. A main concern was the wind. Between the rocks we packed peat until it was generally windproof. The GPMG was put in the sanger with thousands of rounds and all protected from the rain and wind. Grenades placed on the parapet. 66mm rocket launchers too. This was the nominated location to do the sentry duty so it had to be both comfortable and tactically sound. Comfort demanded that a small kitchen area be designed for cooking. This was our first build and we would get very good at designing and creating comfortable accommodation in the following weeks. Also using anything we could find and scrounge became part of the project and great care was taken in the selection of the correct turf or rock. We used everything – peat, rocks, driftwood and detritus from the beach. Anything that would help with the building process. Scavenging at its finest.

'The moving of the boulders was weary and painful work. We came to know every one of the stones by sight and touch, and I have vivid memories of their angular peculiarities even to-day,' said Ernest Shackleton on his adventures. This was also true of our experience.

---

1. Google Earth can be used to locate the small circular sanger. It is still there.

We put some food on and a wet of tea. After eating I went with Bri and Dee for a short patrol around the area just to get acquainted with the land; we carried a GPMG, two SLRs and thousands of rounds of ammo, radio, grenades and 66mm rocket launchers. We called them just '66s' and they are designed for knocking out tanks, but also used very effectively for bunker-busting. It is a tactical requirement to acquaint yourself with the surrounding area. Each fold in the ground must be identified. How close can they get to us unseen from any direction? This started as a clearance patrol but could turn into a fighting patrol at any moment. We needed to know their most likely route of attack. This is based on what we would likely do in such a situation. If you could do it, so could they.

Looking north and slightly east the ground dropped away and came to vertical cliffs. Before the cliffs there is a particular point where there was a re-entrant and a very small river, which was in a dip about 30 yards wide and deepened as you descended to the sea. The bottom of the re-entrant was reasonably flat and grassy with small bog areas, 'wee holes' as a Scotsman says. There was standing water at the bottom just before the beach. A pond. We discussed this as an option and reckoned this would be our preferred route to the Rapier if we were trying to get close to the position before assaulting it. Something had to be done to defend this area. We couldn't spare the men to sit in it; it was too far away from the main position to be of any use.

The answer came in the form of the proffed 'frag' grenade from the San Carlos trenches. A tripwire and explosive device might warn us of attackers. A plan was struck. I used a tin can from the ration pack; it would do the job. The idea was to take the pin out of the grenade and insert it into the crushed can. The grenade's lever was kept depressed by the pressure from the sides of the perfectly crushed can, which was in turn securely attached to a fashioned spike in the ground. The top of the grenade was attached to some string tied off at a post on the opposite side of the gully, so the string acted as a boobytrap/tripwire across the gully at about shin to knee height. Very hard to identify. I hammered the tin with a stone and crushed up the sides so the grenade fitted snugly. It had to be forced into the can to keep the handle depressed. When I was happy with that, I placed the stakes out and attached the can to one stake. It was now that the other two guys decided to go behind a small hillock some 20 feet away: they didn't trust my training/fiddling, and I was starting to doubt it as well. Terry was watching from behind a small mound, grinning through his cam-cream-blackened face. Pulling the pin out to feed it into the can is when it suddenly becomes marginally dangerous and the whole thing can go horribly wrong. Focus is required. Some support would be good. All I could see of the blokes was their blackened faces and green berets topping off big grins leering over the small mound. They were waiting for me to blow myself up, waiting for the laugh. I bet they were already dividing up my kit as I tentatively went through the procedure. It is vital that the mousetrap mechanism in the grenade does not move even the slightest millimetre, or the system will trigger and you only have three or four seconds to throw it at the boys cowering behind the hump. It didn't move and I didn't have to throw it, although I felt like it anyway. I tied off the green string, made sure everything was tight and stood back to admire the set-up. The trap was set and now all we needed was an Argentine commando to come and trigger it. I cannot tell you how gentle I was setting this trap.

We could now continue with our patrol around the headland. We headed down onto the beach area to look at the possibilities of them landing there. They looked very good; the beach was long and fairly shallow, no obstacles and covered in stones. Large stones and smaller stones. All worn round by the violent action of the South Atlantic. It was like being on Cape Wrath in Scotland. The sea was full of kelp. Big thick branches of solid kelp that might help defence. In fact, we decided it was our main defence.

More to the point was the huge whale-bone ribcage lying on the beach off to the left. At the top of the beach. This was good. I'd never seen one of these before and it was bizarre to walk down its spine through the ribs. I thought the ribs might come in useful for rigging overhead cover on the sanger. The bones were bleached white and picked clean of absolutely every morsel of flesh. Interesting yet practical. My perfect world. Makes you wonder how a huge great whale got itself this far up the beach. The storms must be vicious here. Wreck Point is a good name and very appropriate. We continued the patrol and logged the area.

On return, we introduced ourselves to the Rapier team, which was our main reason for being there. They were an Army Artillery outfit and seemed okay. Our job was to protect them, not necessarily be friends with them. Having left them, they drifted into obscurity.

Later on in the day we were attacked by aircraft. This was more like it. They didn't so much attack us – just on their normal route into Bomb Alley to our east. Up and back, same route as normal. One of the planes came very close, so close I could look down from my position with my camouflaged dirty face right into his cockpit and I clearly saw his clean face. It didn't dawn on me to shoot at him with my SLR. Probably because we had a huge set of four ground-to-air missiles on site ready to go. The pilot and I just briefly and impassively looked at each other as you would look at someone who was on a passing bus in the rain. He then banged over the controls to the left and away he went across the Sound. As he was accelerating away, the Rapier went off, *BABOOM!* and away went the missile. This was good, this was very good, in fact it was more than very good. We watched the trail of the rocket spiralling into the distance after its quarry, the spirals progressively getting smaller with distance gained. We held our breath and looked hard, not wanting to miss a thing, trying not to blink. I had never seen this before, none of us had. The excitement grew as we looked on, anticipation of a kill. The rocket went, the plane was going and the missile spiralled ... then a small explosion, like a puff, and the plane tumbled out of the sky. Jubilation. We leapt up and down hysterically slapping each other on the back, whooping and hollering. Almost as if we had something to do with it. Not bad shooting from the Rapier team. My private thoughts in hindsight were, 'I hope the pilot survived'. My thoughts at the time were completely indifferent. The fight was over and we had won. Not sure what 'we' had won. It wasn't our win, but we claimed it anyway. Reflected glory. This was all very new and we felt as if we were in the war a bit now. Just a tiny bit.

Observationally though, we were so remote here in our little position that if the Task Force had decided to go home and call it a day, like they might well have done, we could still be there. Waiting for something to happen a bit like those Japanese soldiers, discovered in the 1970s on the lonely Pacific islands not knowing that the Second World War had finished.

In our new location we still needed to do duties at night. The normal routines must be maintained. The duties here are even more important than at San Carlos because we're here all by ourselves and therefore can't rely on anybody else coming to help us. We are very vulnerable. The lads on the Rapier probably shouldn't be relied on in a fight so here we are, in charge of our own collective and individual destinies. We were not concerned really; this is an expected situation for a Royal Marine. Everything is supposed to be wrong, that's part of being a commando. Everything is supposed to be wrong and it's your job to salvage something out of it. Two guys go on duty at a time to be able to cover their arcs but more importantly to be able to keep each other awake and keep the wets on. This is a group decision. The nights are very long and very cold and extremely dark and it doesn't help being stuck up here on this exposed pimple in the full blast of the Antarctic wind and my goodness was it wet. So, it's good to have an oppo to talk to and drip all over during the long Falkland night hours.

Being in the valley was much warmer, drier and less windy. Up here it was cold, wetter and hurricane windy. It also seemed to have an overwhelming feeling of darkness about it. Not so much physical darkness, just an indescribable darkness. There was a physical darkness. It rained or threatened rain all the time. The other darkness was perceived only, but still had some reality.

Friday 28 May
Day 8
Did two duties last night, rained and wind all night. After stand-to made own bivvy, me and Terry went down to the beach to test-fire his weapon. Grenade was tripped by a little bird. Put up wire entanglement around area. At the moment I am in my bivvy the wind is up to 60 mph and sometimes raining. All kit wet. Now going out to build a sanger. Duty tonight.

As has been established, due to the very long nights and the short days, we had a lot of time to stand guard at night, especially when doubling up the guard. This is never the most pleasant activity of soldiering especially when it is blowing hard from the Antarctic and the rain is being pushed in horizontally, and the rain is so cold, almost sleet. These nights were a real pain, I'd like to give a stoic Englishman's response and say it was nothing, but it wasn't; it was definitely something, especially where we were, stuck out on a headland with no cover at all from any of these extreme elements. 'I'm going outside, I might be some time' was jokingly said many times; it didn't help but at least it did make everyone laugh. The enemy was not our primary consideration. We would deal with them when the time came. The elements were the real, and constant, enemy. The drill was to stand in the little sanger and try to keep warm as much as possible without compromising the effect of standing guard and keeping the surrounding area under constant surveillance.

The sanger was big enough for a few lads to get in it together. Ponchos were slung up to try to deflect the rain. Ponchos are mostly useless but they helped at this time. Even if it is 1 per cent helpful, then it is worth doing. When in these positions you seem to think only of the great times you've had or the good times you are going to have when all this malarky is finished. I am reassured that nothing has changed over the centuries, and I am sure every soldier who ever went to war thinks this way. Quite possibly the 'Universal Soldier' syndrome.

> *He's five foot-two and he's six feet-four*
> *He fights with missiles and with spears*
> *He's all of 31 and he's only 17*
> *Been a soldier for a thousand years*
>
> Donovan, 1965

Donovan had it right. Remarkably perceptive for a civilian. As far as our duties at night were concerned, they were worked out on a fairs-fair system. The nights were long enough so that one or two sets of people would get to have two duties. Our system worked in strict rotation, regardless. It was mechanically metronomic. My turn probably came up more regularly; it seemed good form. Last night I did two and it was painful getting out of the warm, dry sleeping bag or slightly damp or even wet sleeping bag that felt warm and dry, and putting on your wet gear in a windy rainstorm and then standing out in a downpour and feeling the freezing water run down your spine to your belt line – pure purgatory. The water would get to your belt line and fan out round your hips like the freezing fingers of Jack Frost as he gently caressed his hands around your midriff. There was nothing to do about it except live with it and keep smiling. We loved it. It was hard, but hard was good and hard was fun.

That unofficial anthem of 1982 coming from Monty Python's *Life of Brian* again. At the end of the film Jesus, or Brian, is on the cross and he and the two thieves start singing 'Always look on the bright side of life'. We always sang this when life became a bit painful. Consequently, it was sung often. We sang it in all situations, it always seemed appropriate. We were not the only ones looking on the bright side of life. It was an anthem for all the military. Thank you, Eric Idle, you kept the British military smiling and for that we thank you, sir.

The morning had crept painfully over the horizon again this morning. It was almost painful to watch it come up. It was hardly recognisable as having finally come up. We were soaked and uncomfortable. Not too much of a problem as this was still fairly normal for the life of a bootneck. Being wet for extended periods was our job. Being in considerable pain was our job. Smiling while doing it was also our job. We smiled. We sang. We had breakfast and started the day in earnest, slow but nonetheless, in earnest. The main task of each morning was to try to dry everything. Focus totally on this task to the exclusion of almost everything else. If a task is worth doing it is worth doing to the exclusion of all other things around you. All things must be done to 100 per cent of ability. No excuses.

At this time, I was not particularly happy with my personal sleeping arrangement and having been soaked through last night I decided to do something about it. Improvements could be made. Could always be made. Why stay wet and cold; that's not an option for a sustainable future. I checked out the whole area and my remedy was to dig into the vertical side of one of the small peat banks and to hollow it out so I had a small coffin-like chamber underground. The way in was horizontal and just big enough to crawl through on my belly. This had a poncho over the opening to stop wind and rain coming in. It worked perfectly and I was never cold and wet after this, at least in the sleeping environment. The inside of the chamber was tight, probably exactly like a coffin. But I wouldn't know yet. It was just big enough to cook in while lying down. The drawback was that crawling in and out was a dirty business, but this

9 Troop on the Islands. Company Sergeant Major Bill Howie on the left and Sergeant Nick Holloway on the right. Not all the Troop are present. (Troop collection)

Argentinian Marines. Battallon de Infanteria Marina 5 (5 BIM) Easter Day as Father Vicente Torres offers Mass. 3rd Section who occupied Sapper Hill are present. (Permission by Torres)

HMS *Ardent* comes alongside in the Atlantic. We cheer, they cheer and she fires her gun. We are impressed. (Adrian Brown)

Charlie Company, 40 Commando RM at Ascension. Not all the company are present. (Troop collection)

Gun line, Ascension Island with the volcanic dust. Front left Ged Herd then Brian Edmund and then Chris Pretty with fingers in ears. Sergeant Taff Lloyd RM standing. (Adrian Brown)

Adrian Brown, Matt Maloney and Dodger Humberstone on the gun line, Ascension Island. (Adrian Brown)

SBS hand-drawn map of San Carlos settlement. Given to us prior to landing; the perfect amount of information. (Chris Pretty)

After D-Day. San Carlos settlement and Brian Hobbs digs in again and again. (Adrian Brown)

Dodger Humberstone, Matt Maloney and Adrian Brown in their sanger on the Islands. These three men were more dangerous than all the soldiers on the Islands put together. (Adrian Brown)

Chris Pretty, Andy Gaunt and Alex Hepburn waiting … and waiting. The three 9 Troop lance corporals. Friends then and friends now. (Adrian Brown)

War is won by good admin. Joe Garcia pays close attention to his feet, again. The never-ending occupation of a professional soldier. (Adrian Brown)

Blending into a rock-run on a very cold day. Every day seemed like this. (Adrian Brown)

Matt Harris, Joe Garcia and Huey Reed wait. Ajax Bay below. It's a cold day again and something is about to happen. (Adrian Brown)

Matt Maloney, Dick Beasley and Corporal Ginge Wilkins just doing their job. (Adrian Brown)

Corporal Jono Johnson and Sergeant Nick Holloway RM prepare to move. Very heavy loads were the order of the day. Cripplingly heavy. Every day. (Troop collection)

Wreck Point sanger. Chris Pretty at the front and Ged Herd in the sanger. Falkland Sound is behind. It's not raining yet, but it certainly will. This circle of rocks is still visible on Google Earth. (Ged Herd)

Andy Pillar, Carl Bushby and team fly forwards on a Sea King helicopter. Forward to the front line at last. (Adrian Brown)

After 42 Commando assaulted Mount Harriet the prisoners were flown from the base of the mountain back to San Carlos. (Adrian Brown)

Sapper Hill. Argentine Marine's view of the battle. The vehicles are where 9 Troop were. Jono took this photograph in 2007. (Jono Johnson)

Sapper Hill. 9 Troop's view of the battle. View from the track, 9 Troop's drop-off point; it's now a proper road, but the ditches are still there. (Jono Johnson)

IN THE FIGHT. Ged takes a photograph as the bullets and bombs fly. Middle is Carl looking over his shoulder at me on the right. I'm sure this is the moment he talks to me. (Ged Herd)

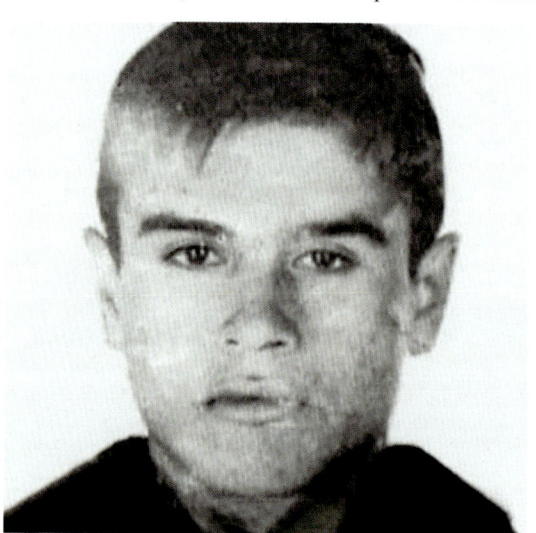

Above: Vince is injured badly. Wrapped in plastic with Graham Hill on the left, Andy Gaunt in the middle and Dee Irving on the right. Blood. (Troop collection)

Below left: Roberto LEYES. Killed in action at approximately 1.40 p.m. on Sapper Hill, 14 June 1982. (Public domain and permission from his family)

Below right: Eleodoro MONZON. Killed in action at approximately 1.50 p.m. on Sapper Hill, 14 June 1982. (Public domain and permission from his family)

Sergio ROBLEDO. Killed in action at approximately 2.15 p.m. on Sapper Hill, 14 June 1982. (Public domain and permission from his family)

Adolfo Gustavo CABRAL. Wounded in Action at approximately 2.10 p.m. on Sapper Hill, 14 June 1982 (Permission from his family)

Midshipman ALEJANDRO KOCH, one month after the end of the conflict. The head of the Navy awarded him the bravery medal HEROIC VALUE IN COMBATE (Permission from Alejandro Koch)

TERCERA SECCION DE TIRADORES

PRIMER GRUPO DE TIRADORES

300.	GUIM KOCH ALEJANDRO		JEFE DE GRUPO
301.	CC62 PEREYRA JUAN *Formosa* 4		RADIO OPERADOR *Pereira Juan Bautista*
302.	CC62 GONZALEZ JORGE *Oscar* 4		MENSAJERO *Chaco.*
303.	CC62 PEINEPOL RUBEN *René* 4		MENSAJERO *Falleció 13/09/11. Trelew.*

PRIMER GRUPO DE TIRADORES

304.	CSIM SINI CARLOS		JEFE DE GRUPO
305.	CC62 LEYES ROBERTO	4	JEFE DE PELOTON +
306.	CC62 PARED JUAN	4	APUNTADOR
307.	CC62 MIRANDA LIBERATO	4	AUXILIAR
308.	CC62 SANTANA JORGE	4	FUSILERO
309.	CC62 CABALLERO OSCAR	4	JEFE DE PELOTON
310.	CC62 BARBONA JUAN	4	APUNTADOR
311.	CC62 OJEDA CESAR	4	AUXILIAR
312.	CC62 ACOSTA PASCUAL	4	FUSILERO
313.	CC 62 CABRAL GUSTAVO	4	JEFE DE PELOTON *Herido*
314.	CC62 PORTILLO RAMON	4	APUNTADOR
315.	CC62 FERNANDEZ FRANCISCO	4	AUXILIAR
316.	CC62 DUARTE DANIEL	4	FUSILERO

SEGUNDO ~~CUERPO~~ *GRUPO* DE TIRADORES

317.	CSIM BENITEZ DANIEL		JEFE DE GRUPO
318.	CC62 LOPEZ ANTONIO	2	JEFE DE PELOTON
319.	CC62 LEIVA RICARDO	4	APUNTADOR
320.	CC62 BORDA PEDRO	4	AUXILIAR
321.	CC62 MARQUEZ SERGIO	4	FUSILERO
322.	CC62 TORRES ISMAEL	4	JEFE DE PELOTON
323.	CC62 FERMIN OLIVEIRO	4	APUNTADOR
324.	CC62 RODRIGEZ GABRIEL	4	AUXILIAR
325.	CC62 GONZALEZ SERGIO	4	FUSILERO
326.	CC62 CORDOBA FRANCISCO	4	JEFE DE PELOTON
327.	CC62 ROMERO ATILIO	4	APUNTADOR
328. 329.	CC62 MARTINEZ JUAN CC62 CONTRERAS VICTOR	4	AUXILIAR FUSILERO

Handwritten notes (right margin):

GPO AMET 7,62
JEPO. CSIM VARGAS M
APRROL OLBENEUYS
ABAST. RODRIGUEZ A
ABAST ROMERO ANG
+ ABAST ROBLEDO SERGI
PZA. AP: OJEDA JUAN
AU: GARCIA DE
ABT: PORTILLO
ABAST PIENEDMAN
FRE

Handwritten notes (bottom):

LZC 3,5"
PIEZA Z: MONZON ELEODORO +
CARG: OJEDA JUAN
PZA 3: SANCHEZ HORACIO
CARG: PONCE TITO

Argentinian Marine nominal list. Those Marines present on Sapper Hill on 14 June. To include Mario SALAS and Ramon CASTILLO. Official Document. (Marcos Basavilbaso)

Argentinian Marine nominal list. Casualties on 15 June at Sapper Hill. Official Document. (Marcos Basavilbaso)

San Carlos settlement for the final time. A scruffy Charlie Company embarks on the landing craft to leave the Islands. (Adrian Brown)

was a small price to pay for the warm dry comfort inside. Anyway, by now our smocks and trousers were becoming blessed by Nature. I was very content with my peat-bank Hobbit hole in the ground. My coffin, my warm Hobbit coffin.

Helly Hansen made blue thermal underwear. A popular Norwegian civilian outdoor company adopted by the commandos. Norway is the Corps' spiritual home and we had adopted many things Norwegian. I wore my HH Lifa top and leggings for the whole time of the war. They were most excellent. It was de rigueur in the Corps of the 1970s and 1980s and I am sure it saved me much pain.

Having completed and perfected the coffin, I went with Terry down to the beach at the north of the point, the one where we had found the whalebones, and we test-fired and zeroed his weapon again. Somehow it needed attention, so we got down to rectifying the problem. Once this was achieved, we decided to test the newly zeroed weapon out on the local sealife.

The large seals here were either leopard seals or at the very least they were great big fat ones, I'm not sure what they were actually. I must have missed that David Attenborough nature programme. I could imagine him here with us … in his hushed voice … 'and here we are … on the rugged islands watching for the leopard seal, this magnificent creature …' *Boom … boom … boom* away go the rounds speeding towards the heads of the bobbing sealife, bootnecks jumping around with joy at the prospect of a clean hit.

They were all very big seals and the leopard seals are particularly nasty, and big. We remembered. So, we tested our weapons on their bobbing heads as they floated innocently on the dark and freezing water about 100 metres offshore among the bulging kelp beds. I remember it well. We missed, but we did find a dead seal on the beach the next day. Not a leopard seal. Terry thinks we had shot it; I'm not so sure we were that accurate. I hope not and I seriously doubt it.

Later in the short daylight, I was on duty in the sanger, which we were constantly rebuilding and adapting. When we were three wets into a teabreak, we heard the muffled thud of the grenade exploding down in the gully. *Crump* … this was excellent. They were here, they were actually here, and we couldn't believe our luck. Let's go and get them! We threw on extra bandoliers and grenades and 66s and sprinted off to the gully ready for a punch-up. Someone took the gun team left to cover our movement and we thundered on to get there before the enemy commandos had time to reorganise themselves. The blood was up, the adrenalin was pumping and we were there to have a good go at them. I imagined, as I ran, that as we came over the lip of the gully we might be skylined, but there wasn't any time for that nonsense; we had a fight to start. We just needed to get there. Over the lip we ran, expecting the full force of enemy fire. Nothing, and nothing again, just silence. Where were they? Had they run? Were they hiding? Where was the injured or dead guy from the exploding grenade? We were collectively and professionally confused.

We would need to do a search. We split up and started to search the area for clues of where they might have gone. Searching down to the tripwire I saw just off to the right of the wire and lying on its back … a little bird, a tiny, little, unfortunate bird. It had obviously landed on the string close to the tin with the grenade, the grenade had plopped out and exploded, taking the bird away with it. I examined the bird; it looked completely whole except for a small hole in the back of its head. It was about the size of a small thrush. Maybe the size of a snipe. All this effort and we'd wasted it all on a small bird. We completed our search and then returned to our position, a bit deflated but having seen the funny side of it. That one small bird had cost me a grenade. 'This parrot's dead!' … 'No, it's resting.' It was a shame. It must be the only bird ever to die by hand grenade on the islands in the South Atlantic. Ever.

The search completed, we returned up the hill and continued to rebuild and modify our sanger. Modifications could always be made, so work always continued with the build. We put out wire entanglements inland from our position; it seemed logical. We had no idea how long we would be here, just like our last location. The weather persisted and we soon came to understand that a southerly wind was the worst. By far. It says 60mph winds. I would not have known 60mph winds then. It was a guess. Probably more, I would imagine. Another day passed on our island adventure. Darkness came early again and the routines of duties predictably started up. It was still wet and cold. Really wet and really cold, and now it was dark and wet and cold. Very dark.

Saturday 29 May

Day 9

My new bivvy is excellent. Two duties last night. It rained – cleared up by morning, however. The wind is now southerly and Antarctic – very cold. Dried my boots in the exhaust of the Rapier. At 15.30 two Mirages came past our position northwards up The Sound. Our Rapier hit the second, it peeled over and exploded. Airman ejected, four men gone to find him at the moment. 2 duties again tonight. A very cold night. Everything froze.

I was obviously very impressed with my first night's sleep in my new hole in the ground; what a way to carry on. It felt very comfortable and very dry. This was a palace. Compact and bijou.

Although all my gear got soaked yesterday, we soon worked out a routine to try to dry it all before nightfall. Life never got too bad with wet gear so long as that sleeping bag didn't get wet. That was definitely the last bastion of hope. If that got wet a Royal Marine just might 'wrap'. To 'wrap' is to 'wrap your hand in' or to chuck it all in, to give up. Wet sleeping bags could cause collective 'wrapping'.

With this in mind, it became obvious that we must constantly keep an eye on our gear to try to keep it serviceable. Admin, admin, admin. If one bit of gear doesn't work, it means you don't work either and here in this environment needless to say everything was covered in mud and soaked. We constantly cleaned things. Constantly repaired anything and everything. The good aspect about the Islands was that the weather did change very frequently, so the wind always blew at some time of the day during a sunny spell, not guaranteed but usually reliable. This meant that it was usually possible to find time during a day, ten minutes or so, when it was both dry and windy. If the tactical situation allowed, you immediately got all your wet kit out and spread it out on the diddle-dee and tried to dry it. This act would mean it was about to rain, so your gear would get wet again if you left it there unattended. But it usually worked if you attended to it. Admin it is called. Get your admin right and you'll probably win. Administration is a war winner. The only piece of gear we had problems with were our Cairngorm boots. They were very thick leather and double lined, so when they were wet through, they really were wet and almost impossible to dry. Most of the time you just lived with it and had either soaking feet or damp feet. We kept them clean and put dubbing on them constantly but they remained wet or damp. They're great bits of kit but required the constant attention that only a Royal Marine can give to his kit.

Terry remembers:

> I suffered from trench foot due to having wet feet from our initial landing at Blue Beach, in San Carlos Water. This was stopped by a visit from a medic on Wreck Point, East Island, who offered me some purple tablets (??) and told me to get them down my neck with anything drinkable. So, I did. A can of Guinness they had brought with the resupply; I was in a state of euphoria! We were also handed, to each and every Marine, a pair of dry Hawkins Cairngorm boots and wait for it, they were made of leather and completely waterproof (well up to the top of your ankles) and required no puttees.

That was the situation until we found that the Rapier missile post had a small generator and out of that generator came an exhaust pipe and out of the exhaust pipe came hot air, very hot air and lots of it. This was not a place to waste hot air. This meant that we could leave our Cairngorms under the exhaust until they were dry. This worked brilliantly and when put back on they were very warm, which then might cause chilblains but it worked. Admin, admin, admin.

Later in the day we had some more visitors in the shape of Argentine Mirage jets. They came on the same path as the one yesterday; we looked at each other again but this time the Rapier was faster. The Argentine pilots were using the same route. It is a tactical rule that a soldier should never use the same route. If you do you become predictable and a predictably obvious target. This applied to the planes in Bomb Alley. Always the same route. I was stood on the lip of the sanger watching what was going on. Buck was with me standing as though we were at a Crown Green Bowls event in Eastbourne, hands in pockets and studying the form. The planes came past, as normal we looked, they looked, as normal ... and *Baboom* ... the Rapier fired again, the missile passing between the two of us and went spiralling off after the jets just as before. This near miss was cause for hilarity again. I don't remember us being too pleased with this but the show had started so we just needed to watch what the outcome would be. Slightly jangled nerves now very quickly restored to normal; the outcome was predictably the same: the plane exploded. One got away but the unfortunate second pilot floated down to earth on his parachute. Four guys went off to find the unfortunate pilot but couldn't locate him. Poor bloke. We informed those that needed to know and forgot about him.

The invincibility we had experienced over the previous week was definitely taking a bit of a shake. There was still no doubt we would win the war, but whether we would be here when it ended was another consideration. It just looked a little less certain now. Too many other people were dying, which must affect the overall odds. Statistically thinking. Evidence was mounting against us and slimming the odds. At the time it was a thought, but not enough of a thought to make any difference. We were still invincible. We had green berets and they automatically made us invincible. We were reasonably sure of this now. Maybe unreasonably.

Tonight was the first of the really cold nights when everything froze solid. This meant that it was inadvisable to leave gear around or even just by itself under cover. It would freeze solid. We always slept with our boots on or with them tucked one under each armpit, or at the bottom of the sleeping bag so they weren't frozen in the morning. If they froze the outcome was self-inflicted pain with no sympathy. Just hilarity.

A clean rifle is the next most important object; actually, it is just as important as boots. As a soldier you are useless in war if you haven't got a rifle that works. This needed to be cleaned several times a day and it was a practice in the Corps to constantly check your weapon for dirt, and I mean constantly. Early onset of OCD and training at the Commando Training Centre Royal Marines teaches you that. Your weapon is your baby and you treat it with tender loving care. Happy, and extremely early predawn, cold Saturday mornings on the endurance course back in basic training comes to mind. Be a clean Marine. If nothing else … then just be clean.

Now with boots cleaned and organised and my weapon cleaned, lightly oiled and duly loved and caressed, I only needed to sort out all the rest of my equipment. This was in three main pieces. The first was the chest webbing, the second the fighting order and the third was my Bergen. There was a quirky nature to our personal equipment. Highly personalised and highly prized. An inordinate amount of time was spent on the creative perfecting of personal kit.

The chest webbing was a set of pouches that hung around the shoulders and as it suggests, it covers your chest and finishes just under each arm pit. Mine carried six spare magazines for my SLR, a survival kit, a small first aid kit, two grenades, a compass and some chocolate (nutty) bars. This chest webbing was worn under my fighting order, which in turn went around my waist so if I needed to jettison my larger and heavier fighting order, I could do it without affecting my ability to continue the fight without sufficient supplies but carrying less weight. That fear of not having enough ammunition again. This was a homemade design and made by Mac McAndrews based on an SBS design.

The fighting order, or webbing, or belt order, goes around the waist and has a yolk that acts as kind of braces, which go over both shoulders. This spreads the load to the shoulders and is usually about 35lb in weight in peacetime, or in training, but had now increased to about 55–60lb, probably more. It is a simple equation of war: whatever you wear in peacetime, just increase the load by double and that is what you will carry on campaign. On the belt I had two sets of Northern Ireland pouches, which are flat and can only carry one magazine per pouch, which meant four in all, these replacing the normal '58-pattern magazine pouches. I always found the NI pouches to be more accessible than the cumbersome regulation '58-pattern pouches, which I had never liked. '58-pattern webbing would swell with water and then retain the water, therefore increasing the weight of the whole thing. I also had two '44-pattern water-bottle pouches, one with mug and water bottle and the second with a rolled-up Arctic reversable waterproof in. We did not bother with waterproof trousers; they are too much aggravation and make too much noise at night when yomping and patrolling, really not tactically acceptable. Not acceptable at all. I had a '58-pattern magazine pouch for my Clansman PRC 349 radio and another for my rations for twenty-four/forty-eight hours. I carried a big Marines Gollock survival knife, a karabiner and a toggle rope and a bayonet. Fighting orders are very personal and adding other bits to it is quite normal. There is no rule. The rule is 'to adapt'.

There is a long-established love affair between the British soldier and his bayonet. One that has lasted the tests of time and the Nuclear Cold War age. But it is definitely a 'significant' relationship. The bayonet is also known to the Geneva Convention. This is the international agreement setting out the rules that we, the British, are governed by when playing war. This does not necessarily mean that the other side has agreed to those same rules. It could also be seen as agreed moral rules for warfare. It seems to be the way of the British that we socially require rules to play by. The apparent ruling regarding bayonets is that your bayonet should not be rusty, dirty or sharpened. We stuck to the rules. I would like to say everyone stuck to the rules, but this may not have been the case.

Our final piece of gear was a Berghaus Roc Bergen. A 75-litre military green, one-compartment, civilian rucksack that the Corps had adopted and had used extensively in the 1970s. Mostly proved in the Arctic. It proved to be the best for the kind of work that commandos do. The Marines had been using them for years before the Falklands crisis and they were tried and tested and were loved by all. It was a superbly sturdy piece of kit that, through time, had thoroughly moulded to my back, even though it was a bit dog-eared and tired. The other option was the Cresta Sac. A framed sac of strong canvas. An SBS-preferred piece of kit, strong and reliable, it could take immense loads. I left mine at home and brought my Roc. All the gear was painted in dark colours with light brown and red streaks to break up the outline of the equipment and match the colours of the diddle-dee. The paint also waterproofed the fabric to some extent. Total all-up weight of our equipment was about 160lb and quite probably more. The weight was inconsequential as a number and was never discussed. It still isn't. It was just more than normal. Numbers become competitive and that is not helpful. It was just immensely heavy.

Such a large weight would mean that staying upright on your feet was of great significance. To get onto your feet required one or two other guys to pull you up. However, the ground was difficult, muddy, tussocks, heather, rivers, rock-runs … most of the time. Falling over did become a bit of a pastime. There were many 'unnecessary rocks'[2] in the Falklands, which made progress very hard when off any of the very few tracks. There are no footpaths. It's tracks or wild. Very few tracks and much wild.

The ground was made up of three main types of terrain. Tussock grass looked just like normal long grass (18+ inches high) but was in fact large clods of tightly knitted humps of grass that had a hidden drop of about a foot on every side of each tussock. Sometimes more. If you missed standing right on the centre of the tussock you slipped down the side and your leg would disappear. This was often mixed with diddle-dee. A large form of heather. Good insulation for sleeping on. Rock-runs were deposits of varying-sized rocks and boulders that streamed down from the tops of mountains and hills. Very unnecessary. Rivers of rocks. Vast rivers of unnecessary rocks. They were sometimes very wide, about 100 metres or more across, and always hugely long. Kilometres long. Complex ground. Walking round them was not an option, it took too much time. Falling between the rocks, especially at night, created a substantial issue and would always cause much giggling at the poor unfortunate who could find himself upended in the rocks and pinned there by the weight. Bogs seemed to be everywhere where the rock-runs and tussock grass were not. This made life difficult too. Good ground, dry, short grass, easy ground was also part of the landscape but we didn't seem to be on this very much now. We had left that behind at the San Carlos shoreline. Short grass was a settlement-only landscape.

Another day had passed and it seemed as though we were going to be stuck here now, miles from anywhere and freezing to death. The other two sections were to our south and we wondered how they were coping. We were left alone. This was generally a good state of affairs, we all agreed.

More duties tonight. The weather stayed the same. Wet and very windy.

---

2. I had been talking about this book to a school group. Chloe decided that the term 'unnecessary rocks' was appropriate. It made me smile, so here it is.

Sunday 30 May

Day 10

A very cold morning all frozen. Now writing this in my bivvy with a small fire going. I am absolutely filthy, my hair is matted and I'm covered in grime. My breakfast was rolled oats. The Rapier team have been told they will leave the location within 24 hrs. 'What a way to spend a Sunday'. Afternoon 19.10 hrs, been for a climb down on the cliffs with Ged. It is still very cold. On duty in OP at 20.30. Tes has just arrived with a wet – goodo. There was one red alert today, but no aircraft sighted. Goose Green has been taken by 45 and the Paras. 1,200 prisoners, 20 dead, quite a few casualties ourselves. Only one duty to do tonight.

The cold weather has really got here now, just as predicted. Summer at home is winter down here. The wind turned again to a southerly direction and blew straight from the Antarctic and the temperature also edged further south. My bivvy hole is proving to be excellent and I have managed to get the small hexiblock fire going inside. When lit, the temperature shot up and I managed to exist in reasonable comfort, well as much as someone can when they are living in a coffin-sized hole underground. Rabbits manage it, Hobbits seem to manage it. I will manage it. The remaining insignificant inconvenience of living in a hole was that of getting in and out. This had to be done on my belly and this was getting me filthy, small problem as I have said and nothing to bother about. However, I have mentioned it twice so maybe it was a problem after all.

Breakfast was the normal rolled oats. These were excellent sachets of porridge that when mixed with some raisins and sugar from the ration packs and other little odds and ends actually resulted in a surprisingly good meal. Breakfast was an important occasion, as were all mealtimes and wet stops. It is funny how the importance of food and drink as a ceremony becomes so magnified in a conflict. It may be something deeply rooted in a soldier. It is not really the food; it is the comforting process of producing hot food with friends. It is the fellowship. It is much, much more.

We had started taking our afternoon tea at 4 o'clock in the afternoon, which had become a regular event, attended by nearly everyone. In the sanger we would gather and huddle up in the wind and rain, stick a brew on and tell inappropriate stories about Winnie the Pooh. These were fun times, bizarre but fun, and we roared with laughter. The stories became more bizarre as people participated and extended the story. If someone were to make a movie about these situations, it would make for a very peculiar and curious scene. I presume this is nothing new. Men in a trench sharing tea and Tiffin chocolate bars and laughing about the utterly ridiculous is probably extremely normal. The game was to keep the spirits up at whatever cost. I wondered what Andy and Jono were doing. Probably exactly the same.

After ten days being ashore it was plain that the section was stronger than it had previously been. Probably ever been. The conditions were manageable and in most situations, everything was quite normal. Mental adjustments had been made and accepted, but clearly the section were physically and mentally stronger and coping really well. Life was on a new trajectory of normal but this wasn't disagreeable.

Ged and I went for another small patrol today, more of a familiarity patrol to see if anything had changed. A scrounging trip. Maybe just something to do. Kit on, checked our weapons and set off down the re-entrant to the beach and then north and westwards around the cliffs. The weather was windy with wet patches. A grey day. A dark day. The cliffs became more sheer and then complete rock. Dark and forbidding. At one point they looked suitable to climb. I had done quite a bit of climbing in my life, with the Corps and in my spare time. I slung my weapon over my back and started off up a route. It was a good one, not too hard but I was carrying all my kit just in case we were bumped while I was halfway up the cliff. I felt great satisfaction to be the first person ever to have climbed on that route; maybe I should have claimed it as a first ascent. I am quite sure I am the only person ever to have climbed there and probably ever will be. That's cool. It was good to do something that had nothing at all to do with soldiering. I came back down by another, easier route and we continued round on our patrol. Nothing seemed to have changed but there were new washed-up items on the rocky shore. Some would be useful for the sanger. We took it all.

By my notes we heard today that 45 and the Paras had just taken Goose Green. In hindsight Goose Green was taken by 2 Para. 45 Commando were nowhere near it. However, again this clearly indicates that the buzz in war is most often incorrect. 'Old wrinkled blanket' syndrome probably. I would never seek to take the glory from 2 Para; it was their fight. But the buzz is usually incorrect, and it was then.

At this stage we were all in a bit of a state. After this amount of time in these conditions our kit was beginning to suffer. Shaving and keeping clean was a significant problem, but was sufficiently maintained to reasonable standards. Still there is no reason to be squeaky clean. So long as all our kit and our rifles worked, that was all we were concerned about. The equipment that needed to be clean was clean. The equipment that wasn't, wasn't. Maintenance and admin again. All day, every day. Discipline and a hard discipline are the answer. Admin. Once you have completed that admin, find some more to do.

The general attitude was changing. Minutely shifting. Almost unrecognisable. Efficiency and discipline were the key. Feelings were irrelevant and discarded. I didn't even consider the casualties 45 were supposed to have taken, not for one moment. Days ago, I would have asked the obvious questions. This war was now full on. A hardness had enveloped us all. Caring for nothing but daily routine and those immediately close to us. Things were getting a little bit harder. Some will recognise this military saying: 'Just stay on the log … stay on the log.'

Chapter 4

We'll Be Home by Christmas

You always want me to give up something. What do you want me to give up now?

Ernest Shackleton's last words

Monday 1 June
Day 11
'Happy Birthday, Annabel'. Stand to was very cold hail and all sorts. It was so cold I had to make my breakfast in my bivvy. Small nap. Captain Pillar arrived by chopper said something and roared off again. Apparently we are staying here now. Weather is very cold and very windy with some sun. Laid barbed wire this afternoon. Now a threat of airborne assault, should be interesting in this wind.

It's June the 1st and my sister Annabel's birthday. For some strange reason I only ever remember her birthday out of all the extended family. The nights were getting progressively and noticeably colder and this morning was another particularly cold morning. We were not only at the end of the world, but also at the end of the end of the world. We could well have been the most isolated section at this time on the Islands. It certainly felt that way, and we loved it.

Captain Pillar, Andy, turned up in a chopper after breakfast. The rotors kept turning. He gave us some information and some encouragement, grinned then jumped back on the chopper and headed off. He had a whole company to see and presumably we were spread out over a very large area. He gave the impression of a frustrated man not being able to get to where the action was, and where he wanted to be. Where he needed to be. His natural environment. We fully reflected his frustration.

He dropped some supplies off for us, more twenty-four-hour ration packs. This was a success for the section. High spirits. Lots of smiling from him and lots of smiles beamed back at him. We were all happy with our limited lot. He told us that there was a very real threat of an airborne assault on the beachhead area in San Carlos. That was questionable with the constant high winds and having to fly through all our air defences to get here. It sounded implausible. We gave it its due attention. Some of us were para trained and we appreciated the problems that they would face should they try such a stunt. It seemed unlikely. We took it on board and then considered the realistic options. Commando raids were more likely in our minds. We discussed this and thought they would land some sort of commando force – it seemed more logical. But still they didn't come. What on earth were they doing? What on earth were we doing? We were just stuck in this remote landscape. Limited information, limited food, cold, wet. Just existing. Exactly how we liked it. The world was perfect.

The weather was its usual changeable self but not too unpleasant; we were getting used to its patterns and we began predicting the next change, and sometimes we were correct. The weather was our main pastime. An all-consuming permanent consideration. We were getting used to it. However, we were still at the very rear of the Task Force. We were even behind the Royal Navy. It seemed everyone had gone forward towards the enemy. Still, never mind, maybe we should be glad we were not getting shot at and be grateful.

When Andy Pillar came, the chopper must have dropped off some barbed wire for us. That was nice and considerate and maybe in recognition of the impending airborne assault. We took this as seriously as we could and started to put out the wire in the areas where we thought the Argentine commandos would come. Not high wire but quite low to stop them crawling up to us. There was not enough wire so we had to be clever. This kept everyone busy. Barbed wire is a complex beast. It really does not want to do what you want it to do. It has an agenda all of its own. The result is inevitably holes all over your smock and trousers. At least we had some proper thick leather gloves/gauntlets delivered too. The wire was set and seemed very permanent. They won't get through that one individual line of barbed wire. It was not lost on us how utterly daft this was. We giggled lots about it. The days continued to be short and the nights continued to be long and cold and wet. Duties again in the rain and wind. Nothing new. In fact, now getting possibly depressingly the same. So much the same that there was little to differentiate the days.

Tuesday 2nd June
Day 12
2 duties last night very cold morning, had breakfast outside however. Had wash and shave, my head is clean. Went on small yomp/patrol around north Wreck Point. Found a grounded missile, reported it back to Tp HQ. Curry for tea, OK. 2 duties again tonight. Rapier here still, we may be here a couple more days. Today was warmer as the wind now from NW and not south.

The dawn crawled slowly over the horizon again. Last night went by with two more cold and wet duties coming my way. Everyone is accepting this established routine. We don't really have a choice, but we do have a choice whether it is insufferable. Another very cold morning. Most of us managed to have a reasonable wash and shave today. Breakfast as normal. This routine seems to be some sort of a rut we are getting into.

Another patrol today, again looking for the enemy, or any sign of them. By this time though it was all wearing a bit thin. We were getting a bit frustrated with our static life. The patrol of four of us went off around the head again. Went further this time. Somewhere down the west side of the point we found a grounded missile in the diddle-dee. It didn't look like one of ours. No English writing on it. I drew a sketch of it in my notebook and we logged where it was. It was about 6 feet long. It had landed pointing north-ish. Using the PRC349 radio, we radioed into our boss, Carl, and told him what we'd found. We were bored and I'm sure the Boss was as well, but it was all we needed as a plausible excuse for inane chatter and sharing information on the radio. It was good to talk to someone new. The day closed with no more activity. A whole day passed with practically no significant activity except established routines. A soldier's life.

What more is there to say. Night came and the relentless duties continued. Every night when there was a clear patch in the cloud cover you could see the satellites coming over nice and slow and steady on a straight course. On a previous military intelligence course about Russian satellites, I had been told that they could take a close-up photo of a cigarette packet all the way from space. Why they would want to photograph a fag packet was beyond us but we giggled about it. We didn't have any Benson & Hedges so every time they came over we dropped our trousers and mooned at them. At this stage boredom meant we could laugh at anything and needed to laugh at anything. We thought the Kremlin would appreciate it. привет пацанам в кремле.

Our isolation may well have been starting to affect us.

> **Wednesday 3 June**
> *Day 13*
> It's 19.45hrs and the sun is out and there is no wind. It's beautiful. This morning it just rained and rained, then it changed. Capt Pillar came today gave us mail, I got five. He also said we're not going to Stanley, everyone's very angry but we're going home soon, some hope!! Anyway the Army Rapier is leaving and an RAF Regiment Rapier is coming instead. CO is coming tomorrow. 2-man tents are supposed to be coming.

Rain, rain and more rain. Andy Pillar came again today and gave us some even worse news, just in case we were maintaining our morale at a level too high for comfort. It is confirmed, we are not going to Stanley. Huge disappointment from the section. As if to offset this news he also said that we would be going home soon. This is a good piece of news but we don't really believe it. We don't want to go home, we want to go forward, please. Depression sets in. He flies off. It continues raining. The days have just got a little bit blacker. The future is bleak. Wreck Point is bleak.

We are sat in the sanger dripping and Ged is about to put a wet on. The tea ceremony starts. The area where he is cooking is a specific area we had constructed, like a small kitchen area. Made of rocks and peat blocks. Just in front of the area is where all the ammo is stored. Maybe not the best thinking, in hindsight. With the ammo are a couple of 66 rocket launchers, a few grenades, some Schermuly flares and other bits and pieces including thousands of rounds of ammunition.

Ged starts his fire and is wearing some big Arctic mitts just to keep his hands warm. We sit in a dishevelled state off to his left and away from the door and out of the wind. Ged fumbles and accidentally knocks over his brew, goes to grab it and sets fire to his oversized Arctic mitts. We burst out laughing and roll around giggling. Ged shouts and screams as the fire spreads; we laugh louder. Ged tries to beat out the flames by flapping his hands on the rocks, which doesn't work and we howl with laughter. The cooker is knocked over in the melee and falls in among the ammo and 66s and grenades, and we laugh louder. Ged changes tack and flaps his hands on his chest to try to beat out the flames; his chest bursts into flames and we nearly die. Ged nearly dies. Ged, with his big Pancho Villa moustache, is going up like a Mexican bonfire and the ammo is about to blow up too. We are all uncontrollably having a choking fit. The risk is finally identified and someone jumps up and kicks the ammo away before it ignites and 'cooks off' and kills us all. Someone else puts Ged out and we continue chuckling on the floor of the sanger. Ged is put back to normal, only slight fire damage, but what a superb laugh! We needed that. A replacement wet is successfully made and we carry on laughing all day. Ged learns to laugh about it.

Andy Pillar says that there are two-man tents coming for us. They have got to be joking. We have never used two-man tents before, not unless you were really up north, or a REMF. I'll believe it when I see it and I bet they don't come. Part of me doesn't want to be insulted by them arriving. Besides we're commandos – we don't use tents. However, if they do arrive, we will use them, of course. He also said that the Army Rapier is going to be redeployed and the RAF Regiment is going to replace them. We are indifferent to this news. Apparently, the CO, Malcolm Hunt, is coming tomorrow. We have heard that he is really not happy that we are not going forward. He's a good bloke, he'll get us forward. If anybody can, he can. More importantly the mail arrived today. I got five letters. Read them, passed them round and burnt them. Letters from Mum and Dad, Granny, local neighbours, that sort of thing. We can reply by writing a 'Bluey'. This is a pre-stamped blue letter for military people. They are free. Write your letter and send it. Apparently, Dad kept my mud-stained letters for years, but they have vanished now. Maybe he burnt them too.

The day goes by and night comes on with all the usual duties and procedures. The days are uneventful now. This is just turning into a survival exercise on this exposed point. However, some of the nights are really clear and you feel as though you can see the whole solar system and everything in it. Peculiarly during the war, you always felt as though the inexplicable could happen. A curious but exciting feeling.

On one of these nights just such an interesting, and inexplicable occurrence happened. I was on duty with Ged and we were stargazing the clear sky when we saw a peculiar sight. A sight I have never seen since. From the south-west two slow lights came across the sky one slightly behind the other almost in a formation, keeping a slow constant speed on a direct course. We watched them come, not very quickly, but at a measured speed, constant. Maybe helicopters, maybe satellites. Then they just suddenly stopped absolutely still in mid-air. They did not slow down to stop; it was a sudden stop. Immediate. No deceleration. They stayed there static for a short while; we looked, our eyes narrowed and we concentrated. We looked at each other. Raised eyebrows. They stayed there for a few seconds then without warning or any acceleration, they sped off at right angles to their previous course at an alarming, immediate speed. From standing still to instant super-speed. No acceleration. We just looked at each other and said something like, 'Good grief, what was that?' How does something do that, go to flash speed from standstill. We discussed it until we were bored and decided to leave it alone. We had no answers. We couldn't even speculate; we weren't that clever. The strangeness of this war was increasing. When on duty at night, sometimes you see the weirdest, inexplicable things. The speed they accelerated away at was as if you put your right arm up in the air out straight and point above you. Then as fast as you can take your arm from vertical to horizontal. That was the speed. But faster. This goes in the weird file and is left alone, and we didn't mention it again. If it was flying saucers from outer space, then I'm sure they were far too intelligent to land here and get involved with this silliness. They go, we stay, it rains and we shrug our shoulders and move on. Total indifference. Strange, but curiously not so strange in these particularly strange days.

During this time, we gave some thought to our enemy. What were they doing now? They must have been suffering as much as we were. The unswerving assurance that we would win was still intact. We would just stay here in our isolation until something really happened. Something would happen, that was sure. What that 'thing' would be was a total mystery, but it would happen.

Thursday 4 June
Day 14
Two duties done again last night, very misty and wet. Moved position 500m north to where the RAF Rapier is. Built new trench and new bivvy. Resupply came today of apples, beer, mail, bread, water and rations. Everyone's morale went sky-high. On duty only once tonight. CO was supposed to arrive but obviously didn't bother, got mail off Sarah, Mr Betty + 2 from Gom + comforts.

We have been on the Islands for two weeks and we are getting used to the idea that our chances of being involved with this war were pretty slim, and probably getting slimmer. We are destined to be observers and passengers in this punch-up. Fatalism's dark tendrils begin to slip into all of us. Last night was wet and miserable, which is normal on our very own and exposed Wreck Point. It is very definitely 'ours' now. We have spent more time here than any human being in history, so we claim it as ours. Belonging to us by possession rights. By the time morning came we were soaking wet with no way of getting dry. No war and now wet and cold and hungry; oh, what a luverly war! The army have gone and the RAF are on site now and have settled in. They are new to this location and there is much to learn about our shared isolation. They look just like the last lot. They select a slightly different location to the army, of course. We therefore have to move to protect them.

The tactical considerations had changed a bit with the change of location for the Rapier system. Dee thought we should move all the barbed wire as well, to protect the new position. This may well have not been the soundest judgement at the time. Tactically sound but not right just at this moment when everyone was in a dark place. Buck and Terry took great offence to this and suggested a better way of dealing with this situation. It would not have ended well for Dee and it was less than helpful too. Diplomacy was needed. Bootneck diplomacy. The situation was resolved but strong words had been said and fists brandished and used. The rebellion was quashed. Time was sluggish now. Time was depressing. I reckoned it was a reaction to being left behind, and the timing of the decision was probably wrong anyway. The boys went back to work and moved the wire a couple of hundred metres, and I watched to see if someone got the urge to 'thank' Dee in his own delicate bootneck way. They thankfully didn't. Wire was moved and we moved on too.

Now everything had moved and we had new trenches, better than before. The section has become extremely proficient at digging trenches and applying the gained experience to sensible trench design. Protection is paramount but now design becomes more of a feature. The boys in Flanders in 1917 would have been proud of us. We maintained the sanger. It was on the only good tactical position. The trenches were more built-up protection, but perfectly constructed from a tactical point of view. More important than anything was the resupply that came today by chopper. Food had been getting short. Fresh rations, what a treat. Fresh rations of white sliced bread and some apples. Also, Guinness beer in cans. Not many but enough. We couldn't believe it. We had some fags delivered, but most of us didn't smoke. The boys had to request fags from the REMFs and they'd be brought up for them. What we didn't know was that apparently their pay was being docked for each packet. A disgusting habit for weak-willed people. But the fresh fruit and bread were excellent and as I didn't smoke, I couldn't have cared less about fags and money, unless they were charging us for fresh rations, and of course that might have also been a possibility.

We heard later on, through a very unqualified buzz, that we didn't get fresh vegetables because it was being hoarded back at the unit QM's department. Apparently one of the guys from our Company HQ stores went back and went into one of the storeman's rooms and the place was full to the ceiling with fresh rations, and this was the first time we had got any. The Quartermaster's Store would often say, 'Stores are for storing; if they were for issuing, they would be called issues'. This was a non-substantiated buzz and could well have not been true. It may even have been a bite. We bit. We bit badly. Being good and well-trained survivalists and knowing how important it is to spread your calories out and keep some rations for future days, we ate the lot in one sitting. We felt better for it. Anyway, we had no idea what was going to happen tomorrow. Probably nothing if we were involved. We were starting to learn to live for the day, live in the day only. Tomorrow will take care of itself.

The mail was good. I had a nice letter from Sarah, my high-school sweetheart. As usual everybody read the letter. We all read each other's letters. It was normal protocol. If it was very personal then it would not be shared. Then it got burnt with everyone else's. I also got one from Mr Betty, Mum and Dad's neighbour who was a Falkland Islander by birth. He was a nice chap and I appreciated his letters. They all got burnt.

Gommy sent some more comforts; crikey, this was like the Western Front. Off with one dirty, manky wool hat and on with a clean, new one. Replacement wool gloves, perfect. They weren't anything to look at but they were warm, and no one cared. I remember she made a very complicated set of brown wool gloves. They were fingerless mitts but with a wool cover that you could pull over the end of your fingers. Just a bit complicated for a Marine, but eventually I cracked it. It was a miracle that they were of normal size and shape. Normally Gommy would knit something and all the sleeves would be lopsided; I say sleeves because it was not beyond her to produce a sweater with two neck holes and three arms and no waist. Even though she probably exhibited the family dyslexia genes in her knitting, they were appreciated by everyone. As a section we are starting to look very … 'woolly' in that very camp 1960s pattern kind of way.

This really was rapidly turning into the survival exercise you would easily imagine. Every day of rain and high winds was making life just a little bit harder. Not unbearable but it required more time to deal with admin and keep everything clean and tidy. We had the time fortunately. That sluggish time of bored people who really want something interesting to happen. That was one thing we had plenty of, time. Days were coming and going. We were here and we were definitely not going anywhere soon. Oh, the static life of a commando.

Friday 5 June
Day 15
Been here two weeks today and am not impressed, wind has picked up, now writing this at 20.00 in torrential rainstorm, all huddled in bivvy singing songs and being too happy. Went for a dhobi in stream, stripped off and jumped in, nearly died. Got resupply but no mail, the rain here is just too much. Duty once tonight, thank goodness.

We thought life had got darker being up here on the Point. However, the really dark days had now started. This was the start of some serious continuous torrential rain that seemed to last for days. It never stopped for a second. With the rain came the lashing wind. All the kit was wet but the work routine still had to be carried out even in these conditions. Working parties, patrols and duties still needed to be achieved. It just made it a little bit less inviting. There is a very unhelpful saying in the military when it is raining: 'Skin is waterproof', said in an offhand, flippant way. Utter bullpoop. It is not helpful and not particularly funny when you are soaked and cold. Skin is not waterproof. Talk to anyone who has had trench foot. Trench foot is a constant worry. It is alternatively known as Immersion Foot. You know when you sit in a bath for too long and your skin crinkles up. Imagine the water you are sitting in is infected. Your crinkling becomes more serious and then your skin splits, allowing the infection in. Disaster then ensues. This must be avoided at all costs. Foot admin is done several times a day. Clean socks, foo foo powder, gentle manipulation of feet. Arctic socks, white, thick and with a red strip at the ankle. Perfect socks for soldiers. Boot care is similar. It all takes time. It is time well invested and is essential. Many lads suffered from this. Sometimes it is uncontrollable. Apparently, Si Poole let Sponner put his bare feet under his armpits to warm them up. This was not unusual, just illustrative.

I remember this day well. I remember it better than most days during the war. The cloud hung low and heavy and forbiddingly dark. Everything seemed to be constantly verging on twilight conditions. The wind was up and I decided that after so many days in the field it was time to treat my body to a dhobi, some sort of serious wash. I knew there was a small stream some distance away so I went with Terry and Ged with all our fighting kit. I forgot it was nearly an Antarctic winter and stripped off naked, ready for a dhobi. The wind blew hard and the skies threatened more downpour. I refused to be deterred and jumped into the tiny stream. Jumped may be optimistic. I ended up under the water and the crimping pain was instant. It was like being gripped in a vice. I left the water at great speed. I remember seeing the lads falling over and clutching their sides, laughing at my obvious stupidity. Having soaped myself and washed my hair, all in about three seconds, I was done. All done and turning shades of blue and purple, the lads dragged me back to my bivvy, dumped me in and made a wet for me. They continued laughing for many hours. I was glad I had brought so much happiness and obvious mirth into their dirty lives. Cleanliness was achieved. Partially. Clean Marine.

This day was the wettest day of the war so far, on this exposed Antarctic point. Some resupply came but it was inconsequential. This is where war becomes mostly waiting. Waiting and surviving and preparing. Whoever can do this best will win. I presumed the rest of the Troop were in exactly the same position. We weren't unhappy. Actually, we were very happy. It was just the harsh conditions. Laughing and joking was still the thing we did best. It was wet and it was miserable. The rain lashed in on high Antarctic winds. But it was still a good day. And we laughed.

Saturday 6 June
Day 16
Wind has died down, put wire out front. CO turned up and said we'd be here till mid-July. Not impressed, no one is. New two-man tents arrived, me and Bri put one up. One very boring day. Much hard work done.

Wreck Point had clearly become our home. We didn't object. It was good to be autonomous and we were in the best of company. Lionel Terray (1961) was a great climber and he created the term *Conquistadors of the Useless*. The title of his book. This applied to us here. The wind had noticeably died down today, which was a welcome change. Still wet though. So much rain in the last few days had soaked the ground to saturated bog conditions. We continued to put barbed wire out and in the middle of this chore the CO, Malcolm Hunt, turned up. We were always glad to see him but this day he did not have good news for us. In fact, he said we would be here until mid-July. The boys are not impressed, in fact we are all 'harry-threaders' about the whole thing. An air of permanence and being totally lost comes over us and to emphasise the insulting point he has brought us the small two-man tents that were promised. This just emphasises the permanence of our sad situation. The sentiment was not lost on us. The tents were an excellent idea except it made us feel like we had really become REMFs. We might be in danger of consolidating our state of permanence if we put them up. Of course, it was a very good thing to do, and ultimately we appreciated it, but it didn't help our solitude and the feeling that we had been left behind. Forever. Useless.

As he landed in his chopper, the downdraft lifted all our bivvies and kit up in the air. This did not help. What more can go wrong? And God looked down on us and said, 'Plenty yet, my son.' Maybe they trashed our bivvies on purpose so it would encourage us to use the tents. The situation made us laugh even more than normal. Hysteria might set in, you know.

The tents were a new addition to us as commandos. Welcome, but new. The section area started to look like *MASH* from the TV, except on a smaller two-man-tent-sized scale. We had not been given tents before; this was new and not really commando-ish stuff and maybe even a bit insulting. Maybe even humiliating. They were just the upper part of the tent. No groundsheet. Made of heavy green canvas and small. With two wooden poles about 3 feet long for each end. The wind whistled under the edges. However, we soon learnt to appreciate them. We embraced the opportunity to humiliate ourselves. But it was practical and that trumps everything. As it says in my log entry, it was a very boring day. Even by our latest standards. By this time, we were filthy dirty and our future had been taken away. This was a day to forget for sure. More duties. More rain and more wind. More dark and more winter. More … just … more.

We gave no thought to anyone else. The world had shrunk again. We were just the section. Nine individuals thrown together by luck of birth. We didn't talk or care about the RAF lads. They were on their own. It was just us. More to the point this world had really reduced to me, Bri and Ged and Terry. It was consolidating itself in its limit. The rest of the world just didn't seem to exist anymore.

We thought this was bad. It was going to get worse. Much worse.

Sunday 7 June
Day 17
It rained all day. Me and Bri lay in our bivvy singing. A very boring day.

Day 17 and this had to be the most boring day of the whole conflict so far. Depression may be setting in, except we don't know what the symptoms are, so don't know how to react appropriately. Dripping is our pastime. Drip, drip, drip. Dripping led to laughing, which led to happiness. Yesterday was bad and God had said it could get worse, and now it did. We dripped and the tent dripped. Thank goodness Malcolm had brought these tents. Humiliating feelings of being classified as a REMF were thrown aside and the tents were fully embraced. It rained non-stop all day. It seemed to have been doing this for days, non-stop. But today it increased in intensity. Me and Bri lay in our tiny tent with Ged, all squashed in, and spent the day laughing and singing songs. Quite untactical really but clearly they were not coming in these conditions. The wind and rain would not allow any landings on the beach and the parachute option was never going to happen. The song I particularly remember was the black and white movie classic of Laurel and Hardy singing 'The Blue Ridge Mountains of Virginia'. During the day, after we had sung it ten thousand times, we managed to be quite good at it. This caused lots of full-on belly laughing and seeing the funny side of this strange and peculiarly absurd situation. Good grief we were bored and we had just about had enough; they cannot treat commandos like this, surely. If something didn't happen soon we were going home. However, we recognised that this was a team game, so we needed to play our small part in this great adventure. It was definitely a small part. Not a speaking part. Whining wasn't going to get us anywhere, but it was funny.

What on earth was going on out there in the war?

In reality, there's nothing else to say about this day, or the days earlier, except it slipped past in a haze of singing and wets, and laughing as loud as we could. It really didn't make any difference that we were laughing loud. The Argentines were obviously not coming. What on earth would they want to do that for? Duties in the sanger were done in downpour conditions. Our own side had forgotten us so why should we care; we didn't, and it still rained … and rained … and rained. Just to make it worse it didn't just rain, it was very thick 'stair-rods' of horizontal rain driven in on the inevitable high winds. This was starting to take on the form of suffering. Proper full-on suffering. We had moved from survival mode to suffering mode. The day never really got to be light; it was dark and forbidding all day. Mordor-ish. The rest of the section were presumably doing what they did too. In their tents and suffering. Not our concern. Our world was the inside of a very small wet green canvas tent with the 'fug' of three damp commandos just passing a day together. Goodness knows what the Troop was doing or even the company. Or even the unit. No thoughts were given to this.

The tents were predictably porous, letting the rain in and soaking us and our kit. Dripping. There is an adage in the military that says, 'Remember that the piece of equipment you are issued is manufactured by the cheapest bidder.' 'Don't touch the inside of a canvas tent.' It makes the water run down inside the tent. I remember Dad telling me and Jules this when we were caravaning as youngsters. We slept in the awning. It made us do it even more. The rule was enforced here too. These tents were quite obviously made by the cheapest bidder. How long can this go on for? How long will we be here for? Bloody rain!

My biggest memory of today, and our previous days, was the laughter. And the rain, definitely the rain. I will remember these days to the end of my days. It was a day spent with best mates laughing and joking and seeing the funny side of everything and anything. Sharing wets of tea and coffee. (Sandy Bottoms, always Sandy Bs.) In some ways it was actually a perfect day. The most perfect day of the war.

Although the world was dark, the mood was light. We had fallen into comfortable routines. This might not last for long.

Chapter 5

At Last! Forward to the Front Line – Terra Incognita

It's no use going back to yesterday, because I was a different person then.

Lewis Carroll, 1865

Monday 8 June
Day 18
Weather cleared up just windy and cold. The helicopter came – a gunship – and we were taken to Ajax Bay. We are now living in a hut in the settlement next to a 1,000lb unexploded bomb. The scene here is untrue all mud, Argie POWs, wrecks of houses and stacks of dead blokes, body bags are seen frequently, being taken to the graveyard. Before breakfast Seaslug brought down a plane at about 12,000ft.

Finally, we were in luck. Somebody somewhere must have decided that we needed to be moved. Wreck Point was to become a memory, and very quickly. Again, maybe disturbingly too quickly. This could mark the end of our misery. Conversely it could also mark the start of new miseries.

On a very cold and windy morning, after the rains, we were told we were going to move. We didn't have much time to get ourselves together when we did get the message confirming our move. We stowed all our kit and waited for the chopper to come. Some of the guys bade a fond farewell to the RAF lads on the Rapier. They were staying and were not our responsibility anymore. The day had started clear, quite different to yesterday. The wind had picked up and the temperature had dropped

126

again. But it was sunny and the rain had stopped for a while. We sat on our Bergens and waited; normality returns. Hurry up and wait again. Eventually the chopper came. It was a gunship; we piled all our gear on board and hauled ourselves up into the dark interior. It smelt comforting, just like home, all the AVCAT smells. It smelt of 'people'. It smelt of 'doing'. Pilot smiled. We smiled. We couldn't believe we were actually getting away from this place. I wasn't fully aware of where we were going, or what we were supposed to be doing, but at least we were going somewhere and that was better than our previous static existence.

The job of a corporal is to assist the lads getting on the chopper. Standing at the open door and helping others. I had spied an opportunity. It was a very slim opportunity, but it was an opportunity nonetheless. The large exhaust of the chopper was unusually pointing down just behind the pilot. I seized the moment, rushed forward and stood in the hot air blasting down and drying me. My altruism was rewarded. Seconds of warmth. We piled on board. The chopper lurched into the air and all the darkened faces split into broad grins. We were airborne and we were away. Wreck Point slid away. It instantly became irrelevant and just a memory. Always looking forward, that's where the war was going to come from.

The journey was warm but very short, unfortunately. We soon touched down in Ajax Bay settlement. We piled off and the chopper lurched again and disappeared. More jobs to do. We were transported from the deepest solitary isolation and deposited in what looked like a small town. We had got used to only seeing each other and the same old scenery, with the same old procedures. Now we were dumped in an area full of people, with buildings and tracked vehicles and all sorts of military paraphernalia. It was like a city to us rural country folk. There seemed to be movement everywhere.

Grabbing our Bergens and weapons, we set off to find out where the hell we should be and what the hell we should be doing. Some of the rest of the Troop were already there so we sat down and put the wets on and caught up with what they had been doing. Jono and Andy's section had not arrived yet. They had been isolated and in a similar situation to us. But it was definitely good to see the lads again. Lots of laughing.

The area was a peculiar sight. It was a set of long, low, grey, concrete, spartan buildings; some had been destroyed by bombs and lay in ruins.

The main field hospital was here and the medical people were here and all the casualties were coming to these buildings from across the Islands, including the Argentine soldiers. The ground had been churned over by vehicles and was deep and muddy. The area obviously needed to be checked out for any proffers lying around. Me and one of the lads decided to take a stroll around and orientate ourselves.

Around the back of the main buildings was a muddy, filthy compound surrounded by head-height barbed wire. In the compound were loads of Argentine POWs. Hundreds of them. They stood in the open, in the mud and cold. They were muddy and cold. We stood and looked at them and they stood and looked at us. Both quite impassive, but both marginally inquisitive. They seemed okay. No real danger. We saw them as a scruffy, dirty bunch, no real spirit, and they didn't seem aggressive either. They probably looked at us in a similar way. We didn't stay long. We smiled at them. It was returned. It had a disturbingly similar feel to the pictures of the German camps in the Second World War, but curiously different. They were obviously miserable. The whole scene looked like a black and white photo. I saw this scene in black and white.

Behind the hospital, to the south, were the bombed-out buildings, pretty much levelled and just rubble. Again, pictures of 1940 blitzed London or Stalingrad came to mind. We had been informed that some lads had been killed here only a few days previously. We accepted the information impassively. Not really having a point of reference to work from. We didn't even ask the names of those killed. Which is peculiar. The buildings were cordoned off with mine tape. We didn't take any notice of that and walked through it and started to have a poke around. It just seemed a practical thing to do; we weren't normalised to the ways of this big city. We figured that there must be some useful gear to proff somewhere in here. What use was it under tons of rubble if we could use it. There were odds and ends but nothing of any interest. We were scratching through the great pile of rubble when a military policeman turned up with his RMP mate. He obediently stood at the tape and shouted at us that 'looters would be shot' or something similar; we stuck our fingers up at him and jumped through a hole in the wall and were away. He came after us but we were fighting soldiers back from the rear-most areas of the war, and we could not be caught. They obviously gave up. We just looked like everyone else. Covered in mud.

Near these buildings there was a small rise with a little track next to it and laid by this were three or four body bags. Great big black rubber slugs laid in a neat row, at attention almost. Absurdly neat. The bags were obviously occupied. There were tags on the outside, I seem to remember. We looked at the bags but not the tags. That seemed intrusive. Just not the thing an Englishman would do. This was all very new. The one on the left had a big lump in it, about the right size for a man, the second one was much the same, but the third had a lump about a third of the way down from the top and the lump was about two to three feet long and nothing else. I looked at it and thought, 'You poor bastard, there's not much left of you.' The fourth was also not a full-sized bloke. The image stuck in my mind like cement and still does. It was still a bright day and they looked … odd. Not scary, just peculiar. I wasn't even sure if they were ours, I presumed them to be. This was a significant moment for me. My feelings of invincibility ebbed away, just a little bit further, melting and ebbing. So, this is what it's all about. I was at the edge of my rabbit hole and I didn't even know I was there. Teetering on the event horizon, getting closer to toppling in. One experience at a time. Being slowly pushed by each new event towards the event horizon. We stood silently processing this scene. Curiouser. We spent quite a while there just looking at these blokes. Not talking. Just trying to absorb the meaning. The meanings must be individually relative, but they were individually elusive. It was very hard to do when you have no point of reference for this. The image stuck and the reality of the situation was not lost on me. We did not discuss it. We didn't have the words and we didn't really know how.

We carried on walking around the buildings and found a bombed-out bunker, so we had a look. It was a mess. We didn't pay much attention to it and continued on our way, not realising the probable significance of it. To me especially. We saw more bodies and more paraphernalia of war, all sorts. We had been away a long time, it seemed. Time may have been quicker here than our sluggish time up north. Much had happened since we had been away. We had an 'air red' at about this time, so we ducked into another low, dark bunker. I don't remember if we were bombed or not; it was irrelevant. We paid no attention. We sat there in the dark for a short while then ambled off to our next adventure. We went to find the lads.

9 Troop had taken over a small, bare concrete room in the back of the main building, not very big, and it was dank. At the end of the room in the right corner was a large hole through the ceiling and hanging through the hole was a bomb, a big bomb. A really big bomb. We had no real experience of bombs but this one looked extremely big. Absurdly big. Bastardly big. It was hanging through the hole suspended by its torn parachute. Apparently, it had failed to detonate. Someone had assured us that it was okay now. What would we know. What would he know. We accepted the diagnosis. But we were told not to play with it. Health and Safety gone mad! We were going to sleep in this room. We figured that if it was going to go off then 1,000lb of explosive would hopefully see us into the next life before we could register it. The choice was stay outside in the cold and wet or live in here with a 1,000lb bomb in the relative dry. We had been outside for two weeks now and were soaked and this dank room looked too good to turn down. We would risk it. The decision felt so natural and logical. It didn't feel like a big risk. My concern was if I was lying under it and it fell down and didn't go off then it might just slowly roll over me. Being slowly crushed seemed a bad thing. A momentary thought thrown away. We got our gear out and brewed up, laid our sleeping bags out and some of the guys got their heads down for a while. Under the bomb. Life was already more interesting than being at home on Wreck Point. In a very short period of time Wreck Point seemed weeks earlier. It was only yesterday. In fact, it was only this morning.

Earlier in the day a plane had been flying really high in a brilliantly clear blue sky. It was just a pinprick in the sky with a long vapour trail running out the back of it. Just like back in Suffolk. We stood and watched, just curious; someone in the know said it was an enemy Canberra; we didn't know but accepted the information. *Boom* … a huge explosion nearby, from a ship probably. It made us jump. Wasn't expecting that. Suddenly there was another circling, clear white trail that left Earth and headed after it. Earnestly. This was like the Mirage over the Sound, only much, much further. Apparently, the matelots had let off a Seaslug from one of the warships sat in Bomb Alley and it was heading after this plane. It was hurrying its way towards its prey. We watched and the murmuring got louder as the missile got nearer to its target. The vapour trail of the missile did what the other one did and became smaller in its spirals as it got closer to the target. We could sense victory, almost smell it. Would it hit? A small puff of smoke and the aircraft vapour trail suddenly stopped at the same point that the missile vapour trail stopped. They met each other perfectly. From this distance they simply lightly touched. Jubilation all round and the lads went mad; we jumped around again, slapping each other on the back and congratulating Jolly Jack Tar. They're good lads and what a great shot at such a high-altitude target. I love the smell of victory in the morning.

The day had been full of new experiences and a real change from being isolated back home on Wreck Point. At least it gave the impression that we were getting a bit closer to the action. This place was a vibrant hub of activity. We also had the chance to meet long-lost oppos from other units. It was like a reunion. Quite an exciting day really. This had been a good day. Definitely better than the continuous rain and wind on Wreck Point.

We slept under our bomb and never thought of it. Warm dry sleep.

Tuesday 9 June
Day 19
Had my 14hrs of sleep last night, breakfast was OK. Beans with sausages. Saw four blokes buried on the hill. The weather is cold but no rain, thank God. Had 'air warning red', 45 got bombed. I heard today Mac McAndrews was killed the other day by a shell in the belly. Another 'air red' has just happened. Jono's section joined us today here in Ajax Bay. About 1600, casualties from the Welsh Guards – 45 Cdo – Paras – HMS *Plymouth* & *Galahad* started to arrive we helped them to the hospital. They were coming in without legs, burnt all over. We worked late with the casualties. It was not nice. It's the first time I've seen men in such a mess. 50 Paras – 50 45 Cdo – 160 Welsh Guards + Ships' Companies.

The night had been long and there weren't any duties to do so we had uninterrupted sleep in our comfortable dry concrete hole. It was perfect. The bomb still hung there, impotent but heavy and looming. But mostly ignored. The nights were getting longer as winter came. We were very much out of survival mode now and back into relative comfort. In the morning we pulled ourselves out of our sleeping bags and cooked a good breakfast. Everything seemed okay with the world. We strolled up to the hill and saw some blokes being buried. Maybe the same guys. By now we were getting blasé about our surroundings. Blasé seemed the best response to all of this, the safest response. It required no immediate reaction. The buildings were in the valley here next to the water of the bay. It was protected from the wind by the big mountain behind it. The one Jono and Andy were on. For once we had a full day of reasonable weather conditions in the valley. The speed of becoming totally blasé to the soldiers being buried was slightly troubling. But it may indicate just how quickly an individual can adapt to extreme surroundings and extreme situations and troubling sights. Again, this might be the quiet, slow personal desensitising process. Unmistakeable, but also unrecognisable. Catastrophically and inevitably gravitationally drawn to the edge of our black holes. Our rabbit hole.

I walked with Spud around the back of the main building and passed the same prisoners in their misery again. Hundreds of them. Doing what they did yesterday. Doing it in black and white. They were huddled in cold groups with very little cover. As we drew level with them, an Air Raid Warning Red was shouted. A casual shrug of 'old soldier shoulders' was our response. We knew what we were doing, and we ambled to the nearest bunker, hands in pockets, and took cover in plenty of time, no need to rush. Bimble. We knew the score. We were old hands at this.

A brief inquisitive glance over my shoulder, southwards. A white Skyhawk jet was skimming the ground and heading straight for us, cannons blasting and large black objects dropping from underneath. Flashing guns. It felt as though it was at roof height, maybe lower. My first thought was to alert Spud. Clearly, he had already seen it. All I saw was a burst of mud as he sprinted away from me with his arms and legs pumping like pistons. I burst into life. I ran. I had nowhere to run, but I ran. My body just said, 'RUN.' The world constricted instantly and closed in around me until all I could see was directly in front of me. It was like being blinkered, super-focused. All else blurred and out of focus. Like looking down a long toilet-roll tube. As I ran, and panicked, I calculated that my speed was not enough to outrun a jet, so I left the ground and dived into a small trench system only about a foot deep to my left; it could have been a drainage system, I didn't care. It was cover. It was full of water and mud. I shimmied along on my belly, still focused on self-preservation. Into my toilet-roll focus and panicked view came a small bunker with a very small entrance. This was the new focus of my life. The Skyhawk had long gone, obviously, but this had not computed. My whole life depended on reaching this small door. Just get inside that door, just get inside said the man in my head. I launched at it. I hit the small entrance at exactly the same time as Mark Garnham from 7 Troop. Our combined force resulted in both of us being wedged together in the small entrance, with legs still outside. Some thrashing. Elbows and knees and a sharp scuffle between us and we were both inside gasping on the floor and giggling like idiots. Possibly some embarrassment allayed by smiles and giggling. All this had probably taken maybe about ten seconds or so but it had felt like half an hour at least, or more. It was significant for me, to say the least. We didn't discuss it. Exhaustion was immediate. Post-fear exhaustion. Post-panic exhaustion. Physical exhaustion but my mind was still racing trying to catch up. My body was here, my mind was catching up and my soul was miles behind also trying to catch me up, again. To say I was shaken up was an understatement. I'm not a windy person and never have been. But this was different. I'm not even sure what I was shaken up about but it had really given my nerves a proper shaking. A jangling of nerves. These new experiences were coming thick and fast now. I was toppling over the edge. I almost felt it happen. Life was precarious. Curiouser and precariouser.

I knew that the Troop were still in the buildings, but I needed to get this sorted. Whatever 'this' was. I probably needed to get away from the buildings in hindsight. Far away. I knew that Adrian was up on the hill behind the buildings. They were in trenches. Autopilot was all I could muster. It became vital that I find him. Imperative, and it became my all-consuming focus. Very peculiar. It would have been more obvious to go to 9 Troop; they were closer but in my confused, yet totally focused state, I totally focused on Adrian. I went searching for him. Possibly frantically. Frantic inside, calm outside. Blasé outside, I thought. I don't even remember how, but I found him with Dodger and Matt in their trench. They were calm and relaxed and we just sat there and chatted. To me I was burbling. Inwardly, I was. Adrian gave me a hot chocolate and after a short while my system calmed itself. The three of me collected together again. Body, mind and soul. The three 7 Troop lads were very helpful and supportive. Probably not realising what they were doing. They were just my friends and were being normal. Having the nerves totally shattered and jangled was new to me, and I felt confused. Consumed. Time had shifted. It had shifted far. Many things had shifted. How could something so short in time seem so long and have such a devastating effect. It was almost irrational.

This was the exact moment I toppled over the edge of my event horizon into my black hole. My rabbit hole. I didn't even know it at the time. Events had brought me here. All I knew was that something had slipped in my life. I determined to myself that I would never mention this. Never. I guess this is what they mean by 'being pushed over the edge'. Maybe this is one version of this saying. It was a strange new world as I slithered down my rabbit hole. At the time I wasn't aware. Too inexperienced to know. Frankly, I didn't know what on earth was happening. Slippage, everything slipped. It slipped in a 3D sort of way, not just in a straight line. It fell away and I fell in.

Outwardly everything returned to normal. I purposely returned it to normal. I knew what outward normal was so it was easy to replicate. Inwardly, it is hard to express. I was suddenly a different person inhabiting the same external, normal body. To anyone else I visually looked exactly the same, probably. Hopefully. Inside, I knew something had happened. I had no experience of this. So I determined to leave it alone and not meddle with it. Life now was much darker. I had reached a Mordor Rubiconic-like boundary.

Johnno and Andy arrived today with their section and we had a small reunion. I was very pleased to see them again. More than they knew. We told our stories over another wet and then carried on doing what we'd done before: scrounging, repurposing and admin. I probably omitted that I had been nearly scared to death.

Not long after they had arrived, we had an urgent message that we could expect many casualties. Very soon. They would arrive by choppers. They asked if we would help. It wasn't our job, but of course we would. We got outside and waited for them, hanging around the helipad area; it wasn't a helipad as such, just a grassy area where they landed. Straight outside of the main entrance on the north side. As we stood there a steady stream of choppers, all in a long line out over the bay, waiting for a landing space, came in, politely and unhurriedly stacked up one behind the other, patiently waiting their turn to land. When their turn arrived, they came in at full speed, doors open, hit the deck, skidded and before they had stopped, the crewman was already booting blokes out onto the ground in a trail of men lying in the chopper's wake. They were just landing in a heap on the grass. A long heap of people. The chopper lurched back into the air and went off for more. We rushed forward and started grabbing them and dragging them off to the main building. As soon as we'd delivered one, we turned round, sprinted back out and got another. This went on for what seemed ages and we brought in loads of blokes. They were in a hell of a state, all sorts of injuries. Andy said he'd grabbed one, hauled him up and his legs dropped off. Speed was the word. Be gentle but be swift. The smell. The smell of burnt flesh was everywhere. An odd, sweet smell. Pungent. Eventually the last chopper arrived; it seemed like hours since the first one had come in. We emptied it and got the injured lads inside. Our smocks had changed colour.

The inside of the bare, concrete building was a different world, a very different world. There were blackout blankets on the doors and the light inside was very subdued and dark. There were bright lights over some of the tables where earnest men were operating but the rest of the room was in darkness. Dark corners where who knows what lurked. Urgent work. The room was quite big and noticeably warm. Body-warm warmth. There were piles of casualties everywhere. Much blood. Much pain. No screaming or crying. Stoicism maybe. Shock, probably. We decided to stay, maybe we would be of some help. We offered. It wasn't so much a decision as a compulsion. We were allowed to stay. The rest of the day and the night was spent helping the injured with the medics and the surgeons. Time became no object and the injuries were ... well, horrible. From extreme burns and penetration wounds to more simple injuries. But they all needed some sort of help. Misery was everywhere. The things in the dark corners smiled and beckoned. The place seemed to function perfectly; the guy in charge must be a bloody good bloke. Rick Jolly at the helm. I didn't know who it was at the time; clearly he was doing a great job. Everyone here seemed to know their own job. It was dark. Dark in so many ways.

Later in the evening when things had slowed down a bit, we were stood and sat and slumped around the room in the dark by the light of the small paraffin lamps and having a wet when the blankets on the main doors parted and this solitary person stood there before us. He had long hair that was standing up on end and facing back at about 45 degrees. He didn't have any eyebrows or any facial hair, his eyes were bulging, his slack mouth hanging open. He stood there, wrapped in a blanket and looked at us. Somebody went forward and sorted him. Strangely, it was a peculiarly amusing thing to happen after a very long, bloody, hard day. A striking part of the day was the smells. The Argentine POWs smelt of a very strange odour. One I had never smelt before, or since. The smells of the burnt casualties and of the inside of the hospital. Peculiarly strong memories. Not bad memories. Not upsetting. Just another memory to add to the pile.

Somebody told me today that Mac MacAndrews had been killed a few days earlier in a bunker around the back of the buildings.[1] He'd been firing his GPMG at the plane till the bomb struck him. This hit me like a hammer blow; he had been a bezzie oppo. Was it his bunker I'd been in? Was it him I'd seen in the body bags? The mind does silly things sometimes. I was horrified that Mac was dead. Horrified. These new experiences were mounting up, and fast. Processing them was sometimes easy and sometimes more complex. There was a simple answer for all of them. Just don't talk about them. Just don't talk about them, at all, ever. It's easier not to express them. Especially when you don't have the correct words. My mind wouldn't shut down when I went to my hanging-bomb room for sleep. But sleep did come, and it was peaceful.

Today was a sharp shunt along the spectrum of war experiences. It had been relatively slow until today. The experiences had seemed to progress at a relatively constant speed, until today. But this was a sharp jump laterally along the slide rule of war experiences. Emotions

---

1. Further confusion about Mac. It was about ten days ago that he was killed. I leave this in the text just to show how confusing this can be at the time.

had been stretched tissue thin, but peace was found by close of play. Tomorrow would be fine.

The Troop slept.

Wednesday 10June
Day 20
Up, had breakfast, packed and moved out of the settlement up onto the hill where we dug in/built up, our bivvy was huge. CO came to see us, we might be reinforcing the Guards at Bluff Cove, so we could be on the move soon. My feet are OK, the weather is good, and now we're safe on the hill am going to write to Parents.

Less sleep last night for all sorts of reasons but breakfast made up for it. Squatting in our concrete room and brewing up in semi-darkness was not bad at all. Comparatively speaking, it was still like a hotel to us. The bomb still hung there. It was inconsequential, almost a friend. A very heavy impotent friend.

We had been told to get our kit together. We were moving up onto the hill where Adrian and the rest of the company were. The company seemed to be coming back together again. Bergens on and all the gear collected, it was beginning to weigh a ton. We were indifferent. We took the small yomp up the hill in decent conditions even though the strain on the backs was telling. We had again managed to accumulate more ammo from somewhere, so weight-wise the Bergens were groaning. Still not a problem and no different from usual. Life went on, mostly. Our lives went on. We still had no idea when this whole thing would finish. It didn't feel like it was going to finish any time soon.

We got to our assigned Troop area and found a decent place for the section to organise itself. We had been on the Islands for what seemed like years and the state of us probably looked that way as well. We were sick of living in small, tactical, uncomfortable places, so we decided to build a massive bivvy for most of us to get in. One that would be a palace, a very comfortable palace. One that would demonstrate our newly perfected construction skills combined with our growing indifference towards this war. So that was exactly what we made. We built it using all sorts of kit we had proffed from down at the refrigeration plant/hospital area. It was excellent and all the section got in no problem, including kit. There's no use in being uncomfortable when you don't need to. We deemed we didn't need to. We even perfected a small door that was completely watertight and airtight. Our expertise was improving. Much time and creative design were invested in our new home. Long discussions on design and practicality. It was complete. To be creative you need to be at the top of your game.

Malcolm came today and told us that there might be a possibility that we were going forward to reinforce the Welsh Guards who had all those bad casualties yesterday. This was really good news for us, but none of us believed it. Not a bit. Of course we didn't. We had turned into cynical old men already. How come they got to go forward when we were held back in the rear? This was worrying; I thought we were a good unit. Still, he was quite convincing, but not quite enough for us. Maybe they'll bring tents again to placate us. It would work again.

Apparently, Malcolm had threatened to resign if we didn't get forward to do something – good man, I'll resign too; that'll make them stand up and think. Malcolm's resignation was the buzz going round the unit. Probably untrue, but we wanted to believe it. So, it became our convenient truth. Like many things.

As far as the rest of the day went, it was just the normal round of wets, checking feet, cleaning weapons, getting each other on bites, laughing and writing to Mum and Dad on the bluey. Generally just preparing for the next event. It is a curious thing in war that none of it is your choice. You just get on with what you have to do when it is given to you. No choice. We had no choice to be here on this hillside, but we were. It was quite fatalistic, and we were okay with this. But it was kind of fun too. Fatalism and ambivalence were a safe place to be.

We have been told that me, Andy and Alex are going forward with Nick to recce Bluff Cove, ready to fly in the Troop. We are ready and waiting but as usual it turns into a hurry-up-and-wait scenario. We sit at the bottom of the hill waiting for the chopper to come, and it doesn't. After what seems like hours, we are told to return to our previous positions and wait for the call. Andy, Jock and I get our kit on to yomp back up the hill, not a great distance but far enough for it to hurt. Nick decides that he has to see someone at the bottom of the hill and asks Andy to take his fighting order up the hill to the position. Andy says no problem and the kit is slung on top of his Bergen and we start yomping. The hill is steep at this point and the added weight to Andy's kit was beginning to tell. Andy is a strong bloke, I mean really strong, ox strong, but this extra 60-odd pounds did for him. Alex and I exhibited no empathy as we watched him crumble under the weight. Andy thinks this is the moment he started having a bad back. We got to our position and Andy collapsed. I don't blame him. He started to complain about his lower back; apparently it was giving him some real problems. We could have helped, but it didn't seem to dawn on us. Wets were put on and tea was taken.

So our day's activity so far has been to walk down the hill with all our kit and then a walk back up it with more kit. Someone's got a sense of humour and I still suspect we're not being used to our maximum potential. The grand old Duke of York came to mind.

Back in our positions we are informed that an SAS patrol[2] has got itself in trouble and might need some assistance, so we are all put on stand-by. On with all the kit again and prepare for a quick move, anywhere. This is a bit more like it, but we sit around in our sticks waiting for something to occur. Time passes by. At its normal speed. Obviously, the SAS patrol has got itself out of trouble and we're now not needed. So here we sit doing what we've perfected, waiting and waiting and waiting. I could quite easily become paranoid and think someone's got it in for us. 'Infamy, infamy, everybody's got it infamy.' I try to console myself by convincing myself that people are actually getting seriously hurt and killed up at the front and after some considerable introspection I don't fancy getting seriously hurt or even killed. But as much as I try to convince myself, I still want to be away from this rear echelon and up at the front. It is our natural space to be in. I don't particularly look forward to getting fragged but the thought of staying here is probably even worse. We all agree on this and try to look forward to a decent move.

Jono remembers this stage:

All the Company/Troops movement was conducted at night, move by night, harbour up and rest by day. I will not

---

2. In hindsight this was probably John Hamilton's patrol out west. He was known as either John or Gavin. I knew him as John.

try to recall days or dates, only approximate times of the day when the events I can recall happened.

It was decided after the loss of the Welsh Guards at Bluff Cove that they would be reinforced by two companies from 40 Commando RM. Charlie Company consisting of 7, 8, and 9 Troops was one of the companies chosen to go forward, the other being Alpha Company.

We began our advance out of San Carlos leaving from the Red Beach area overland at night.

During a halt, lights were observed below our rest stop that were duly reported. Some of these lights were seen to be moving about. Due to this report the Brigade back at San Carlos stood to, fearing an enemy move during the night to attack the bridgehead. But it turned out to be the Scots Guards who had stopped well below us and were cooking and making wets.

The advance continued during which we witnessed an Argentinian reconnaissance aircraft being engaged and destroyed by a Sea Dart missile from one of the covering ships in the Sound. The aircraft came down in pieces, the main body of the craft fluttering down in flames until it disappeared from view.

A helicopter move saw us flown a few miles forward where we landed behind a ridge being held by some Gurkhas that was being sporadically shelled; here we joined up with what was left of 1 Welsh Guards.

A night move forward, our first in company with 1WG.

Waterproofs, they all wore waterproofs, all the time, whether it was raining or not. These were not the modern Gore-Tex of today, but the camouflaged jacket and trouser set as issued by the military, known as teabags because you got as wet from sweat on the inside as they were from rain on the outside. We avoided them completely and many lads had purchased their own dark-coloured civilian waterproof kit. The problem with the issued ones was the noise they made, especially at night, a sort of swishing sound as you walked, so you can imagine 150+ blokes trying to move tactically at night with the swish and rustle of those damn waterproof suits.

A typical incident I experienced while moving with my section at night in a long line or snake of blokes advancing in single file. It is pretty dark in the Falklands at night, no ambient light, even darker if the stars are obscured by cloud, so we tried to maintain a tactical spacing at the same time not completely losing the man in front.

During this night we had been yomping maybe an hour or so over typical rough Falkland terrain, when suddenly the man in front stopped, so I stopped and went into the kneeling position, which was replicated down the line behind me. After about 5 minutes I could vaguely discern a small group ahead of me, which I took to be some sort of briefing going on, so I slowly moved forward to find out what the hold-up was. I came across 3 or 4 WG lying on their backs propped up against their Bergens, with a sergeant knelt by them. All I could hear was them complaining they could not continue; they were tired and needed a rest, the Sgt was pleading with them to carry on and get moving. I enquired where the next man in the column was and it turned out they had let the blokes in front continue, so we had lost contact with the rest of the unit. I quickly grabbed my section and we continued at a fast pace to try and catch up and regain contact with the advance. Thankfully, we could just discern a faint path through the wet grass and gorse where the rest of the unit had passed. We regained contact with them after about 15 minutes, I have no idea what happened to the WG we had left in our rear.

We were briefed for the forthcoming attacks on the hills surrounding Stanley. We were to be reserve for 42 Commando's attack on Mount Harriet. We were to move forward and secure their start line. We were given a route to follow that had supposedly been recce'd; unfortunately they briefed us on the wrong route, which took us the wrong side of a large lake, which would have devastating consequences. We set out around 2200 that night as lead company, lead troop and after making good progress for a couple of hours my section was walking point. Behind us somewhere in the rear there came a sudden sound of a muffled explosion, a sort of *crump*; it went deadly quiet for about five seconds then came this horrendous scream almost like a wild animal in absolute agony; it was chilling to hear and it kept going for what seemed like a long time, but was probably only a few minutes, just long enough for a medic to get to the casualty and plunge a needle of morphine into his arm. Then all was silent. Word came forward that a grenade had detonated in someone's pouch. We all took our Bergens off and sat down on them, each man facing out covering their arcs waiting for word to carry on.

Then came a message nobody ever wants to hear: 'Minefield! Don't move.' Blokes drew their legs up closer and tried to get them onto the Bergen as well; somebody suggested feeling around for anything unusual or uneven ground around you. This was quickly rescinded as a stupid idea, but in stronger terms. The screams from the casualty had been unnerving and a couple of the lads were discussing making for a track marked on the map about 300 metres away. This again was quickly disregarded when a second *crump* came from somewhere behind us; again, more shouts of pain then silence again. We could hear some armour moving along the track mentioned previously, presumably Scorpion or Scimitar armoured vehicles moving up to support the attacks. The company commander, Captain Pillar, then moved forward and briefed us that we had two casualties and were waiting for a casevac and engineers to lead us out. We began to receive sporadic shelling, presumably called in by an enemy observation post that had spotted the two flashes in their minefield. All we could do was hunker down and try and make ourselves as small as possible.

Eventually we could hear a helicopter approaching to our rear; a Scout helicopter flew in very low and he came in on a single green torch, shielded upward, and hovered over the casualties, not being able to land due to the mines, but he hovered low enough for the casualties to be lifted onboard, all this while we were under sporadic shell fire. The pilot, a Royal Marine, was later decorated for that act.

A little later some figures appeared coming up from our rear; they had covered torches low on the ground and were laying out white tape, lads from 59 Commando Royal Engineers, cool as you like, laying a path for us to follow. We were quickly instructed to stay within 1 metre to the left of the tape and try to walk in the footsteps of the man in front. Not an easy task to complete but we eventually reached the edge of the minefield and got safely out; the advance continued, but by now we were well behind time.

Vince remembers the minefield:

I don't remember much of the minefield incident. To be honest I was so tired I think I slept through some of it. We were patrolling when I heard an explosion and then a constant scream. I remember considering the options, mine, hand grenade gone off in someone's pocket or a direct hit by artillery. I remember seeing Alex's tin helmet toppling off and rolling away. Fearing that would trigger another mine I covered the parts I wanted to protect and hoped for the best. Shortly after, there was a second explosion and now we had two casualties needing immediate casevac. It is quite scary being in an area with mines who knows where, when its pitch black and then to top it all we were being indiscriminately shelled. Very inconsiderate of the enemy. I will be eternally grateful to the Engineers that got us out of that minefield after several hours and just before daylight. We would have been sitting ducks.

Jono continues:

We reached the lower area of Mount Harriet and the attack had already begun, tracer lit up the night sky and naval gunfire crashed overhead and landed on the upper ridges of the mountain. A duel between one of our gunners on the lower slopes, red tracer flashing up, to be answered by one of their machine guns, green tracer flashing down. This continued until after a long burst of red tracer there was no answering green tracer.

Another enemy machine gun opened up from what looked like a very narrow cleft in the rocks; red tracer answered it and bounced, spun, and ricocheted all over the place, but still the green tracer continued to spew out of the rocks. A flash to our rear then something glowing, tracking up the hill toward the cleft in the rocks, the glow disappeared into the cleft followed by a flash, explosion and screaming, then all quiet. One of our Milan anti-tank rockets had taken it out.

As it drew closer to dawn the firing began to die down. I was stood next to L/Cpl Andy Gaunt when we noticed a light moving at speed from further up the coast and moving away out to sea. At first it looked like a nose light of a helicopter, but it was travelling way too fast. Suddenly the horizon was lit by a huge flash and explosion, we thought we saw an outline of a ship in the flash; something had been hit by something and was now on fire. Later we realised we had witnessed the land-based Exocet attack on HMS *Glamorgan* that had been providing naval gunfire support to the attacks.

With daylight came the job of searching the slopes and rounding up Argentinian prisoners of war, some who had been missed during the attack and had now crawled out of their hiding places to happily surrender. They were searched then taken down to an assembly point; from there they were loaded onto Wessex helicopters and flown to the rear. The injured were given treatment on the spot then priority on the helo lifts.

I recall an aircrewman assisting Argie troops into his Wessex holding an entrenching shovel in his hands and letting them know any problems and they'd be on the receiving end. Most were just happy to have survived the night and still be alive. As it got lighter we got down to the business of breakfast and a good old mug of tea. As I sat in among some rocks getting ready to boil some water there was this smell that I couldn't figure out, a sort of pervading stink. I had a quick look round hoping I hadn't settled into an Argie latrine when I spotted the remains of a body, obviously Argentinian from the remains of the green parka and helmet, probably hit by shell or mortar fire. I marked the place and quickly relocated.

That night we spent at the bottom of Mt. Harriet guarding a group of prisoners still waiting to be sent to the rear. It was a bitterly cold night as the weather had deteriorated toward winter. We had to keep moving to generate some warmth, so we got the Argie prisoners to walk in a circle anti-clockwise, while we walked in a slightly bigger circle clockwise, which seemed to suit everyone. Now and again a prisoner would walk away from the circle to squat and relieve themselves; some were suffering from bad bouts of dysentery.

I got talking to an Argie medic, red crosses on his helmet and armband. He spoke good English with an American accent. He said, at first, he couldn't believe we were English troops. He was a reservist who had been called up and had arrived at a transit barracks in Argentina. Sometime during the night, they had been told they were going to the Chilean border as there were tensions between Argentina and Chile. They were driven to an airfield in the dark and loaded onto a C-130 Hercules. They arrived, he now knows, in Port Stanley before dawn and had been immediately deployed into the hills. He had no sooner got to his assigned unit when the attacks had begun and he was captured. He was convinced they had been fighting Chilean troops.

By now most of the hills around Stanley had been captured during those night attacks: Mount Harriet, Two Sisters, Mount Longdon were all in British hands. The Scots Guards were tasked with capturing Mount Tumbledown and the Gurkhas Mount William. Then the Welsh Guards were to push through with us attached and capture Sapper Hill, the last high ground overlooking Port Stanley.

We moved forward to a small gully and took up positions for the day. That night the Scots Guards would attack and once Tumbledown was captured we would move forward onto our objective.

That day was spent checking kit and resting. In the afternoon I had to attend to a call of nature so weapon and shovel in hand I took myself off round a small rocky outcrop. I found an excellent spot, out of the ever-present wind and in some sunshine, and with a view of the coast and out onto the sea. I had just settled down, weapon and shovel next to me when I saw a black speck appear travelling right to left as I looked out at it along the coast. It was travelling very fast and low. I quickly recognised it as a jet, tracking along the coastline, but whose? It drew opposite where I was sat and it was probably several miles away when it suddenly turned left and flew straight towards me. Whoever it was, I was mightily impressed they had spotted me among the rocks having a crap. Nevertheless he continued to bear down on where I was sat, so I grabbed my rifle and tried to squirm between two large boulders; bringing the weapon up on aim, I prepared to defend myself from this eagle-eyed aviator. As it drew closer, and with some relief I recognised it as one of ours, a Harrier; it got within a few hundred yards of my position then climbed very rapidly at the same time as a dark object released itself from the underside of the aircraft. The Harrier half-rolled and dived back down to hug the ground again. The object continued to fly in an arc and disappeared behind one of the hills, quickly followed by a large explosion.

I witnessed another attack similar to this a little later: one Harrier would fly in low and fast from one direction, then climb to expose itself. Meanwhile, a second Harrier came in from a different direction, climbed, released its payload and both would then dive down to low level and exit the area in different directions.

That night was another bitterly cold clear night and as we stood around waiting to move off, we could see shell bursts ahead of us; some looked like air bursts over one of the marked tracks. The section commanders and 2ICs stood having a chat and then the word was given to prepare to move out. We shook hands and returned to our sections.

We had been moving for maybe 3 or 4 hours over very difficult terrain, rock-runs, frozen marshland etc when the word came forward to halt. It appeared the Scots Guards were taking longer to achieve their objective and were meeting some stiff opposition; we had to go firm for a few hours and wait. Sentries were posted and the rest just unrolled their sleeping bags among the bracken and got in them fully clothed; everyone was exhausted from the yomp and the bitter cold. Sometime before dawn I got a shake to get up and ready to move. I tried to open my eyes but found I couldn't. I felt around my face and my eyelashes had become frozen to my cheeks, and about 3 inches of snow had fallen and covered the landscape. We quickly got organised and the lads were up and ready to go in record time. The section commanders were again stood waiting when the Company Sergeant Major, Bill Howie, a man well respected by everyone and who had made sure the Company was fit to fight during the long voyage south, appeared out of the dark. 'Why are there still people in their sleeping bags, you were told ready to move five minutes ago. Get them up now.' It was gently pointed out that the ones still in their bags were not Marines, nor members of Charlie Company, and in fact the lads were stood in single file ready to move just behind him.

It transpired that it would be daylight before the Scots Guards secured their objective and we would be out in the open, so we moved into a series of gullies where we could not easily be observed and waited for darkness to continue our move forward.

Things would change very rapidly in the next few hours.

Chapter 6

Battle Preparation and
Scary Monsters

*You have everything but one thing: madness. A man needs
a little madness or else – he never dares cut the rope and
be free.*

Anthony Quinn, *Zorba the Greek*, 1964

Friday 11 June
Day 21
Up early, really cold clear morning, packed kit and flew by chopper
to Bluff Cove to join with A Coy & the Welsh Guards. Packed kit
i.e. 1 Bergen between 3 plus fighting orders. At 20.00 we started
yomping to Mount Harriet where 42 put in an attack. The night was
very cold. We arrived, got heads down for a couple of hours at the
start line, ice everywhere. Then moved position to a gully. Mount
Harriet was pounded all night, very impressive sight. 15 K in 9 hours.

The new stage is set. New players and new stage sets will arrive. New
experiences are going to come thick and fast during the days ahead.
Recollections become confused and the timeline has slipped out of
synchronisation completely. The notes I took at the time are quite
probably incorrect regarding incident times, or even days. However,
the incidents are all true. The order in which they happened may be
questionable. The order they are written here may also be questionable.
It would be possible to correct all of this in hindsight using official
reports; however, the evidence is left uncorrected. This clearly indicates
the way time slipped for us all. Nothing more and nothing less.

Back to Ajax Bay. After we had been stood down the night before, we were now ready to move again. The game was afoot. This time though it was for real and we were to be choppered forward to the Bluff Cove area to reinforce the Welsh Guards. There was no recce. We were all going as a company. Alpha Company was already there. Apparently, the Guards had lost the equivalent of two fighting companies worth of men and we were going to fill those gaps and become part of the Welsh Guards. We weren't particularly pleased as we'd rather be under control of our own Commando HQ. But beggars can't be choosers as they say, and any fight was better than no fight. Even if it was someone else's fight.

We flew forward in a Wessex that was grossly overloaded with guys and kit. The doorman had a bright orange balaclava on under his helmet, I distinctly remember that. The first real colour I had seen in what felt like years. We hadn't seen bright colours for some time. Just subdued colours. Black, brown, green and blues and this was a bizarre colour to be seen down here. But welcome. Antidisestablishmentarianism maybe.

We flew into a wide valley and jumped out. Kit on and away up the nearest mountain. There was all sorts of activity in the area. I remember looking down the mountain at a small track and seeing two motorcyclists charging along this track. We figured they must be Guardsmen. As they travelled artillery was falling all around them. We laughed and waited for one of them to be blown to bits. They dodged through all the fire; one fell off, got back on and they both made a clean getaway. Much cheering. The Guards seemed to be in the valley and we were in the mountains, which again made for fun when the Argentines shelled them. Some rounds came near us but only enough for us to shout obscenities at them. Probably 155mm artillery, we were told. They were big, very big.

At about 2000 hours we made our last meal and stowed our kit in one Bergen between me, Ged and Bri. As we had the gun, we had to carry the great loads of ammo plus spare barrels and all sorts, so our loads were quite heavy. No tripod. By choice. As gunner, Bri had the gun, Ged had ammo and I carried the Bergen plus extra ammo. My ammo fear still gnawed away at me. I figured this weight wouldn't be too bad. It was deep, dark night when we set off in a commando snake, one behind the other. We yomped for hours through rock-runs and rivers. The rock-runs were the worst. They went on for hundreds of yards and in this kit, it was really hard graft. Rock-runs, peculiar to the Falkland Islands; great swathes of big, jumbled rocks hundreds of metres wide and thousands of metres long. Almost impassable. But not. Grit your teeth and get through. Some laughing and giggling. It's awful, but not too bad.

As a note, carrying about 160lb of kit in a civvy Bergen isn't too dreadful. But most of our kit was carried in the military way: it wasn't all in one Bergen nice and neat and tidy and all the weight on the shoulder straps and hip strap. The bandoliers of link for the gun weighed 12lb and were slung over each shoulder. Many of them. The tape they were hung on was about half an inch wide, which soon worked its way down to about 5mm and this 5mm took the whole weight and worked its way into the side of your neck. These were slung around your neck and sat underneath your arms; as you walked, they began to slowly close together and choke you very slowly.

We had gone a considerable distance, or at least it felt like it, and I began to feel distinctly faint. Weakened. Nick was walking up and down the line encouraging all the blokes in the dark; as he came to me, he saw I was struggling a bit. I remember his words:

'It's not like you to struggle, Chris. What's up?'

I replied: 'I must be ill or something because I feel terrible; this lot is really heavy.' I was genuinely bewildered as to why I was struggling so much. No problem, just keep going, it's only pain anyway, and pain is only in the body, so separate it from your mind and keep going.

We went through the night, stopping and starting, stopping and starting, resting on our weapons and sending duff buzzes/messages up and down the snake just to keep everyone giggling. Chinese whispers. It was very cold and all you could see was the line of blokes ahead of you in the dark.

As we were yomping along, we kept on coming across .5-inch machine-gun barrels and working parts and ammo. Big things. These were being dropped by the Guards up front. We were still in proff mode so we picked them up. They must have had problems and so ditched them. They were super-heavy but we still took them. Maybe they were left there for others of their regiment to follow up and pick them up; too bad, we'd got them. We could give them back to them when we got to wherever we are going. The night went on and I continued to struggle along.

After a long time, we arrived at the base of Mount Harriet and joined a huge group of milling blokes with huge Bergens on. Nobody really knew what was going on except one young officer who was trying to sort out who should go where. He was stood in the dark and was under some obvious pressure. We played a harmless trick on him. It made us laugh. He didn't laugh. The officer pointed out that we could have jeopardised the whole battle. We smiled at him blankly. There is a saying in the Corps that goes something like this: 'Sir, I think you've got me mixed up with someone who actually gives a shit.' We walked away to our allotted area. Some minor giggling. Tactical giggling.

Life has changed considerably. The colours of life have changed. Life has become dark, now darker even than the previous dark. The time now has slipped all over the place. It was hard to keep a handle on it. It was hard to know how long you had been involved with certain events. Or when certain events happened. This was becoming strange: not a problem, but recognisable and acceptable. We had all the time in the world.

I realised that my weakness was due to drinking bad water. Ged had found some earlier. I had drunk it. Logic dictated that the only way out of this situation was to use the hoarded water-purification tablets. I had hundreds. It occurred to me that if I took some tablets directly, they might flush out the system. I took a big handful, a really big handful. I was peeing chlorine for days, but it worked. Don't try this at home kids. I was okay again.

There was white mine tape laying across the ground, which seemed like a good idea in a tactical situation. We seemed to be on a start line. A bit like you'd expect in the Boer War. I didn't pay any further attention to it and we started getting our kit organised. Ahead of us in the dark was a huge mountain. In an archetypal mountain, triangular shape. Perfect mountain shape. This was Mount Harriet. We got our spades and pickaxes out and dug small shell scrapes. All this time the moon was full and very bright and sat just behind the mountain peak. Nothing too different yet.

The world shatters and all hell breaks loose and shells come screaming over from our side and impact on the mountain. It's started. Flares are fired by the big guns in the rear and float down, completely illuminating the mountain. Naval gunfire support starts with high-explosive shells. This is outstanding. We knew that 42 were attacking the mountain tonight and we were reinforcements should they require it. We reckoned

42 must be up there doing it now. We knew we wouldn't be needed. We stand by and watch with big grins on our cammed-out faces waiting for more action. I'm not quite sure what is going on except 42 are going for it and the guns are pounding the mountain to bits. The *whizz* and *sewww* of shells overhead is superb. Electrifying.

The scene is us down in the valley with the mountain rising high above us and looming over us. The shells are illuminating the surrounding area. Massive explosions going off everywhere. The artillery and NGS come in waves. A great pounding and then a quieter period. This same process repeated and repeated and then repeated again and again. We notice that after each wave subsides there is an Argentine soldier, about three-quarters the way up the mountain on the right-hand side. who pops up after each wave and uses his GPMG to spray everyone in the valley. It sounds like a GPMG not a .5 or the smaller FN heavy barrel. Tracer everywhere. We watch him and then watch the fall of shot of the next fire mission wave. Did it hit him? Occasionally it seems to come very close but he still pops up again and continues firing in the next lull. Every time he does this, we start cheering for him. What a good chap he is. Our concern for this soldier increases as the night wears on and we start to like him. This great furious anger continues for some time, and we are getting very concerned for him. Finally, later on, they bring in some Milan wire-guided missiles and after a few shots they put one straight into him as he is firing. We cheer the Milan shots as they are fired, not loudly. He pops up again and he is hit. We are a bit unhappy about this. We felt it was uncalled for. He was a good soldier and should deserve a medal for what he did. We appreciated his determination. He didn't move from his position at all. We could have sworn we heard him scream, maybe not.

The battle wears on and the shells keep on coming and the supporting lighter arms also put heaps of rounds into the mountain. I didn't think a mountain could be pounded so much. It was the most extraordinary sight at night. I have never forgotten it. To our left we can see Two Sisters being illuminated and fought for by 45 and then further north Mount Longdon where 3 Para is having a hard night of it. The world is alive with fighting. Everywhere people fighting on all the mountains. An absurd night.

Before all this we decided we weren't needed, so we took off our Bergens and started to relax a bit. I had taken my chlorine tablets and was still questioning why I had been so knackered on the yomp in when I saw Ged open the top of the Bergen I had been carrying. He started to pull out belt after belt of GPMG ammo. When we had been getting our kit together for the yomp a few hours earlier I had thrown out loads of tins of peaches and stuff, which Ged had sneaked into the Bergen; I wasn't going to carry all that for him. But when I wasn't looking, he must have put all this in, so no wonder I was knackered. Andy said the last he saw was me chasing Ged with a shovel above my head away into the darkness. I wasn't sure what I was going to do with the shovel once I'd caught him, but I was mad. Probably actually mad.

We settled down again to the fireworks show and started to get our heads down. Some Argentine artillery shells landed close by but after a few we got used to them and just got our heads down and didn't worry. The night progressed and 42 were successful, and we were not needed. Of course. We woke in the dark with a sharp frost over ourselves and our kit. Snow. The night had been clear and cold, colder than we'd thought. It was really getting towards winter now.

Up and away again. We moved to a new position a bit further away from Harriet into a small gully. Here we rested and started sorting our kit out and putting wets on. We were out of sight of the hills so a small, covered hexi stove wasn't a problem.

The battle for Harriet was the most amazing thing I had ever seen; the sheer spectacle of noise, explosions, light and sound was just awe-inspiring. The sheer violence. This was a real battle, full on and no holds barred. It was nothing like the battles on TV; this was real. The smells, the colours, the explosions. The idea that people were being killed up there just added a bit of extra strangeness to the night. An oblique night.

Alejandro was still on Sapper Hill waiting. His recollections:[1]

> The days pass and the permanent version circulates of abandoning the static positions until that moment adopted by the unit, this is to mobilise the Battalion in the direction

---

1. Alejandro has written the original text in Spanish. It has been translated by Marcos. However, for accuracy Alejandro's Spanish version is at the back of this book, unaltered, should you wish to read it. It may even read slightly differently.

of San Carlos, going from a strictly defensive posture to another that would have to be offensive.

On this occasion, I volunteer to go to that point with my Section, being ruled out such a possibility by the head of company.

In the course of the days, the advance of the enemy troops, after their landing, is permanent as well as the continuous siege of the naval artillery, air from very low altitude, and already in June the ground artillery is felt, with an even more accurate degree of precision.

We also watched with astonishment in the early morning of June 12, the launch of the MM-38 Exocet missile, located near Puerto Argentino, its luminous trajectory of more than 29,000 meters above sea until it hit the ship HMS "GLAMORGAN", a unit that although it was not sunk, was out of combat and disabled to attack its own positions.

According to Marcos, Alejandro's troops were part of Marine Infantry Battalion No. 5 Ec, a unit of the Argentine Navy belonging to the Austral Marine Infantry Force-Río Grande, Tierra del Fuego Province, Antarctica and Atlantic Islands South. They were suffering just like us. Just like us they wanted a fight.

Life was speeding up. New sights and sensations seemed to rush at us at every minute. Time seemed to be speeding up but curiously felt as though it was slowing down. Very peculiar. We went to a gully and stayed there.

Saturday 12 June
Day 22
At new gully, set up, had wet, were bombarded by 155mm, impressive. I found a small Argie sack of grenades, Energas etc. It is a beautiful day, however is very cold. Suddenly called to help Argie prisoners at Mount Harriet. Got to position and put about 200 on choppers. We then had to march the rest (116) to our position 3K away. Retreat from Moscow. Guarded them at night. Temp -18°C last night.

The big 155mm Argentine artillery found our range and start to shell us again. These are impressive explosions. We learnt quickly how to count the shell into our positions. Apparently if you can count to 8, then it is going to hit you. At about 6 you pay attention and hit the deck. This is some complicated mathematics for a Royal Marine, but it became a good game and seemed to work practically. It was even possible to distinguish between different calibres by the pitch of the scream of the shells. You learn quick when you need to. Life is very different to a few days ago on Wreck Point. A few years ago at Wreck Point. Life has completely changed. We now inhabit a world at war. It is all around us. The scenery has changed. It is mountainous and rugged beyond belief. We exist in this microcosm of enormity. This absurd little corner of the world. The days are bright and cold and the clear nights are even colder. The moon is very large. No sleeping bags, limited food and water but our world is good. You couldn't fault it.

We set off on a small patrol just to check the area. Formally a clearance patrol but again more like a familiarisation patrol that could turn into an immediate fighting patrol if we bumped the enemy. We needed to know the lay of the land. We found a small Argie sack just laying on the diddle-dee. The diddle dee is very thick around here. You need to lift your legs high to move through it. High stepping. Like deep powder snow. After a quick discussion we decide not to grab it in case it is boobytrapped. The lads sit down and I go forward and attach a piece of string to it then we all retreat to a suitable distance and take cover and I give the string a sharp pull. The bag moves about a yard. No bangs or explosions. It's not boobytrapped, so we go forward and take it to bits. Inside are several Argentine grenades, quite different to ours, and a few Energas, which are grenades that you fix to the end of your rifle. You can fire these greater distances than the handheld ones. The Energas are no use, but the hand-held grenades are. They are distributed around the patrol to the lads and they are stowed away. With this minor interest over we return to the Troop and start sorting kit out again. Quick clean of the rifle and we're ready for the next event. Things are moving fast now. The chess pieces are moving rapidly. We are pawns. We are happy being pawns. It's our job. We return to the Troop. Nothing to report. The bag has a nametag on it. Typewritten name: Ramon Gauna. Sold. Apy/2/A/RT 12. I have it here; it hangs in my study at home. I always wonder whether he survived. I hope so.

We wait for things to develop. Just when we think that we're on for another wet we are called to go forward and sort out 42's prisoners from the mountain battle last night. As a Troop we go forward till we reach the road. A small gravel track. Approximately one Land Rover's width wide and raised slightly above the surrounding area. About 6–8 inches. This is the first solid ground we've been on since we landed. It feels odd in many ways.

Prisoners are coming down off the mountain and are being handed over to us. They are de-robed and searched and put into sticks under guard by a few of our guys. They sit in ill-disciplined rows waiting. Nothing is said. Nothing needs to be said. They are filthy and have that 1,000-yard stare of scared people. Most are like this, some are not. We go through the group asking if anyone speaks English. A couple do, so they become willing interpreters for us. The rest are a sorry bunch, as you would expect. It's sunny, cold but windy and they have just lost a battle. Some seem to be really young, or look it, but some are much older and have that Latin hatred in their eyes. Quite a motley crew really. The smell of the prisoners is very particular. It seems they all smell the same. It is very strong and exactly the same as the POWs at Ajax Bay. Maybe we smelled just the same to them. I remember thinking at the time that if I ever smelled that again in my life, I would recognise it immediately. The choppers land one at a time and the sticks of prisoners are sent off still with their guards. Andy goes off with one group as their guard and returns later. Now Andy is a hard man and he said that on the journey there was one Argie who looked so hard he even put the willies up him. I didn't know there was anybody anywhere who could do that. We laughed. We keep on sending off these prisoners until we are finally stopped. I don't know the reason the choppers stopped coming but here we were with a huge bunch of prisoners in the middle of nowhere, with nowhere to go. Bizarre and still slightly absurd.

New orders come through and we are to take them back to the gully that we were in last night. We counted them and the total came to 116. We formed them up as a big loose squad in three very loose ranks and set off over the diddle-dee. They vastly outnumbered us. We had decided that if any of them decided to run, then they'd be appropriately stopped by us. To limit the chance of crossfire we formed up on the right side of them only. We are in the middle of nowhere. Where are they going to run to? We thought it was logical though. Off we went across the diddle-dee; they were stumbling and falling over and generally having a very bad time of it. We waited for them to make a break for it. They must have had such a pounding on Harriet that their courage must have left them. None of them ran. Of course they didn't. They really were well beaten. 42 must have done well up there. Maybe these lads were so far down their own private rabbit holes they couldn't move. Or were reluctant to move. A forced immobility.

It took us quite a while to get back to the gully and the whole experience was like the 1970s Leo Tolstoy movie *War and Peace* where the Russian prisoners are escorted back from Moscow in appalling conditions. The season had changed overnight. Winter was on us. We got to the gully just as the light had gone. Carl remembers that it was early/late evening when we started the march, albeit with some moonlight. The temperature was also falling rapidly. The prisoners had to be kept somewhere, so we found a large hollow. We put them there. Unfortunately, the hollow was also a small marsh/boggy ground and acted as a cold sink. One of the prisoners was a very nice man. A dentist from Buenos Aires and we quietly talked together for a while about the war. He seemed to be an excellent chap, very educated and polite and a very nice man. We reflected his politeness back to him and we laughed together. I think I shared my tea with him. Sippers. Not someone you'd expect to be sat out here with all of us. He told us there was an officer in the group of prisoners and that the other soldiers were quite keen to do some damage to him. The officer was found and taken to one side and told to sit on a small hillock with a Marine guarding him. He was a belligerent little man with fire in his eyes who made it clear that he should be treated better than his men. That did not happen and did not sit well with us. We asked him if he spoke English; he indicated that he didn't. Our dentist had told us that he did. We didn't say anything to him and left him thinking he had fooled us. He was isolated and cold. Having a conversation near him in English saying what we would do to them all in the morning spooked him a bit. Specifically, we might hand him back over to his own soldiers. He was arrogant, but also a bit windy. He was working hard at keeping it together maybe.

Once he had been separated from the group, they all seemed to settle down a bit. I thought this was a bit peculiar really and couldn't understand why. A bit like getting a fox out of a chicken coop. Each section had to do POW guard duty that night. This only seemed fair and we needed a full section on because there were too many of them. We stood around in the cold and watched them watching us. If we made a wet, we would often let them have some if they were really struggling. It wasn't worth being antagonistic to them. As they would say in all the small 'Commando' picture books/comics, 'For them, the war is over.' It certainly was. I think they were glad. Shattered, but glad. They seemed good lads. No need for hatred here. The night passed without further incident, except it was absolutely freezing, and the marsh started to freeze up. The bright clear night, the big moon and the damp made this an uncomfortable night for all of us.

At this stage of the war everything now seems even darker. All our business is in the dark now. Things are moving faster and the stakes seem much higher. This is quite exhilarating. It's only been forty-eight hours but it could have been weeks. Or minutes. Or maybe seconds. Time had slipped further and a kind of madness has come over the land. Not a bad madness, just madness. Maybe we need the madness.

Sunday 13 June
Day 23
Up at 0730 to guard Argie POWs, temp still in -0°C. Had scran, bombarded again. Had warning order as for attack on Sapper Hill. Spent day preparing for attack. The sun is out and very clear but is very cold. Guns are bombarding Sapper Hill all day. [written next day] As I write this I am absolutely knackered in my slug on a diddle-dee mattress in the open. We started yomping at 22.30 to cover 2 K to start line, on the way we had to go through 3 minefields – Mr Allen and Mac McGregor had their feet blown off – I have never heard screaming like it. Advanced to FUP – arrived 05.30 – took about 8–9 hours to cover 2 K. Left FUP at 10.00 on Monday and went back to old position.

We had pulled the early morning cold shift for guarding the prisoners. Of course, it still wasn't light; it didn't get light until about 10 a.m. Of course, it was freezing too. When it did get fully light, we were hit by shellfire again. Not enough to cause a panic but close enough to get the shock wave. By now we really had got used to it.

The Argentine prisoners were in a sorry state having sat in their freezing marsh all night. I was now in danger of feeling sorry for them. They were covered in mud and filth and that strange smell still hung in the air and clung to everything. We were covered in mud and filth too. What a bizarre sight in the middle of nowhere.

I am informed by someone, and I can't remember who, that the belligerent Argentine officer needs to be taken to the Welsh Guards Battalion HQ for interviewing/interrogation or whatever Guardsmen do to their prisoners. I select Paddy to come with me and we approach the isolated form of the officer, who is still sat on his rock. Paddy puts on his cold weather clothing, his pusser's grey blanket with the hole cut in the middle; he ironically looks like Pancho Villa. Again.

We nonchalantly stroll up to him and I politely say, 'Right pick up your stuff and come with us.'

He doesn't move and continues his non-English-speaking stance. I'm tired by this time and I'm not up for someone giving us a hard time.

Again, I politely say, 'Pick up your stuff and come with us.' He looks at us like we are lesser mortals. Again, I say, getting a bit frustrated, 'Pick up your f*****g gear and come with us.' Giving him my best Paddington Bear Commando Hard Stare and he still doesn't move. How can he stand this pressure? He's continuing to play the non-English-speaking role. We grab him by the scruff of the neck and pull him along.

'Now come along, old chap, you really must come with us,' we urge him in our best British commando-ish way.

He resists, slightly. Enough to claim his resistance. He is gently encouraged to walk with us by the timely and gentle application of a Cairngorm boot. He still shows some reluctance. We don't hurt him, we needn't do that; all we want him to do is move, then we can go back and have a wet. I'm not sure what he thought we were going to do. Maybe he was judging us by what he would have done. It takes us a while to encourage him towards the HQ, which is away round the small spur and up a small grassy gully. The sun is up and the air is still very cold. We individually stink so as a group of three individuals, we collectively pong of people who have lived in the field forever. We have all probably already seen too much.

What I see next nearly takes my tactical breath away and makes me weep internally with frustration and laugh with queasy admiration. Imagine the scene. It is a bright morning and we are very close to the enemy and we round the bottom of the gulley and ahead of us about 100 metres away is a great big green tent. Probably a military 9 x 9 tent. (nine-by-nine) This is what REMFs use. Outside the tent are some chairs and a small collapsible table. Arranged correctly. A gentle scene is being enacted by the players on this extremely curious stage. There is a lad running around like a mess-man or an MOA (Marine Officer's Attendant) in our Corps, serving stuff to clean-looking men who are sat cross-legged at the table, blue Bergens lying around in a heap on the ground, seemingly uncared for. We stand motionless and dumbfounded by the sight, our jaws probably flapping in the gentle breeze. Here we are on the front line and these people are having a picnic. We have not been resupplied and are suffering. We are suffering tactically and calorifically, down in our shared frozen marsh. This is clearly the Mad Hatter's Tea Party and I am very clearly at the very bottom of my rabbit hole. I have met the Mad Hatter. Maybe I am the Mad Hatter and don't know it.

As we near the tent a tall, regal officer with blond wavey hair and red gloves waits for us. He looks down his nose at us as though we are undesirables. He is everything a Guards officer should be: tall, dashing, handsome in a posh way, and still wearing his red gloves. RED! He is extremely clean. Oddly clean. He manifests regal and in a strange sort of way I am kind of impressed. In a Raj, Indian Mutiny, Ladysmith kind of way, not in a Falklands War way, an oddly captivating scene.

'Here's the Argie officer you wanted.'

Tall, clean, regal officer says, keeping his distance: 'Good God, he's a bit of a mess, isn't he?'

'You'd be in a bit of a mess too if I'd just kicked you all the way here.' (Swearwords omitted).

Officer looks very unimpressed. Guards Officers can do that very easily. 'I don't think – then you shouldn't talk,' says the Mad Hatter quickly. The Argentine officer recognises fellow officer spirits and naturally gravitates towards them. We don't object. Our job is complete. We shrug and turn round and leave this scene of Henley-on-Harriet. What sort of war have we got ourselves involved with here? We shrug and stroll back to our position and put on a wet of tea and wait for the next episode of madness to unravel. It doesn't take long. It never seems to take long.

We get a warning order that we are to put an attack in on Sapper Hill. Bill tells me to get the boys ready. Being good soldiers who know how to do battle preparation, we immediately put a wet on and start preparing. The rest of the warry kit is ready anyway. So it is just prepared a little bit more and is ready to fling on and go when we are needed. However, we don't hold our breath. We have learnt this response. Hurry up and wait.

The hills over the back of Harriet are still being bombarded. At one stage we stand and watch as a Harrier comes screaming in from our left as we look north, flying very low and very fast; just as it comes to Harriet it flips up vertically and a long, large bomb is flung off the bottom of the plane. The bomb doesn't fall vertically – it flies horizontally and continues flying over the hill. The Harrier roars off and the bomb disappears over the hills. Lobbed. We wait about four or five seconds and there is a huge *crump* and shock wave as it goes off. Crikey, that's new, big too. It was brilliant, I've never seen anything like it.

Later in the day we are given orders to move position ready for the attack on Sapper Hill. We are not to cover too many miles, so it doesn't seem like too much of a problem. It's dark again and we get our kit together and form up at about 10 o'clock at night. The weather is clear and we are tasked to lead the Guards into the form-up position. (Note: I accept that this incident may have happened before this day and I wrote it up incorrectly.) We are all in one long snake again and we are at the front. We start yomping and the snake concertinas back and forward. One minute sprinting and the next almost at a standstill. All unit snakes are like this and there's not a thing you can do about it. Ged and Bri are near me as usual. The stars are bright and the kit we are carrying still seems heavy. We have everything. Everything we need for a fight and no more. My feet are still in a reasonable state thanks to these Cairngorms. We are in good form. We have got stronger.

After some time, we round a small hillock and start along the side of a small valley. In the bright light of the moon, we can see an armoured vehicle across the low valley pointing in the same direction as us. It's static. No movement. Using our heavyweight night vision kit (IWS) we can make out in the green glow that it is one of our Scorpion tanks. What is that doing here; are they lost? Still at least it's ours, so we forget it and keep moving.

We continue further in the darkness. Heads down with the weight of kit, we are in the rhythm but keeping alert. We are not far from their positions.

Whump!

A muffled explosion and immediate earie silence.

After about three seconds came a screaming like I have never heard. It was so high pitched my first instinct was to turn to Big Ged and say, 'What the f**'s a woman doing out here?' The sound was awful and kind of put the willies up us all.

We started to quietly discuss what it might have been. A very strange sound. We had stopped by now and we assumed all sorts of possibilities. Based on our limited experience. The screaming continued. Some were serious considerations and some weren't; in fact, most weren't. We grinned. Somewhere back down the snake there had been an explosion. We walked around discussing our theories in expansive gestures. We thought it might have been a grenade in someone's pouch that had accidently gone off; we came up with several ideas but the one thing we hadn't identified was the possibility of a mine.

Word came forward that Mac had stood on an anti-personnel mine and it had blown his foot off. According to a 7 Troop lad, the foot had come off, gone over the heads of some guys behind him in the snake and had hit one of the blokes in the face several men back. This had freaked that bloke out and all in all the Troop behind us was having a bit of a trauma. As soon as we heard it was a mine we froze to the spot. Minefield. The night was freezing and there was ice forming everywhere and Mac was not a happy man. They had given him morphine and he'd settled down and was quiet now. Surely the Argentines had heard us. This incident occurred 20 metres or less behind us in the commando snake.

Lieutenant Paul Allen, Mac's Troop commander, walked back along the line to find out what was going on. He recognised it was his job and he needed to be there. He stepped on a mine and he had his foot blown off as well. Another *whump*. However, there wasn't any screaming this time. Apparently, he was very calm about it. He said later that he had made a decision not to scream and alert the enemy. Morphine was administered by Andy Pillar and Ken Hames, who were first on the scene.

There we were near the enemy, in the dark, illuminated by the moon with all sorts of explosions happening around us and standing in a minefield. They were bound to see us soon. They did too and soon we had shells coming down around us.[2] However, that wasn't our primary problem. The focus of the problem lay beneath our feet and underground. We were still frozen to the spot, afraid to move. No, let me rephrase that: Marines are never afraid, just a bit apprehensive.

Apparently, M. A. Black, our Royal Navy commando medic, had dealt with all the problems on the scene. He was an ace bloke, the best I've ever seen. Our medics were Royal Navy commando medics. A breed apart. Anyway, the casualties were dealt with and the artillery had calmed down a bit. After some time, we got fed up with this sticking-to-the-spot stuff so we started moving around. If we were going to get blown up, then so be it. Prodding around for them with your bayonet seemed daft as well. We threw our Bergens on the ground. Dramatically. They didn't explode so we sat on them, in a small peat cutting. Ged sat next to me and so did Brian. We talked quietly for a while about nothing in particular. No more explosions. Just waiting again. Someone will solve this.

The Commando Assault Engineers from 59 Commando came through us checking the ground. Good lads. They are experts at this, they truly are. They laid some white mine tape for us to follow and away we went as a company, minus Mac and Mr Allen. They had been recovered by a Wasp helicopter flown into a minefield at night and under fire. Brave stuff.

We were still at the front of the whole unit snake. Following the white tape. We eventually arrived at the end of the white tape. The guy at the front didn't know what to do so he stopped and we all piled up behind him.

He was squealing, 'the f*****g tape's stopped, the f*****g tape's stopped' and pushing back on the guys who were piling up behind him.

We pointed out this was the end of the minefield. Continue. By this time, we're getting a bit threaders with the whole thing. We'd been yomping for hours and hadn't got very far at all. The story of this affair is recounted by one of the Royal Marine Assault Engineers who came

---

2. Subsequently discussing this with Andy Pillar he said there was no artillery falling on us. I am still convinced of this and so is Jono. I would imagine Andy was consumed with concentration while working on Mac and Paul to worry about a trivial little thing like artillery shells landing near him.

through us and cleared the field for us. Apparently, the AEs came up and started prodding the ground and clearing the mines. After some time, they got threaders and in good bootneck fashion decided to rap. They sat down by the side of their handiwork. Our front guy, seeing them sit down, stood up, said cheers to them and started walking, assuming that the job was finished. The AEs were horrified but couldn't stop us. We all filed past saying cheers in a suitably tactical voice and disappeared into the dark over the unfinished minefield. We continued through blissfully unaware of the mines and got through unscathed. We continued through two more minefields but by now we were old hands; they were inconsequential and we didn't lose any parts of our bodies.

We arrived at our destination early and after some rest the tactical decision was made that we should return to our gully. This was normal military procedure. A story by one of the company lads says that Bill said he didn't know how to tell us all. How would we take being told to turn round. He was at the front. He says he turned round in the dark and all he saw was the whole company down on one knee looking up at him. He says he was nearly overwhelmed with affection for his lads. We were happy to follow Bill anywhere, so all was well. The affection was returned.

Apparently, we had all walked over the mine that had eventually got Mac. The ground was so frozen that the pressure pad only went down a little bit at a time as we all walked on it. Unfortunately for Mac it was he who applied the final pressure required. Maybe this was the case for Paul's mine as well.

Sometime during this night, we were looking off down to the southeast across the bays and islands. The ground was flat and open and the moon was out and big and bright. The night was clear and cold and we could see for miles. We could see forever. Over to our left and a long way off there was a big *kaboom* and a missile passed in front of us, some miles away, from left to right. Very low across the landscape, skimming. Fast. Seeking. We watched it in seemingly slow motion across the landscape, skimming the ground with a big orange tail to it. It definitely seemed to know where it was going. We stared and followed it away and into the darkness. There was a distant explosion. We wondered what it could be. Just another weird thing in our new lives. One of the lads said it was an Exocet, maybe it was. In hindsight it was the Exocet that hit the *Glamorgan*.

Chapter 7

Sapper Hill – A Fight for Our Lives

Alice: How long is forever?
White Rabbit: Sometimes, just one second.

Lewis Carroll, 1865

Monday 14 June
Day 24
In the gully, arrived there at first light. Gurkhas and Scots Guards are still fighting for their objectives. The Arty and ship fire is incredible. The weather is so cold even all lakes are iced up, -20°C.[1] Got my head down for about an hour, called suddenly to get ready so we readied and headed for the choppers, 9 Tp flew first and we were dropped right next to Sapper Hill, right into a firefight with the Argies on the Hill, it was just like Vietnam, the firefight lasted for 10 mins and Vince caught it up in the arm, we were mortared on the edge of the road, where the mines were, eventually we got comms with HQ and found that Stanley had surrendered, we had done it, we all then marched to Stanley where we set up on Sapper Hill. Dropped 5.5 K forward of other elements, we think it was planned. 4 kills to us at least.

We yomped back to our gully, again. No one dripped; this was normal for us. The Gurkhas and the Scots Guards are still on their objectives giving the Argentines a hard time. Many things are becoming confused today. In fact many things have been confusing over the last few days. The temperature and who did the fighting and probably much, much

---

1. These temperatures are clearly incorrect.

more. Our supporting fire is extremely effective and we are quite used to the sound of shells going over our heads now. It is no longer anything to be acknowledged; it just feels normal and would probably seem strange if it was not there as a backing track.

It's still dark and me, Terry and Ged have got ourselves wrapped in a poncho like a taco on the thick diddle-dee and are staring up at the sky again. No sleeping bags. It's got even colder and our shared warmth is doing us some minimal good. The inevitable is starting to become obvious. The thought of going into a battle is something we talk about but not for long. This is a subject to be talked around rather than discussed directly. Equipment is frozen this morning. The ground is frozen and white. We are covered in white frost and snow.

We sleep for a short while but are woken and told to get our kit on and meet up in the gully. Bill tells us we are going forward and to make sure all the guys are ready. Down we go and form up into sticks. It is a short wait and immediately the choppers land, we pile on. Normally we've had to wait for them, but not this time; someone is in a rush to get this over with. Our Troop is the first to emplane on two Sea Kings, 'Pingers' or helicopters rigged for anti-submarine warfare. Just before we take off Andy and Jono are told by one of their lads that his feet are too dodgy to last him through the coming battle. He is left behind.

We pile on and squat with our weapons at the ready. Suddenly this has got extremely serious. The idea is that we are to be flown forward to Mount William, which the Gurkhas have just secured. We are to secure the start line for the composite Welsh Guards battalion to form up and advance to battle on Sapper Hill. The battalion now consists of one rifle company of Guards and two of 40 Commando including the Guards Support Company. Our Support Company had been split up and sent to 45 and 42 and even further afield.

Securing the start line is no real problem; in fact it means we will probably stay there while the others pass through us to press on to the objective and we will come up in the rear and do our bit. Undoubtedly, we would get some sort of a fight. Remember it's a team game. There's no real tension on the chopper; in fact it's a bit like a normal move in the UK except for a few minor twists. It is broad daylight, the sun is bright and we are hurtling along at a speed that I have not travelled at in a chopper before, especially at this height. We seem to be at ground level, hugging the terrain and doing a thousand miles an hour. The guys are looking at each other with pure excitement in their eyes; this is fantastic. I share a glance with Rick and we beam big smiles at each other. We start to whistle and hum the tune from *Apocalypse Now* when the First of the Ninth Air Cav go in to the village in choppers: 'Ride of the Valkyries' soundtrack. This felt just like that and everyone was hooked into it. We laughed and sang. However, I remember looking out of the nearest window and thinking, 'We've been going for a long time, haven't we, and fast as well?' Big beaming smiles through blacked-out and filthy faces. We were well used to using choppers. In fact, as commandos we were never out of the things and you got used to the feeling of speed and time. This was fast and we'd been here a long time, maybe a bit too long as far as I could calculate. I was not an expert by any means but you know when you know. Time and distance are not too complex.

The thought started to vanish as we came to a screaming, flaring landing. We knew what came next; what we'd do was get out and start our work in the normal fashion under the watchful eye of the Gurkhas on the mountain above. Before we had got the chance to land properly, the whole of the left side of the chopper seemed to shatter with bits and pieces flying everywhere, the noise deafening. Debris flew everywhere. I remember seeing the sky and a hillside clearly through the side of the chopper; most of it seemed to be missing. 9 Troop was in it again, well and truly dropped in it, right up to our necks. The chopper had thudded onto the deck and guys started spilling out through the door on the right-hand side. Smiles gone. The rotors were still going full blast and guys were going everywhere.

We had landed on the small, light-coloured gravel track just at the base of the rocky spine of Sapper Hill, and the choppers were being shot to pieces. We were still inside. We were being shot to pieces. I remember someone shouting, 'It's okay, it's only the Gurkhas on Mount William.' Blue on blue. I didn't believe it. Time shifted and slipped again, minutes became hours and seconds became lifetimes. Exit, road and think. I remember the tail rotor being very close to me as I crouched on the road. The choppers revved up and leapt into the air. I remember seeing them lift off with bits coming off them and banking away to the right and away they went. My mind said, 'Ba**ards.' My head was spinning to make sense of this and we were still being shot to bits. I couldn't believe the choppers had left us. The noise was phenomenal. Normally when choppers leave, a true feeling of peace descends. Quite the opposite now; suddenly the sounds of battle crashed in around us. I remember standing there on the track and throwing guys off the road and into the cover afforded by the slight camber of the road, that 6 to 8 inches or so. The bizarre, intrusive thought of the line from *An American Werewolf in London* jumped to mind: 'Stay on the road and stay clear of the moors.' I remembered that someone earlier had said that the road was mined on both sides but this didn't seem to be relevant at this stage; it seemed a much better option to be in the minefield than on the road in broad daylight without any help or cover. Vince knelt at my side and with his GPMG in his hip, sprayed the hill just behind us. The enemy were only a short distance away, and seemed much closer than they probably were.

Once everyone seemed to be in cover, I decided to leap into the minefield too. There was no space left for me. The only option was to go further into the minefield behind the line of lads already there. I leapt. Vince stayed for a moment longer then he went too. I sailed over the top of the other lads and found myself in mid-air with bullets zinging all around me and thinking, 'Sh*t, I'm in mid-air. If I survive this I'm only going to land on a mine and get blown back onto the road.' Time slowed and sped up and slowed. Slipping left and right. I landed and waited for the now familiar thud. No thud, thank God. I look up and Sponner was in front of me, with Andy next to him, then Elvis and the Boss a few feet away to my right. The noise of the incoming fire was tremendous and deafening. We started to return fire as a Troop and … I froze; not just froze – more like I was literally petrified to the spot, nothing was working, only the brain. I lay there with my head buried in the snow, thinking, 'This is definitely it, I haven't got any cover, nothing, I'm going to be killed.' This feeling of being petrified has never left me. I was absolutely rigid. I'm not even sure if it was fear; it was literally the body doing its own thing. There was no panic. I remember looking at the snow in my face and under my helmet and thinking quite logically and coolly, 'Right, I'm going to will myself underground now. I'm actually going to move my body underground without moving a muscle.' Andy said he looked over his shoulder at me and thought I was dead. I must have been there for only a short time but it felt like an eternity and all the time I was waiting for the inevitable tug of the bullet and the warm feeling. I had this overwhelming certainty that if I raised my head I would receive an instantaneous bullet between the eyes, a third eye. My mind became preoccupied with this notion and my head became reluctant to move. I was not a religious man by any means before this moment. I remember calmly saying to God, 'If you get me out of this I'll believe in you till I die.' You're apparently not supposed to make deals with God. I did. I also remember logically thinking if this is it, really it, then what happens? I knew all my kit would go to Andy but what would happen to me? If I died now, would I just be dead and that's it, nothing else? I couldn't compute this as a concept. I couldn't believe that I'd die 8,000 miles from home on this piece of scrappy, snowy ground. My body would be stuck under the ground and I'd be gone. This was when I realised that there must be more to life than just us, just our bodies; there must be something else inside us. Maybe that soul that Irish poets talk of. It sounds crackpot and I accept that. I make no excuses. It was a weird sensation and one that I had not been prepared for. This all happened extremely quickly. It was logical, calculated and calm. I'm sure it only took seconds. Maybe it didn't. I had probably hit the bottom of my rabbit hole. That would seem logical.

Terry remembers:[2]

> During my time in the Falklands War, days seemed to blur into one as did events. What was hours seemed like minutes and minutes might have been hours. What happened in relation to time, in reality is difficult to gauge. When your life and your close friends' lives are at risk, time does not matter; it is events that make outcomes and these outcomes/actions are what we recall. In the 'fog of war' people will become confused and become separated from others. In the following sections I will recall what I witnessed and my emotions at the time. Others, whom may have been in the same location may have different views; both can be correct from the protagonist's perspective.

---

2. Terence Victor Barnes. (2021) *Before, During and After my Falklands War*. All contributions by Terry are taken from his book.

All these sensations and feelings happened very quickly and before I knew it, I was back to normal and fully functioning. This must have taken seconds to compute. Maybe it took longer, who knows. Who cared but time had truly slipped to one side. It was like snapping out of a dream state and suddenly finding yourself back on earth. My thoughts of a third eye had completely gone. Thoughts of death had gone, they'd all gone, just evaporated without any thought process from me. I was not afraid, and that was weird. Cold clarity. Maybe I had resigned myself to the inevitability of being killed so it wasn't worth worrying about. So just concentrate on your job. It'll happen when it happens. I remember lifting my head and looking up and seeing the lads again. The rounds were still coming thick and fast but I wasn't concerned anymore. They even mortared us and the clods of earth landed all over me. I checked my body just in case some foreign object had found its way in without me knowing. I couldn't feel any holes or any wetness so I was probably okay. Again, I wasn't concerned; it was now just a job to get on with it. Maybe I was concerned that I wasn't concerned. Cold logic returned.

I looked over the backside of Sponner and Andy and saw the hill clearly above us in strong, clear sunlight, everywhere white with snow. My focus was back. I could clearly see some heads moving around up there between the rocks, not far away on the skyline on the spine of the ridge. On the stegosaurus ridge. I remember taking aim, very carefully and calmly; I waited for a head to reappear where I had seen it go down behind the rocks. Sure enough, it predictably popped back up again. I took a slow breath, released some breath and I remember releasing the round at the head. That was easy; I hope they're all that easy. As I released the round, I saw Sponner's buttocks momentarily clench as the round passed over them by a couple of inches, which amused me somewhere inside. Looking off to my left I could see a tight knot of lads, Elvis one of them, half-kneeling. Apparently, Vince had been hit and the boys were trying to sort him out. There wasn't any noise, nothing at all coming from Vince; the wound was a really nasty one. Andy was blasting away and the Boss was taking charge. Another head appeared. Clearly silhouetted. I calmly released the next round and the same outcome as the last one. This was a doddle and Sponner's arse flinched again. I heard some screaming off to my left. One of the guys was screaming, 'I've been hit in the arse, I've been hit in the arse.' All the guys were giggling by this stage, the ludicrous position we were in causing considerable laughter. It was suddenly quite cool. One of the blokes crawled over to him. Apparently, a round had passed down his back and gone into one of his rear pouches on his webbing, coming to rest on his backside. The round was red hot and he rightly thought he'd been shot. Quite a few of the guys had their pouches shot off them, which became a subject of further amusement. I think Nick had two pouches shot clean off; he was a lucky man. Mind you, Nick was invincible; everyone knew that. He was a huge man; how had they missed him and only hit a small pouch. Improbable but possible. Things were moving very fast.

The first stage of the fight seemed to be over.

The second stage of the fight began. Strangely enough, the firefight started to rock backwards and forwards just as we had been taught it would. First, they would fire with all they had and we'd get our heads down, then we'd fire with everything we had and they'd get their heads down. This socially accepted agreement went on for some time, rocking backwards and forwards.

Alejandro was on the hill looking at us:

Already on the night of June 13–14 and during the early morning of this last day, we observed the continuous lines of fire of the attacker, which flowed and converged in 'Tumbledown'. It was really a Dantesque spectacle that came to completely illuminate the closed night.

In the early hours of June 14, we were violently surprised by ground artillery, with a precision hitherto unknown, the impacts occurred literally on the location of our positions, leaving in view craters of singular proportions and made all the surrounding terrain tremble.

After this attack, late in the morning we began to see the movement of own troops perched on the main road in the direction of Puerto Argentino. Slowly but inexorably we see the passage of members of different units.

With such a panorama and in the absence of specific orders I go to the company command post, at about noon;

there the Chief himself, imposes on me the order to retreat my Section under the concept of establishing the final defense on the perimeter of Puerto Argentino.

With that idea in mind, I descended from the hill in the direction of my own positions. There the personnel were outside them, expectant about the orders to be given, when I was very close, we received the alert regarding the proximity of enemy helicopters; The first of these, a 'Sea King', remained practically static for a period that seemed like an eternity, without its pilots guessing the course to follow. It is in that period that my paintings [soldiers] ask me what to do and so after making sure that it was an English helicopter, I ordered by means of the signal of rigor to open fire, an order that was finally fulfilled by the entire Section.

The helicopter continued to be suspended for a few seconds, until it made the decision to fall towards its starboard in the direction of the sea, and a few meters away proceeded to disembark infantry troops without completing their landing. After that and already smoky from the impacts received, you can see its landing in a southerly direction. Those troops immediately take linear position, getting a brief cover in a terrain accident and begin firing profusely on our positions.

By the time I fired my rifle at the helicopter, he had locked himself, crawled down to retrieve a backpack in which he had collected ammunition of all kinds and approached the position of one of the MAG machine guns, to verify why he was not firing. I found shooting; It turned out that his pointer had been wounded and I considered him dead, so I instantly decided to operate on it with my own hands.

I started shooting and immediately perceived the accuracy of the enemy fire response, the projectiles literally grazed my head, so I decided to look for a more covered firing position, this is simply lower, as more protection could not be obtained as the front of the position was built with peat. I also used brief seconds to rank the raise according to the distance I estimated the enemy was.

The Cabo Segundo IM SINI, office of shipper. There were many bands that were used in combat.

The very appreciation of the time taken by the action exceeds me, in that there is a total and absolute loss of notion of it I only know that it shoots continuously, beating the sector of British soldiers from left to right and in reverse on repeated, successive and continuous occasions, in every possible way. I remember changing the piece for a better shooting location and burning the palm of my right hand due to the temperature of the barrel tube, a product of its continuous use.

It was evident at that moment the offensive impulse attacker, as one of the enemy soldiers set out to lead it managing to cross the road that led to Puerto Argentino, reaching a distance very close to us, being thus killed by multiple shots of his own.

This sequence continued until the fire ceased from the place it came from. It is at this moment that I get rid of the piece and start my own retreat. I was the last soldier.

In my retreat, I find lying the body of Private Robledo, which moments before had been loaded by Corporal Segundo IM Sini, in an attempt to move it to his own line, I adopt in the event identical posture, I charge it on my shoulders and begin to move it. A few meters I perceive his body already lifeless, with multiple visible impacts on his chest and abandon the attempt.

I continue my retreat, in search of the command post of company, for this I had to ascend the southern slope of Sapper Hill, in search of support while, constantly, I am the object of shots whose projectiles surround me; its impact on the undergrowth that surrounds me is clearly perceived, they coming from another place, that is from a course further west, corresponding, as I would later learn from troops who would have disembarked from other helicopters in that sector.

As I retreated from the hill, the helicopter that first approached our positions, lands steaming as I said, a few miles to the south, another helicopter of similar characteristics was also hit by the fire of our weapons.

In relation to these events I always had the question, what was the real reason why, the helicopter or the infantry transported in it decided to lock themselves in combat, since having radio communication, they knew that the hostilities had ceased.

It was very evident that the commander of the aircraft hesitated to leave the area when he realized that his presence was the object of gunfire and why he came so close to our positions. They are all unknowns that still remain in my thoughts.

Without prejudice to this, there is one that I could eventually clarify and that is the following. The English helicopter was not armed, therefore its proximity in terms of concrete attack was not perfectly defined and strictly speaking it did not represent in that context either a threat and / or imminent danger, however, I ordered to open fire on it; Was that correct? I have been assimilating the answer for several years, but today I am convinced that I have acted as the situation demanded and according to the information I had at that difficult time.

I received a final order to retreat my Section to stand in defense at a point further north;

It could have avoided confrontation with the heli carried troops, surely it was, but the decision made was totally consistent with the previous order given: DEFEND and that could be done there or elsewhere.

In fact I was the last man to remain on the battlefield, this as a simple objective assessment and without claiming any merit of his own.

The second part of the fight was moving fast. Looking left, I saw Neil Pleasance with his Clansman 351 Radio trying to get help. The original plan was to advance to contact. Neil had rightly put on a trailing antenna. This was a piece of trailing wire instead of a solid aerial sticking straight up and advertising his importance in the Troop, making him an obvious target. Unfortunately, the range of the set is dramatically reduced by using this dangling wire aerial. He had to get this aerial upright somehow. I remember seeing him with his arm stuck up above cover holding the end of the wire as high as he could to try to get reception. The look on his face was comical, a squint saying, 'I'm about to lose my arm.' I remember internally squinting too and waiting for it to happen but hoping it wouldn't. Apparently, he couldn't get comms at all. The firefight continued back and forth unchanged, as the rounds flew both ways with a vengeance.

In the middle of this I remember the Boss calmy looking over his shoulder and looking right into my eyes and quietly saying, 'Chris, I could order you to fix bayonets and charge now … [long pause] … but I won't.' I was relieved. If we had stood up at that moment we would have lost three-quarters of the Troop in one go. I was absolutely sure of it. Many others were convinced of this too. In the pause between 'now' and 'but' I thought, 'Good grief, Carl. You're actually going to do it.' His decision saved lives. It may not have been the commando response required by our 'system' but we saved many lives that day with a very sensible decision.

Off to my left Nick Holloway and Jono and another couple of guys leapt up and raced across the road. I couldn't see where they were going but I thought, 'Uh oh, we're on the move … get ready.' But nothing happened. Were they dead? I couldn't see them. Crikey. 66mm LAWs were being fired from our side. Sam banged a couple of 66s off at the ridge. So did Dee. 7.62mm and .5 inch was coming back at us in a wall of metal, red hot metal. Probably white hot.

At some odd moment during this and without any orchestration, the whole Troop started singing Monty Python's 'Always look on the bright side of life' and we started giggling again. The situation suddenly turned into a comedy where we all simultaneously found the silly side of it. It wasn't so bad after all; at least we were with all our mates. The roar continued from both sides. We sang and shot at the enemy. They shot at us. I always wondered if the Argentines could hear us singing. That would have been bizarre. This was a very odd moment in the battle, but it seemed to turn the tide.

Time had gone from super-speed to slower, then back to super-speed. In the super-speed moments, there is no panic but it all feels … fast.

In the slow-motion moments it is in super-slow motion. Maybe the brain is working so fast and that it makes it all feel slow. Time was super-slipping again. There seemed to be no control on which you had and when.

As I looked at the hill from where I was, the left of the hill was a spine of rocks but the hill tapered off to its right, my right, onto slightly easier ground. I have always known that 'don't just look to your front, don't just look to your front … they'll come from somewhere else'. It's what I would do. Do the unexpected. I looked right. Around this exact point came about fifteen or so Argentines in a formation, a loose sort of formation, more of an extended line, not really a formation but a loose group. They were trying to attack us! Cheeky and good effort. I informed my gunner. Bri saw this and immediately shouted for more belted ammo for his gun. The air was instantly full of green bandoliers floating towards him. They all landed on his back and pinned him to the deck; there were so many of them he could hardly move. We all laughed. It was comical. He was dug out and the ammo was sorted and as one, all our guns started up together. Terry had taken Vince's GPMG and was doing a fantastic job. He switched fire too to the advancing men. It wasn't really necessary for us to use our weapons, we needed to conserve our ammo; the guns could do the work. The targets fell and ran. Skinhead went mad with his gun, a manic grin on his face as he blasted off belt after belt and seemed to drop loads of them. Wikipedia says that 'Marine Midshipman Marcelo Davis's 1st Platoon from M/BIM 5 attempted a counterattack but were beaten back.'[3] It was a good effort and we appreciated it. The ones who were still standing ran. Good thinking. It must have been the last attack that the Argentine Army did in the war and well done to them. It is professionally possible for one soldier to admire another soldier's actions, enemy or not. Good effort, lads.

The firefight continued, backwards and forwards, backwards and forwards. Ged was to my left and took a brilliant photo of us in action. At the time I was unaware of his creative streak striking him but later when I heard what he'd done I was quietly furious that he wasn't shooting.

---

3. It is accepted that this source may be weak and therefore may be incorrect, but it is an interesting insert.

However, now I have this prized photo in my album, I am very glad and pleased he did it. Good decision, Ged.

While all this was going on, Neil P had retained his arm and somehow had got comms with the rest of the company; he'd heard that there was a white flag flying over Stanley and that they had all surrendered. We'd done it, we'd done it, us, 9 Troop had won the war. Just us, all by ourselves. Little old 9 Troop. Euphoric.

Of course, it wasn't and we hadn't, but it felt like it. The firefight slowed down and seemed to peter out. The Argentines seemed to disappear. I just remember someone saying, 'Make safe and stand up' in a range-day Platoon Weapons Instructor-type of voice. I remember thinking, 'Not on your nellie, I'm not making safe for anybody; I've just nearly been killed.' But no, the order was correct: 'Unload, unfix bayonets and make safe, it's all over.' We looked at each other through unbelieving, narrowed eyes. Are you sure? Do they know? How do we know they know? Do they know we know?

I remember very slowly getting to my feet. Ready to drop back down again instantly. This is bound to be a trick, I thought, and we're all going to get killed by a trick. We all stood up, in very, very slow motion. When I was finally vertical, I remember turning to Carl, who was also standing, and saying, 'I'm never doing that again.' He smiled. I smiled. I meant it.

It was finished. We got together as a Troop and I remember Andy comparing how many rounds we'd fired. He said he had used nearly all his. I was slightly embarrassed that I hadn't fired off that many. I didn't mention it at the time but I did feel quietly secure that what I had fired had probably counted. My father trained me in precision and perfection and that's what I applied to my shooting skills. It all came back to my main fear. I felt that I needed to conserve as much ammo as possible for future possibilities. That was my theory and my irrational fear. I could always give Andy some of my rounds anyway if we had been tasked to take Stanley. Things had cooled off. The firing had stopped and we were stood and taking it all in. Off to our left Vince was lying on the snowy ground, still being dealt with by the lads. Blood everywhere. Alex had a head injury and was down as well, being dealt with. That's all I could see from where I was. I remember being relatively unconcerned and detached; our section seemed okay, thank you God. Jono asked if we could go up and do a body count, but he was refused the opportunity.

There is that unhelpful offhand saying at times like this. 'What doesn't kill you, makes you stronger'. Sublime.

7 Troop had been landed some kilometres to our rear and had heard that we were in trouble and Adrian and his guys set off down the road at a sprint to get to us and help with the fight. Adrian said it was a manic run at full tilt, knowing that we were in trouble. Unfortunately, they were just a bit too late to get involved. We were overjoyed to see our oppos and very grateful they had all made such an effort to get to us. Friendships seemed to solidify further.

Strangely, time became peculiar again around about now. I had been either on super-fast time or super-slow motion during the fight but now everything was slowing down. It was slowing down slowly and at a constant speed. My head was having problems calculating the changes. I checked over my body again and we checked each other; this was a miracle, how the heck had we all got through that. Time became dreamlike and more detached for a short while and seemed to drift like smoke. Quite irrelevant, but an interesting sensation. Guys were everywhere on the little road in the snow. 9 Troop and 7 Troop.

The next thing I knew there was a small tank on the road right in front of me. A bright sunny day, snow all around. Soldiers on the tank riding. Not Marines, clearly. I remember being quite unimpressed that they wanted to get past us and I was immediately suspicious of their intentions. Another imperious officer in the tank turret said something like, 'Get out of the way, my good man, we're going on up to Sapper Hill to take it.' I remember disagreeing with him and saying that we took this hill and we were going up first. The disagreement progressed to an argument. I stood in the middle of the road feet firmly spread apart with some of the Troop lads with me and the tank crew grinning down at us. They clearly thought they had the upper hand. We collectively decided that they shouldn't pass. Pointed rifles at the man in the tank might convince them. I wasn't quite sure what the long-term intention was. It was a bluff of course. I thought the argument was won by this action. The argument became a bit more animated, and they slowly rotated the turret and pointed their long-barrelled, high-velocity 30mm L21 RARDEN cannon straight at my face. Ah, I thought, staring up the barrel, you win. Bluff duly called. One thing I have learned is never ever say 'or else' unless you actually have an 'or else'. We moved and let them pass. We were not pleased with them, but we accepted their argument gracefully. As gracefully as we could when we were clearly outgunned. The tank roared off up the track. The incident was soon forgotten. Not a loss, just a learning point. We formed up in a staggered file and moved off behind the tank heading along the road and up the hill. Always remember, this is a team game. Even when you think it isn't.

As we walked, we found several bodies on the road. They were obviously new kills and we were curious. As we turned north at the back of the hill, the devastation was apparent. The place was like something I'd never imagined. There were dead blokes and bits of abandoned gear everywhere. Mud and shit, just mud and shit. It reminded me of those black and white pictures that my Grandad, Father Tom, had of the First World War and which I used to look at on Saturday afternoons at his house while he puffed on his fags. The world was monochromatic. We continued up the road in slow time, more of a bimble than with any speed; being tactical had just about gone out the window, but it was loosely maintained. We found one body without a head. We couldn't find the head; it had vanished. It had been taken off quite cleanly and had disappeared. Poor chap. It was a curious sight among many curious sights at the time.

We came up the hill from the south, through the mud and shit. I use the word 'shit' because clearly they had had no toilet facilities or toilet discipline so the word is exactly, descriptively correct. The smell was overpowering. That Argentine smell overcame us again. A Unimog vehicle had been abandoned and was half sunk in the mud and leaning to one side. As we passed, we peered inside and there on the gearstick was a bright red beret, a nice one too. Dee and I looked at it and between us, we leaned into the wagon, being careful not to touch anything in case of boobytraps. With a weapon we fished it off and got it out. Dee took it. It was a roof. It was a good roof. I was envious. We continued walking up through the mud and continued looking for proffs. There was so much equipment lying around in the mud. So much to roof. We heard that one of 40's Assault Engineers had been badly injured jumping into a trench. The enemy had laid boobytraps. He was a friend of us all. Nasty, and after the fighting had finished too. The story was probably aimed at putting us off scavenging through the trenches. It worked. While we were there, we liberated a whole stack of Argentine fags.

For some inexplicable reason I started smoking for the first time in my life. It seemed such a natural thing to do. First one then another and then many. I was not a smoker and never had been; my life was governed by physical fitness and I knew what these would do to me but I kept going and kept finding something comforting in this ritual. Now I was a chain smoker.

Suddenly, or was it slowly, the world had changed. My world had changed, in what felt like an instant. Maybe all our worlds had changed. I felt quite sanguine about the whole thing. The war was over. There was no more fighting to be done. Sapper Hill was empty of any live enemy soldiers. They had all gone. The detritus of war was everywhere. It was like a smelly landfill site. In the last day my life had moved significantly. I wasn't even sure how this would affect me. I wasn't even sure where I had moved to. I was definitely above myself. A subtle change and we had moved from aggressors to occupying forces. It had moved from survival in war and the fear that comes with it to survival in the landscape. Just a survival exercise again. We had no intention of going to Stanley; it wasn't even discussed as a possibility. Our immediate concern was the oncoming night and the cold that would come with it. We immediately reverted to scavenging mode. Some of the lads were tasked with finding food from the trenches. Others were given the role to find anything we could build with. We selected a cutting in the peat facing north where we could build a huge sanger. We could see Stanley in the half-light down below us. About fifteen minutes' walk away. We needed cover, warm food and water. We were in a semi-non-tactical mode so we could build big and comfortable. Food was found and shared. All our creative efforts were applied to this building project. Fully focused on the task.

The fighting had finished and we never spoke about it again. I had probably been to the bottom of my rabbit hole and in hindsight it seemed I was slowly coming back out of it. Time seemed to return to some normality and the correct colours seemed to return. The darkness lifted. Night was coming and we needed to move our fingers and get building. Urgency and application. Forget what happened today. Jono remembers this day:

> We were in a harbour position when suddenly I became aware of a lot of frenetic activity in the Company, Troop

commanders being called to the Company HQ position and mini briefings taking place, a definite sign things were about to happen. The Scots Guards had secured Mount Tumbledown and the Gurkhas had secured Mount William; the only high ground left was Sapper Hill, which overlooked the only tracked road into Port Stanley.

Our troop commander Lieutenant Carl Bushby called all the section commanders together and gave us a very quick set of orders. Basically 9 Troop were going to be flown forward to Mount William in advance of the company where we would become a fire support company and would give fire support to the attack on Sapper Hill.

We were told to get as much ammunition as possible and extra GPMGs. There was a hive of activity as kit was distributed and extra ammunition issued, then we waited for the helicopters. Very soon we could hear the sound of rotors and two Sea Kings appeared flying low and fast towards us. We noticed something strange about these two, they had humps just rear of the rotor blades, not the usual Commando Sea King troop carriers we were used to. When they landed it became apparent that these were anti-submarine Sea Kings being utilised due to the shortage of airframes. We lined up and clambered aboard.

The Troop was split in half with Troop HQ and the Boss in the first helicopter; we were in the second aircraft. Inside was a bit of a squeeze due to there being a sonar operator's position within the seating area. I moved up behind the two pilots' positions and put on a set of headphones to have comms with the crew if needed. Normally from this position I would get my map out to check on the route and identify landmarks, but I could see the crewman positioned by the large cargo door through which we had boarded had his map out; also the co-pilot in front of me had a map in his hands, so I stuffed mine back in my side pocket. We lifted off and followed the front helo.

Our flight time had been given as about ten minutes up to Mount William, which was being held by the Gurkhas, and we had been warned not to stray too far off the track where we would be dropped off because of mines. We flew very low and fast, contour flying about 500 metres between each helo. Ten minutes came and went and we were still hugging the terrain then we banked sharply left and picked up a track which we then followed.

Looking out over the pilot' helmets, I could see a small hill coming into view with the track running up to its right; then I saw the front helo start to flare and begin to descend toward the track some way short of this hill. We followed suit and looking out of the crew door immediately behind and on the left of the pilot's position, I could see through the small, hatched window figures dressed in green jumping up and scurrying away; there were also a couple of small fires burning that looked like they had been cooking. I assumed these were Gurkhas getting out of the way of the downwash from the rotors, which was throwing small pebbles up onto the aircraft's fuselage. Our crewman slid back the cargo door, which was facing away from the hill, in preparation for us to land and exit; the lads had stood up ready to go.

I suddenly became aware of flashes coming from the hill where these figures had scurried away, then realised these were not in fact Gurkhas but Argies who were now engaging the helicopters with small-arms fire. I glanced at the pilots who were sat passively waiting for the crewman to tell them we were off, completely unaware of what was happening around them; presumably with their helmets on they could not hear the pinging going on around the aircraft, I turned to face down the aircraft as the first few lads were jumping out, and began trying to shout above the noise to warn the rest, who from inside the fuselage, couldn't see what was happening. Just at that moment a string of tracer rounds passed through the cabin from right to left as I was looking, passing just in front of the crewman. His eyes took on the size of dinner plates and I saw him start to shout frantically into his helmet mike. The lads who saw it needed no more encouragement to get out quickly and I could already feel the helo starting to lift. By the time I got to the door the aircraft was lifting and beginning to bank away from the hill, and I jumped from a rapidly increasing height to land just at the side of the track.

I rolled over and became quickly aware of a tremendous amount of incoming small-arms fire. It was like being down range in the butts. Looking around I could see Marine Rick Miller to my left, the space between us erupting as rounds impacted around and threw up stones and pebbles. We were quite exposed with only the small rise of the track in front of us, and we quickly tried to push up some rocks in front to give us at least a degree of cover.

My recollections through this contact were of Corporal George Porthouse suddenly shouting he had been shot in the arse and watching him do the best break dance I'd ever seen, Lance Corporall Jock Hepburn rolling over and shouting he'd been hit; then I saw Sergeant Nick Holloway suddenly jump up and tear off his webbing. I thought he was bugging out but then I saw smoke and flames from his pouches and realised he had taken rounds through them; he got up and dived across the road into a ditch that was on the other side to us. I can recall shouting to my right, where a couple of lads were lying with GPMGs, to get the guns going and quickly heard the comforting sound of them opening fire. At this point the Troop were now engaging the enemy furiously and starting to win the firefight. Marine Sampson knelt up and fired a 66mm light anti-tank weapon up toward the enemy positions, then a couple more were fired.

I heard the Boss shouting to his radio operator Marine Pleasance – they had obviously been separated during the scramble out of the helos – to move to his position with the radio; at this point there was still an intense firefight going on. Marine Pleasance shouted, 'Boss if you want the radio come and fucking get it.' He did move to where the Boss was lying but he only had a battle antenna fitted, which was basically a piece of trailing wire, so the boss had him lying on his back holding the wire antennae up in the air while he started calling for artillery support.

I decided the ditch on the other side of the road was much more preferable to where we were so warned my section to move over the road into the ditch where Sergeant Holloway was. I got up and quickly dived across the road into the ditch holding a white phosphorus grenade, which I intended on throwing to cover the rest of the section across.

As I threw myself into the ditch, I quickly realised there was a stream running down it that was ice covered. I broke through the ice and splashed into knee-deep water, as the grenade bounced out of my hand and skittered across the top of the unbroken ice, luckily with the pin still in place. I crawled down chasing the grenade and smashing the ice. I quickly grabbed it, pulled the pin and threw it forward; it burst into a huge plume of instant white smoke and the rest of the section moved into the safety of the ditch and resumed firing. By now the firing from the enemy had decreased rapidly and the occasional figure or head would appear among the rocks above us and attract our fire. Sometimes they reappeared, sometimes they didn't.

It eventually became clear that the enemy were withdrawing in front of us, and this was the reason the Boss was denied his fire mission. The Boss called the ceasefire as it was now obvious that a complete retreat was happening, and we had to conserve what ammunition we had left. I had exited the helo with 9 x 20 round magazines for my SLR and I had 1.5 left, yet I can't recall changing any magazines throughout the entire contact. All my spare belts for the GPMGs had been given to the machine-gunners.

We had several wounded to take care of, the most serious was Marine Vince Comb, who had laid on the open track engaging the enemy positions with his GPMG while the Troop exited the helos and took cover. He was eventually shot through his upper arm and thrown back off the gun, at which point Marine Thorburn had crawled forward and began firing the GPMG. By the time we got to Vince he had already self-administered his morphine ampoule, so we dressed his wound as best we could and got him into a survival bag to await casevac. Corporal George Porthouse had been lightly wounded by a round that had gone through his rear pouches, smashing his boot brushes and creasing his backside. Lance Corporal Jock Hepburn had been hit in the head by a ricochet or a stone thrown up from impacting rounds.

Considering the amount of incoming fire, we had been very lucky.

It was then obvious to us all that there had been a map-reading error on the part of the helos and we had in fact been dropped off at the foot of Sapper hill, in full view of a very surprised company of Argentinian marines. We had flown 3 km forward of the front line at that time and landed.

One of our company medics, Doc George Black, ran forward about 2 km to reach us when he heard we had casualties. Once the casualties had been sorted and Vince had been casevaced, we slowly advanced up the track leading to Sapper Hill, and from there we got our first sight of Port Stanley. Argentinian positions were well sited on Sapper Hill, in depth and mutually supporting, and many still had a lot of abandoned kit in them that some of the lads liberated. The surrender negotiations were in full swing below us in Stanley, and although the Argentinians on the Falklands has surrendered, the mainland had not so air raid precautions still had to be observed.

We spent two very cold nights on Sapper Hill, but we did have the luxury of a tent we had 'liberated' from an Argie position. The first time we had slept with overhead cover in six weeks. From there we were flown back to Bluff Cove and then to San Carlos where we had a couple of days where most of us caught food poisoning from the excellent central feeding kitchens.

Vince recollects the battle:

June 14th, as we jumped from the helicopter onto the track at the bottom of Sapper Hill, we were already under fire. We had surprised the enemy who were dug in at the top of the hill by landing where we did in broad daylight. It was also a huge surprise to us because we were in a totally different LZ than planned. There was no time to be scared, the training kicked in and you just went about doing what you were supposed to. Everybody just started doing their bit in whatever role they had.

Paul Rogers and I ended up in the middle of the track that was slightly higher than the surrounding area. We were giving covering fire while everyone else disembarked. After a short while, we realised we were on our own and everybody else had had the good sense to get into some sort of cover allowing them to return fire. Paul and I were very exposed where we were, and enemy rounds were landing all around us. I shouted to Paul and told him to cross the track and get into cover with the others and I would cover him. He told me to go first, and he would cover me. It then became a bit of a friendly argument, Paul saying he was slightly older than me and he basically had seniority. My reply while laughing nervously was that my gun was bigger than his. Paul eventually crossed and found good cover and then I followed suit. While returning fire I noticed two lines of dirt being hacked up very quickly towards me from two different directions, basically, with me laying in the middle. There was no way of avoiding the impending impact. In fact, I think I probably started shouting expletives at the Argies before the bullets even hit me. I somehow landed on my back after being thrown through the air. By the time I hit the ground, I had already got the morphine that we carried attached to our dog tags in my hand. However, the wind had been knocked out of me and I lost all energy. I couldn't even tell precisely where I had been shot, just guessing it was somewhere on the left of me. From where I was laying,

I could see our signaller waving the antennae about trying to get a good signal but desperately trying not to get shot in the arm himself. It looked quite comical at the time, but he did a great job. Mick Thorburn aka Elvis got to me and injected the morphine and applied a field dressing. He had no regard for his own safety and did a great job. There were many events in this short firefight that probably went unnoticed, this being one of them, I guess.

Then, suddenly it was over; the noise stopped. It was then that I was told my good friend Alex had also been hit, in the head. It turned out to be a ricochet luckily for him. These things happen when you lose your tin helmet in a minefield and don't retrieve it. Andy Gaunt my section 2IC removed my watch from my left wrist and pocketed it. He didn't realise I had also been shot in the wrist. When the watch was returned to me, I noticed a small crack on the face and wondered whether the watch had slowed some of the impact. I then remember three of the lads laying on the ground around me and trying to prop my head up and asking me to smile. It was surreal but Elvis was taking our photo. I remember trying to smile but then sort of going back into unconsciousness, probably shock and relief. The medics had been dropped at the correct LZ quite some distance away along with the remainder of the lads. Upon hearing there were injured Marines in need of assistance, they ran to get to us even though they believed the track to be mined. I recall begging the medics when they arrived for more morphine. Not because of the pain, but the actual feeling of it. I was laughing and giggling like a schoolchild. The rest of the troop continued with the objective along with the rest of Charlie and Alpha Companies, leaving Alex and myself at the side of the road with the medics. As the Marines filed by, one of the lads in Alpha Company threw a slug [sleeping bag] at the medic so they could put me in it before I went down with hypothermia as it had started to snow.

When the casevac helicopter came in to land to take Alex and me to be treated elsewhere, I joked with the pilots that I could fly the helicopter. They placed a stretcher at my side and when asked to swing my legs over onto it, I couldn't even feel them due to the morphine and other pain relief. Hilarious. The next thing I knew was when I woke up again and thought I was in a coffin. Surely, they didn't think I was dead, did they? I looked up and saw a sign that read something like 'DO NOT PANIC, YOU ARE A CASUALTY OF WAR AND IN A HELICOPTER POD'. There was a little Perspex window directly above and I saw the pilot look down, smile and give me the thumbs-up. Great news, I'm alive and they know it. Basically, I was on a stretcher affixed to the side of the helicopter. Not exactly something you do every day.

I don't remember anything else until I awoke once again, and this time found myself on a sort of makeshift operating table with medical equipment all around. There were Marines and soldiers on stretchers and green slugs on the floor around me. It must have been night-time because red light was being used and it felt very dingy with stale air. I shouted out in a confused state not understanding where I was. It was then I heard Alex say that I was okay, we were in a field hospital.

Next time I awoke I was in the field hospital at Ajax Bay, the infamous hospital known as the Red and Green Life Machine, so called because of the colour of beret that the medics wore, red for Paras and green for Commandos. The former abattoir had been bombed by Argentine jets a couple of weeks before and the medics had continued working with two unexploded bombs lodged in the roof. A medic was removing my mountain boots as I woke up. When I asked him what he was doing he simply replied, 'You don't need them anymore, do you?' I agreed with him, and we did a deal. He got my boots and I got a mug of tea. Fair swap I thought at the time.

From Ajax Bay I was airlifted once more on a stretcher over to SS *Uganda*, a merchant ship that had been converted into a HOSPITAL SHIP. As the Sea King landed on deck,

I was greeted by what I could only think at the time was an angel, so pure and white. On land we had been living and sleeping in trenches and shallow scrapes, we hadn't showered in weeks and were very filthy and no doubt quite smelly. Now here was a ward sister to greet me wearing what appeared to be the cleanest clothes I had ever seen plus she smelt so fresh. She had a big smile and welcomed me aboard telling me that I was going to be looked after. There were also two immaculate stretcher bearers, both RM bandsmen who take on this role during times of war. With them was a male Royal Naval nurse who had a big smile on his face until he lent over me. I was still wrapped in the slug that I had been given a day or two earlier. This young sailor, who was probably older than me, was intrigued to know where I had been hit. However, in his excitedness he leaned over me and unknowingly lent on my injured arm. My uninjured hand was still functioning, and to his surprise it swiftly grabbed him by the scruff of his neck and pulled him in close. The Bandies quickly calmed the situation down and I was persuaded to let go of him. I was then stretchered to a patient ward and provided with a bed. The first proper bed in about four weeks and it felt like heaven. The last few weeks had been spent living in trenches and shallow scrapes dug out of the Falklands peat. Now I was warm, comfortable and, very importantly, dry. It was then I considered the rest of 9 Troop and wondered whereabouts they were and where they were managing to get their heads down. Life on board was really great. We were well cared for and well fed; no more rations! Most of the injured were in good spirits, considering the appalling injuries to many. This was just a testament to British troops overall.

The first ward I was on had beds around the edge with patients' heads nearest the side. Down the middle were a further two rows of beds with patients being head-to-head. Immediately to my front there was an injured Argentine soldier who smiled at me constantly. I wasn't comfortable about this, and I admit to having some very bad thoughts as to what I wanted to do to him. Only once I could sit up, I noticed that the patient head-to-head with me was also an Argentine (so I thought). Because I was unable to get to 'Smiler', I decided to take it out on this chap secretly. He had rather a lot of skin missing from his stomach and things were quite visible. I decided to give his bedhead a knock whenever there were no witnesses. As he groaned and complained, it became quite clear that he couldn't speak English. The following day most of the unit COs came onboard to visit their wounded. Lieutenant Colonel Malcolm Hunt visited me and we had a chat about my future career and going home. To my surprise, a senior Gurkha officer visited the chap that I was head-to-head with. If he ever gets to read this … I am so, so sorry. I truly am.

One afternoon a nurse come to find me and informed me that it was Mac's 18th birthday and wanted to know if I would visit him. I went and sat with him for a while and we discussed what had happened. The nurses had very kindly had a cake made for him but he was not in the best of moods for celebrating, not surprisingly. In a nearby bed was Lieutenant Paul Allen. Both had had their injured feet amputated. I really felt for them, both still so young with their whole lives ahead of them.

After a few days I was deemed as walking wounded and transferred to the lower decks. Now in smaller cabins and in bunk beds. There was a real mix of regiments down here and mostly we had a ball. One particular person was a merchant sailor with a sad tale as to how he got to be among us. He introduced himself, saying with a smile, 'I might be gay but I'm not interested in any of you.' He became a great asset because he knew exactly where to get items that we struggled to locate, like Arctic socks. He'd previously had problems with alcohol and had apparently been dry for quite some time. This was until the Paras heading south on SS *Norland* persuaded him to have a drink or two. A few weeks later he was in a poor state of mind and his superiors, thinking he was suicidal, had him put on the hospital ship. He would do anything for anybody and was always cheery. One example was when the sea was rough, he always made sure he helped all the injured on the lower decks get their scran before he had his. It was near impossible to queue for food with arms in slings or legs in plaster while trying to hold on to whatever you could to stay upright while also holding a metal tray for one's meal. He was also able to source us bits of uniform that we desperately needed. We were permitted to watch a movie every afternoon and I recall one day the film was *Endless Love* starring Brooke Shields. He was shedding tears and we were playfully teasing him. He was laughing and crying at the same time, but the banter was all in good spirits.

About three weeks later I was transferred to one of the smaller hospital ships and ferried to Uruguay where we were then driven in a heavily armed convoy to the airport and flown back to RAF Brize Norton. When we landed, we were put onto coaches (more serious wounded were in ambulances) and driven to RAF Wroughton Hospital nearby. It was here that our families were permitted to greet us and welcome us back home. On the coach I was seated next to our 'great asset' who had helped us immensely. All of a sudden, he started to cry. I asked him why he was crying. He said that he felt a fraud; he believed that he was coming home to a hero's welcome and he didn't deserve it. I told him that everyone down there had done their part and he had no reason to feel ashamed. That was the last I saw of him. On the day of the Victory Parade in London there was a small story in *The Sun* newspaper saying that he had committed suicide.

The last leg of my trip was the convoy of ambulances that transferred us from the RAF Hospital to Royal Navy Hospital Stonehouse in Plymouth. The ambulances were full of beer, and we could just help ourselves. This meant that we had to stop at every service station en route for loo stops. At one of the services, I was aiding Mac who was on crutches. It had just started to rain as we entered the service area and I watched as Mac went to move forward the rubber suckers on the end of each crutch stayed stuck to the tiles. This meant that as he placed the crutches down again it was metal on wet tiles. One crutch went left and the other right and Mac fell on his fresh stump. The pain must have been unbearable, and he cried out. In true military humour we all laughed until I realised that nobody was helping him. The civilians that were all around us had no idea who we were. We were not dressed in proper uniform and all of us had some sort of injury. We probably looked quite intimidating. I asked some civvies to help him up as none of us were in a condition to do so. To this very day, if I see someone on the same type of crutches, I always wince.

The Argentinian casualties during this battle are identified below by Marcos. With the greatest respect for each soldier, the text is unaltered from the original.

Adolfo Gustavo CABRAL

RELATO DEL INFANTE ADOLFO GUSTAVO CABRAL continued walking, only when I heard the bolts of their weapons did I stop. and they check me noticing that my clothes are bloody and they take me to be cured by an English doctor from the paratroopers 2 who just reached Sapper Hill from Monte Dos Hermanas, who lays me down on top of a stone and extracts me with a I knife the bullet lodged in his back, he sutures me and then he sends me to the hospital in Puerto Argentino. With the help of the veteran photographer of the English army, Paul R. G. Haley, in 2019 it was possible to know the name of the doctor who saved the life of the Marine, Adolfo Cabral. His name is Steven Hughes and, although we had the description of the doctor recorded by Cabral, who said that he was dark-skinned, with a beard and spoke to him in English, but descriptions of the English fighters is that Dr. Steven Hughes was permanently with his camouflaged blackened face that was difficult for him to recognize from his own companions.

Roberto LEYES

The infant who fell in combat ROBERTO LEYES, came from a family from Ciudad Corrientes, from fishermen, in the Malvinas, he looked for food going through the minefields, he had the charisma of a leader and a great companion, he had a daughter when he went to the islands. In combat he encouraged his companions to shoot, he walked from position to position, that is where he was mortally wounded with a shot to the chest.

Sergio Ariel ROBLEDO

The Marine SERGIO ARIEL ROBLEDO belonged to a family of 11 brothers from the province of Buenos Aires, on Sapper Hill his function was to supply the Mag machine gun, he was wounded in combat in the chest, in his position and transferred by Midshipman Alejandro Koch climbs the hill for a long distance and is left on the ground for not having signs of life. it was approximately 2:30 p.m. on 06/14/1982

Eleodoro MONZON

The Marine ELEODORO MONZON came from the city of Quitilipi, province of Chaco, his family had a small field and animals, in Sapper Hill his function was to fire a rocket launcher, in his combat position he unprotected his body to be able to visualize the firing zone and he is mortally wounded in the chest.

Marcos' words:

> For many years, I had this question. What prompted these defenders of Sapper Hill to defend it to the death? The answer was very clear in the retina of their eyes of the survivors. the images in his mind of the patriots of the air force that like avenging eagles attacked the fleet with little chance of returning, an armed fleet that bombarded them for months with no chance of defending themselves. That heroism of the Argentine aviators fallen in combat and the love for the family, for the country, defended the Hill when everyone had laid down their arms.

Terry recollects that day:

> After what was called by one officer I overheard as the 'worse night of his life' (and mine too), I returned to a re-entrant and put on a wet with Chris Pretty, Ged Herd and Brian Edmunds. Because I was so drained, the effort of putting a match to a hexi block caused me to set light to my Artic fingerless gloves, turning them to an even darker brown and black, the original white having disappeared weeks ago. I couldn't give a toss. I was so tired, so we just pulled a poncho over our heads for cover; I wasn't even bothered about the artillery barrages flying over our position in both directions. I slept 'spooning' with my SLR and 66mm LAW. In what seemed a blink of an eye we were stood to and told to prepare for an attack on Sapper Hill. I thought it was a joke; what I would have given for a few more minutes of zeds. My Section, 33C, loaded onto the first Sea King helicopter and to be honest with you I was just so pleased to be out of the cold weather conditions. The aircraft followed the contour of the land; at one point when it banked at such a steep angle and speed, I looked out of the door and could almost touch the foliage/heather. Suddenly the engines screamed and the nose of the craft almost pointed vertical then came down to land with a bump, port side facing up hill. I could hear cracking noises and 'crumps' but thought nothing of it (I was later to learn that these noises were small-arms fire from the Argentines coming through the fuselage and the 'crumps' mortar rounds landing nearby). The navigator seemed to be in a bad mood; he grabbed me by the arm, pointed up the hill and then almost kicked me out – I thought, 'What's his bloody problem!' I was third or fourth person out of the leading Sea King. With my SLR, I took up a firing position looking up the hill. The roar of the engines was deafening as the Sea King took off; the pilot was in no way hanging around. I watched the second helicopter offload the rest of 9 Troop and also do a quick disappearing act. We had been dropped off almost on top

of the enemy's positions, not, as briefed some 5 km back for an advance to contact! Cracking and deep thud noises were happening all around us. We were on a track on the side facing uphill and it was difficult to see above the gorse and tussock grass. I can recall someone telling us to cross over the track, so I did. We had very little cover from the incoming rounds, only the convex shape of the track that gave us about 8–10 inches protection, I felt very exposed to the rounds coming in. We were also very conscious that on each side of the track antipersonnel mines had been laid and because of Charlie Company's previous night's experience of being stuck in a minefield, with casualties, we were very apprehensive on venturing too far off the hardcore. I lay in a foetal position, experiencing such strong emotions of fear and butterflies that I had never had in my 19 years of life. It was like being a child locked in a cupboard under the stairs with only total darkness for company and no escape. I just wanted to be somewhere else right now, anywhere but here, a different place, a different time. Help! It was, for me, an overwhelming sense of fear, a time of ultimate dread. Suddenly an image of my mother and home came to mind. I promised to myself that if I survived this, I would go to church every Sunday (if you were brought up a Roman Catholic, I am sure you can relate to this). Having these recollections and thoughts gave me the incentive to refocus, start getting involved and then all that training kicked in. I thought that if I was going to die, I wasn't going to do it laying down. I heard an order given by an NCO to our left to another Royal Marine from the troop to get his head up to which he replied, 'If you think I'm putting my head up there, you can f**k off.' This annoyed me, W***er, especially because he thought he was the tough man of the Troop and to think that he was just as scared as me; this made me even more determined to act.

In a bizarre move, Corporal Dee Irving (my section commander), laying next to me on my left, started fiddling in the top pocket of his windproof, pulled out his ear defenders and casually put them into his ears as if he were on a Sunday pheasant shoot. Mne Mick Thoburn aka Elvis was laying on my right in the same position. Dee said, 'You two aren't doing much good there.' So I looked up the hill and saw three Argentine soldiers in their grey uniforms, hoods up, standing up in a trench with white granite and quartz rock behind them, at about 100–150 metres to my 11 o'clock, three-quarters of the way up the hill. One of the Argentine soldiers always sticks in my memory because, unfortunately for him he was fat, and had a huge black moustache and therefore made a bigger target. I just fired as many rounds as I could from my SLR in their direction. However, I had a problem; my bloody weapon would not reload. So, I fired a bullet then would have to cock it to put another round in the chamber. I knew exactly what the matter was: the gas barrel had come loose previously while zeroing our weapons at Wreck Point and I, with a colleague, had stripped the casing off and fixed it by screwing it back in. Trust it to happen again at such a crucial time. During this part of the firefight, I can recall Dee Irving asking me to pass the 66mm LAW, so I did and thought nothing of it. A few seconds later my whole world went black. I thought I was gone, dead, only to regain my consciousness to see that Dee had fired the 66mm LAW at a target. I was not so much annoyed with him for not warning us and taking into consideration the back blast from the rocket, but what really pissed me off was the fact that I had carried and slept with that 66mm LAW from day one and never got to fire it.

I can remember seeing Vince Comb slightly higher up near the centre of the track, with little or no cover. I can also recall a deep thud of a .5 gun being fired at us from a position off to our left. I could hear bullets passing just above our heads and stones ricocheting. Then I heard a thud and a crack, looked up and saw Vince had been knocked back and was, with sheer determination and courage, trying to crawl back to his gun. It was obvious he was in pain; I could see that his eyes were watering and some blood was seeping through his sleeve. Dee told Elvis and me to help. Elvis was slightly closer to Vince; with some effort Vince had moved closer to where we were laying. Elvis started to patch him up and I had to do one of the hardest things I have ever done. With all the willpower in the world it took me to overcome the fear of being shot, I crawled up on to the track and recovered Vince's GPMG. It would have been so easy for me to just carry on firing my SLR. With a mixture of fear and anger – the anger I used to motivate me – I made a move in the second most terrifying situation I had ever been in the last few minutes and slowly edged forward. I placed the bipod on the top of the track and fired at anything or anyone on the hill to the left. Slightly closer at 1 o'clock, I could see a sanger-type construction, with a green-coloured poncho for a roof and corrugated iron on the side. I fired several rounds into this. I was conscious and scared that I was running out of link and shouted for more. At this stage I looked down to my right and saw Elvis and Dee patching up Vince. The injury on the top of his arm was oozing deep red blood like a sponge being squeezed and soap suds pushing out. Dee, cutting cartilage, muscle and clothing away, placed several first aid bandages on the wound to apply pressure and prevent any more blood loss. This ad hoc surgery was performed with a pusser's knife. Out of the corner of my eye at about 2 o'clock, I noticed some Argentines jumping through a heavily foliaged area, taking cover every so often and firing FNs at us, trying a right flanking manoeuvre on us. So, I switched fire and let loose at them. I could see by my tracer rounds that my fire was slightly too low, so I raised the sights and continued firing at them. Having picked out individual targets, I let go with bursts of three to five rounds, stopped, looked up over the sights, saw that the targets had disappeared (whether I had shot them or they had merely taken cover I could not say for sure) then moved on to the next; I was trying to preserve ammunition. Dee asked me if I had seen them to the right and I replied, 'Got them.' At this stage I believe (remember the fog of war!) I saw a very brave act. Lance Corporal Chris Pretty, taking his gun team, made up of Mne Ged Herd and Mne Brian Edmunds, to the furthest right flank of 9 Troop under fire with absolutely no cover, facing away from the main enemy. This action was carried out without any direction from a superior and showed an excellent awareness of tactical importance while under fire and leadership qualities unique to the Royal Marines. The right flanking attempt seemed to slacken as I saw some Argentines disappear over the horizon and out of site. So, I switched the gun back to the sanger and trench to my left. I could not see any enemy anymore but continued to put bullets into these targets to keep their heads down. At this stage there was a call from the right, where our troop commander Lieutenant Carl Bushby RM and Troop Sergeant Nick Holloway RM were, to cross the track moving up hill towards the enemy. They moved first while we gave cover then we followed. After this the firing from the Argentines ceased. I can remember seeing a guy from another troop's gun team in C Coy 40 Cdo RM, on the track a few hundred metres away to our left completely exhausted and swearing because he had run to catch up but missed the fighting. We thought the Argentines had gone to get some support and would be back. One of the lads to my left (Mne Griffiths I think) pulled out a tiny Union Flag and started to sing 'God Save the Queen' followed by others joining in.

After this I can recall a Blues and Royals Scorpion light tank with a couple of Welsh Guard's officers arriving and saying something about taking over from here using the tanks to their advantage and getting to the top of Sapper Hill first. Lieutenant Carl Busby and Mne Ged Herd gave them (the Pongos) a mouthful of what we and the rest of 9 Troop thought. So, we ignored them and continued advancing along the track towards Port Stanley, passing a dead Argentine body on the centre of the track, facedown with some congealed blood visible having leaked from his head. Sticking to the path and advancing up the track I was thinking, 'Bloody hell, they're going to start firing at us.' As we got near the top, I was deliberating about the peak with its rock formations, almost vertical cliff faces and how they could have wiped us out with such good defensive positions. Seeing the coastline and waves crashing on the rocks in the distance, bizarrely, made me think about going for a swim when this had finished. Getting to the top of the hill I could see many Argentine soldiers, looking dejected, some stumbling as they walked, facing away from Sapper Hill, heading east towards Port Stanley, with no interest in us or what was happening behind them. I wondered what was going through their minds. Fear of being prisoners of war and what treatment they would get, especially when returning home. Sadness at the loss of friends. I felt no pity for them, only anger because they had tried to kill my friends and me only hours ago.

Later, on top of Sapper Hill we were happy to meet Royal Marines from 45 Commando, yomping in from our left (west). The first night on the hill we put together a makeshift sanger made of tarpaulin and oil barrels attached to an Argentine position. It was freezing with a blizzard blowing and we had no sleeping bags or refinements – somehow, we had grown accustomed to this by now anyway – only our battle order. Finding some Argentine long-sleeved T-shirts, still in their plastic wrappers, we put them on under our windproof tops and lay close to someone to keep warm from their body heat. Although it was a very cold, bitter night and I can recollect shivering, I did get some sleep. Some Argentine ration packs we found were a godsend; I can clearly remember eating some biscuits that were very similar to TUC crackers and finding cigarettes and a box of matches that I placed into my mess tins and stored back into my kidney pouches (I still have these today). The next day, with some relief we were flown off the hill by helicopter to Fitzroy, where we were put in a barn, cramped like factory chickens, but at least out of the appalling weather.

> **Tuesday 15 June**
> *Day 25*
> The whole section built a sanger on Sapper Hill, spent the night there and next day were flown out by choppers to Fitzroy where the whole Unit + Guards + Engineers were sited in one barn – the night was cramped to say the least.

The night had been very cold again. Our creative skills had produced a fully sealed sanger. The scene was of absolute devastation, with mud and filth everywhere, bits of kit and more mud. The smell was strong enough to grab the back of your throat and twist it. It was that very distinctive, overpowering smell again. The morning was cold. The shelter roof was made from wriggly tin and ponchos, peat on top to insulate. Cut peat stacked to make the walls. Holes stuffed with mud to keep the wind out. We'd made the door out of a scrounged frame. From this we hung an Argentine poncho, which made a secure airtight door. It had snowed overnight. Antarctic winter was here. Early morning and one of the guys had put a wet of tea on and passed it round to us all as we lay there in the warmth of our home. We were stuffed in like sardines, but this just made it warmer. Other lads had come and knocked on the door for refuge. They were admitted of course. Some of the lads had proffed some Argentine rations. We cooked some. Most of it was huge tins of corned beef. We opened them and ate it straight from the tin. It was good.

The night had been spent in luxury, warmth and comfort. Sleep had come easily. The weather outside had been foul; it had degenerated into minus temperatures with snow and sleet. The inside of the shelter was boiling hot with all the bodies crammed in together. We had some hexi cookers. The lads were cooking and enjoying themselves. Big beaming smiles through cammed-out blackened faces. We had slept a night of warmth although comfort lessened as more guys came in and the size of the sleeping area became smaller for each person. It was cramped but for the first night in ages we had a warm night.

Rick had an experience last night, which he recalls in the aftermath of our gunfight at Sapper Hill:

> The Troop re-org'ed and bivvied-up adjacent to the enemy position while we witnessed the men of 45 Cdo RM

advancing on our position in the far distance from the west after their long, hard yomp across the Island engaging Argentinian forces in hard-fought battles along the way. Anyway, we'd stumbled across a cache of Argentinian food, including large tins of peaches and pears that we gleefully & hungrily tucked into. As I devoured a tin of pear halves, I heard someone outside going around the position asking if anyone knew me. Suddenly, a strange, camouflaged face appeared in the bivvy uttering the immortal words of 'Hello Rick ... got any spare scran?' It turned out to be a guy called Mick St. Pier who was in 45 Cdo RM at the time. He was the older brother of a school classmate of mine and was the person who introduced me to the Royal Marines in the first place! I was soon to leave school and was around my friend's house playing records, when he said that his older brother was home on leave after doing 6 months in Cyprus with the Royal Marines (with the now-disbanded 41 Cdo RM). His brother (Mick) then showed me his phots of Cyprus and of the runs ashore in Ayia Napa with his oppos, etc. I curiously & excitedly asked him what the Royal Marines was all about as I'd never heard of them before. I was absolutely hooked after he'd told me about the training and of the life as a Royal Marine Commando ... and the rest is history! That day on Sapper Hill, the day of the Argentinian surrender of the Falkland Islands – 14th June 1982 – was the first time I'd seen him since the day he first introduced me to the Corps!

The morning was cold and we woke and started to sort our kit out. Back into the swing of admin. As I emerged from the front of the shelter; I was facing approximately north-west towards Longdon. The weather was clear and very cold. I got out wearing just a Norge shirt, Helly Hensen undershirt and trousers. For the first time in what felt like years I was comfortably warm. I looked out over the area as if this was my new estate. It was still devastation. No change.

As I looked over my left shoulder, I saw a sight I will always remember. There, stood in the lee of our 5-foot-high, dark and dripping peat bank, were two gentlemen. They were in bad order. They were obviously wet and cold. Clearly, they had suffered last night in the open. One was an officer, quite young with dark hair; the other was older and was a sergeant with a big black moustache. They were a sight and were clearly not Marines. At the time I thought they must be Welsh Guards. They had been suffering all night and were still suffering now. Behind them was a poncho pegged to the top of the peat bank. It was obviously not doing its job of protecting them from the elements; it had come loose at a couple of points and was sagging. I was warm and dry and they were cold and wet. For the briefest moment I was sorry for them. If they had come to the shelter last night, I'm sure we would have let them in. They would have been welcome. I pitied them but I was also shocked that they hadn't done anything to help their situation. Shrug and move on.

The new day began with cleaning up. We checked trenches and all the Argie equipment, finding all sorts of gear that we kept and repurposed. Their boots were very good and so were their thermal underwear and over-jackets. We wore these just as extra protection. The scrounging continued. It's as if the fight had never happened the day before. It had become an irrelevance already. Only irrelevant because there were new tasks to get on with.

Later in the day we are flown back to Fitzroy settlement, to the big shed there. Like a barn. Probably a barn. We were on our way out of here and heading to the rear again. Having a proper barn roof over my head was a bit disturbing and I found it quite hard to get used to. I felt vulnerable in there. I felt as though I should be outside; I felt really uncomfortable inside. We'd been living outside for about a month now. Supposing they kick off again. Adrian slept outside.

We started to sort our kit out and got a wet on; the place was filling up quick. We found our own little areas of space. I found a place high up on some packing cases and this is where we made our initial home. Away from the many bodies on the main floor below. We came back down when all the moving around was finished. We slept the night sat up on the concrete floor. There wasn't space to lie down. I was perched against Jono from 7 Troop and we soon became comfortable leaning against each other's backs, knees tucked up. Too little space to lie down. We were packed in like sardines. I wanted to be outside. The following day we are flown back to San Carlos by chopper in an uneventful move.

Back to where we started from.

Wednesday 16 June
Day 26
In the day we were flown to San Carlos, to live in a tent, drink Pepsi, see Ben and live like lords. Weather is freezing and wet – had photos taken.

Having flown back to San Carlos and back to where we had started, it did seem strange to see all the lads here again who hadn't been and done the things we had just been and done. It seemed like a lifetime away when we were back here, inexperienced in the ways of war. Nobody knew what we had done and it wasn't discussed. Nobody cared. It just seemed natural, so no need to talk about it. I went to find my old flatmate Ben to see how he was getting on. He must have been aware of what I'd just been through – the grapevine must have done its work. Somewhere inside I was sadly disappointed that he knew nothing of what had happened. Never mind. It's okay.

I found myself drinking Pepsi with Ben in a nine-by-nine tent, just like the one the Welsh Guards had at Harriet, and he didn't have a clue what we had been through. How could I blame him? We were sat in the nine by nine when a Para warrant officer came into the tent. He looked experienced. He had a huge moustache, like Ben's. We offered the other moustache a Pepsi and we started chatting. He seemed like a decent bloke. Obviously, he had had quite a war and he wasn't bashful to tell us all about it. He said he had been at Goose Green. He told a story that remains untold here. I would learn to keep experiences to myself. It was strange though; after all my experiences I now felt as though I was totally different to Ben. Not better, just different in a strange way and I couldn't pin down what it was. I felt as though I couldn't actually tell him about our most recent experience with the Argentines. I wanted to tell him absolutely everything about all the ins and outs and how I felt and exactly what had happened and how we'd flown in to a full-on battle and taken casualties … but I feared that he would just not understand. A new fear. I'm sure he would have understood but it was a worry at the time, and I didn't understand what was happening to me. So, I didn't say anything and it has remained unresolved since then. This was the beginning of not being able to talk to anybody about what went on. Maybe this is why the guys from the Second World War won't talk about their experiences, maybe.

After a while of being in luxury, I decided that I needed to be somewhere else, anywhere else. I didn't really but I really did need to go and find some of my own guys. I actually felt a bit uncomfortable in such luxury, and uncomfortable that my present company couldn't understand my experiences. It was me and definitely not Ben.

I strolled back through the mud and the gloom back to the boys. I found them back in the sheep shed down by the bay. They'd put a fire on in a 50-gallon drum and it was burning well. We just sat on the bales of wool and laughed. My overriding memories of this period are of darkness, wet, mud, cold, warm fire, larking around, laughing, group photographs and an overwhelming feeling of 'it's over'. Not in the sense of 'Phew, it's all over' but just 'It's all over and we can go home', quite matter of fact. No real emotions. None at all. No thoughts of home and what was going to come next or what my next move was going to be in life. Just the simple fact that it had finished and here we were now ready to move on to the next thing, whatever and wherever that was.

We got our heads down among the bales of wool and had a relatively good night, although we stayed awake for a long time. Now it was over there wasn't the reason for sleeping at every opportunity. The urgency of living ready for battle had left a big hole in me. It sounds dramatic but I can't explain it any other way.

It was today that Andy and I had a quick look round our old area. We came across a Bell Huey helicopter, an Argentine one. It was just sat there on the grass doing nothing. Probably waiting for us, we presumed. We stood there and got into a very serious discussion. Would we be able to fly this thing? We reckoned we could. We could definitely get it off the ground. The only problem would be getting it back down safely again. We were so serious we very nearly attempted it; we were so close to trying. I can't remember why we didn't but I still reckon we could have done it. Besides it would be a great proff. What a giggle. We moved on and left it alone and instantly forgot about it.

The next day the landing craft came and picked us up. The Troop was back together again. The whole company back again in one landing craft. Old friends found and congratulated, hands shaken, big grins. Back to HMS *Intrepid* for a day or so. Then back on to *Canberra*. Clean and civilised. We were dirty and uncivilised. It took twelve hand washes of my wool jumper to get it clean. We were going home. The journey would take two weeks. Pleasant weeks together.

The *Canberra* had been used to transport Argentine prisoners back to Argentina. Taking over our old cabins again, we found a neatly placed dollop of human excrement in every cupboard and drawer. Everywhere. We roared with laughter. They had got us back and we truly appreciated the sentiment. Good work, lads. Just brilliant. This is how it all finished.

Chapter 8

Coda – A Reflective Future

A man must shape himself to a new mark directly the old one goes to ground.

Ernest Shackleton

It is hard to create a final scene for this adventure. A conclusion seems somewhat inappropriate. It has not yet finished. The complexities of human character and of the war make it seem unjustified to formally conclude it. Nonetheless, I am stood alone on that same empty, dark stage that we have all been on for the last months. The adventure has reached its finale and everyone else has exited the stage. I am alone. The curtain has come down behind me and some final words must be said.

This was a great adventure. The Troop was closer than ever. Strong. Friendships solidified forever. Sadly, for some it was more than an adventure. More of a misadventure. The adventure we had together could almost be classified as a Homerian adventure in its character. These particular Homerian characters went out on a quest, were successful in the main part and they mostly returned home as heroes. Recognised by a grateful nation as heroes. No one felt heroic. It was our job. It was expected by England. The outcome was always inevitable as far as the Troop was concerned. Always certain of victory. Uncertain of the process to achieve it. Invincible. But the journey was not what was expected. I guess it never is. An important point to note is that it was an enjoyable experience. It was great fun with the best oppos you could possibly have. It was the greatest fun. Infinite fun, 99 per cent fun and 1 per cent fear. Percentages may vary. The peculiarity of this adventure was the lack of an end date. It could have lasted forever as far as we were concerned. For some it did.

For some it has. It was a strange time. Time was strange. However, time seemed more irrelevant as the war progressed. Conversely, and weirdly, time became more critical as the war progressed. Time was slippery. It was always critical to focus on the 'performance and not the outcome'. Every day was a sole day of infinite time. Every day was a performance-driven day. Concentrate on your own little tasks every day and do them to perfection. Presuming that others were doing the same. War is a team sport. Do the little things well is the mantra of the perfectionist. Admin wins wars. If every day was good, then the outcome would also be good. Logic dictates that successful small targets must equal successful big targets. Always set small targets, every day. Always be successful. Set another small target, repeat.

Time proved to be as slippery in these weeks as at any time in our lives. More so. Many events were oddly timeless. They could have lasted hours or they could have lasted seconds. It is all in the perception. All in the dilation. What is time anyway; surely it is truly relative? Relative to whoever is measuring it. Time goes fast and time goes slow, but it is still real time to any other observer. Relatively speaking, slow motion is a very real thing, the brain speeding up to calculate and compensate for the situation and consequently making the world seem slower. Seemingly slow actions being fast. Confusion with time is acceptable. Time is a confusingly slippery eel. Be grateful of peaceful non-slippery time.

This slippery time was a major part of the whole experience. Colours were magnified, as were smells and sensations. New points of reference were developed every day. The proposed rabbit hole effect may be just a metaphor. It may even hold some credibility. Maybe not academically, but experientially. The rabbit hole is our own very private experience. Another slippery thing. Events happen and we get nudged over the edge of the event horizon into our black hole. At the bottom of which all things are distorted. Again, the time slips. The colours accentuate and the smells are magnified. Many things change down here. Maybe this hole has no bottom, maybe it is something totally different. Maybe there are levels. Depths. But you know life has definitely changed. It is a mad place to be. That known point of reference has been shifted. Possibly forever.

Once in the hole there may be three proposed recovery options. The first is that we come back out of the hole just as we were, complete. Maybe even better and stronger for our experience. Emboldened by our suffering even. Sublime. The second is that we come back out of the hole but we leave a residue of ourselves in the hole and that never returns to us. Leaving us like a ship without a rudder. Unsure what has happened to us but our direction has faltered and we know we are missing something. The third option is darker. Maybe some of us never come back out of the hole and we are still there. Having never moved. Immobile in our darkness. Lost to the world and lost to ourselves. Just lost. Maybe the weight of our souls has changed.

These observations are exactly that. Observations. They are not fact. They are observations of experience only and are probably filled with nonsense. Experience is, as they say, 'a brutal teacher'.

On returning to the UK, our lives progressed. Often in different directions. The Troop have stayed loyal to each other and we see each other regularly. Speaking every day on social media. Our lives continued on our separate journeys and we parted ways at some point. Some stayed in the Corps and some left the Corps and progressed to other careers. Many went to the police. Some into academics. Some to prison. Some to work in prisons. Jono, Ged, Andy and Graham/Pusser went into careers in the police force. Rick went on to a very long and prestigious career in the Royal Marines. Nick became a Royal Marines officer and now works with the Royal Marines charity. Jono also became a Royal Marines officer before joining the police. Terry went into academics and wrote his own book about the Falklands War. Graham/Pusser became Dr Hill and gained national renown for investigating crime. Sponner went into the business world and Spud became a commercial diver. Alex went into the Prison Service and Vince became an intelligence analyst. Si became a drill instructor in the Royal Marines and completed his time. Bill continued his illustrious career in the Royal Marines and Andy became a highly respected brigadier in the Corps. Ken joined the SAS and became a major. Carl went into business and is now an accomplished musician. Paul suffered after the loss of his foot, as did Mac. Adrian became a professional photographer and an academic. Ben left the Corps and joined the RAF and became a senior officer and an author. Many of the Troop made great successes of themselves.

Elvis died in Hong Kong a few short years after the war. Phil Marshall also died in an accident at his home. Dodger died, as did Matt. They are all missed. They are all remembered.

We spent our lives together. Leaving the Corps, or any military, can be a dislocating experience. Dislocation of expectation. The Corps takes thirty-two weeks to create a Royal Marine commando. The new creation is often completed by producing a new Frankenstein creation. Not a bad Frankenstein, just that the Frankenstein was made of many learned 'attachments' not belonging to the original 'authentic self'.

Imagine a pile of Lego bricks. The standard-sized ones. Four by four. The pile is multicoloured. After your birth you start to create a base layer of your character and personality, your likes and loves. The things you like to do and your interests. This is the lowest line of ten bricks all in a row. The colours signify your interests and what you love and who you really are. The second row of eight is placed on top as you get older, also signifying your developing character and personality and skills and loves. As you get older the third layer of six bricks is laid, and so on. Just like Maslow and his 'Hierarchy of Needs' theory. When you join the Corps, or any regiment, they spend time methodically removing your multicoloured layers until a similar base level is reached for all. A very base level. They then start to place their own green ones. Their green Lego blocks. By the end of commando training, this probably means your brick-wall pyramid is now nearly totally green. You go on to have a successful career. You leave the Corps and enter civilian life and you wonder where that young multicoloured boy went. The person you were before you joined. Those things you loved and the interests you had. Gone and replaced. You leave the Corps with their green pyramid intact, your own colourful blocks strewn all around. Lost. No wonder we feel lost. Lost boys. Return to those things you loved when you were young.

Again, this is an observational hypothesis and is in no way the truth. It is only a thought experiment for you to play with. Of course, this is not gender specific. Or war specific. Probably we all have this issue. Seek out someone who will quietly listen to your story and listen to your 'authentic self' talking. Listening is the key. People who offer their advice may not be experts. You may regain some of your childhood's colourful bricks. Regaining just one would be a major success. Good luck, my friend.

Finally, an observation about the truth. The truth. Maybe as slippery as time itself. Who decides what that truth was, or even is. Some truths are easy and some not so easy. Some convenient and some not so. The scenes we witnessed together may give each of us a totally different memory. This is not bad. Healthy research may suggest that it is totally normal for this to happen. It also seems to be okay. Just know that it happens. It might even be fun. It is the linear core feature of this adventure story. We all saw it differently. Maybe just a comedy of errors.

Harris, so correctly observed in his *The Recollections of Rifleman Harris*: 'All I can do is tell the things which happened immediately around me, and that, I think, is as much as a Private soldier can be expected to do.'

The final scene of this play is at an end.

Exeunt.

Postscript

Post-Traumatic Stress Disorder

Mental health is fully recognised now. The military has learnt that it too must recognise the issues surrounding the good mental health of their people. They now recognise that they have a responsibility for this. PTSD/PTS is a dreadful situation to find yourself in. It should be said that it is a disorder that is not unique to the military. Military PTSD is not unusual in its many forms and it is a totally normal reaction. This book has been all about memories. About the smells, sounds and sensations that happened during the war. This writing may stimulate and provoke reactions after reading this book. I am not a fan of the word 'trigger' but it is the one used at the moment in the Veterans' world.

If you have found this book to be provocative in this way, then please seek professional and qualified medical help.

First you must
My advice would be to initially talk to your NHS GP doctor. Be very open about what you feel. They will be very kind to you.

Second you should
Contact SSAFA. SSAFA is a military charity that gives extremely good help. Please phone them. www.ssafa.org.uk/get-help/mental-wellbeing/dealing-with-mental-health-challenges-and-stress

PTSD and DSM-5

In 2013, the American Psychiatric Association revised the PTSD diagnostic criteria in the 5th edition of its *Diagnostic and Statistical*

Manual of Mental Disorders (DSM-5; 1). PTSD was included in a new category in DSM-5: Trauma- and Stressor-Related Disorders. All conditions included in this classification require exposure to a traumatic or stressful event as a diagnostic criterion. DSM-5-TR was published in March 2022 to include scientific advances since the release of DSM-5. No changes were made to the PTSD diagnostic criteria for adults in this update (2). www.ptsd.va.gov/professional/treat/essentials/dsm5_ptsd.asp

Appendix A

Alejandro Koch
Spanish version – unaltered original

ALEJANDRO KOCH
GUARDIAMARINA DE INFANTERIA DE MARINA – JEFE DE
LA TERCERA SECCION – COMPAÑÍA MAR – BATALLON DE
INFANTERIA DE IM Nº 5

Mi nombre es Alejandro KOCH y pertenezco a la Promoción 110 de la
Escuela Naval Militar. Egresé a fines del año 1981 luego del viaje de
Instrucción en la Fragata ARA Libertad.

Junto a otros cuatro compañeros fui destinado al Batallón de Infantería
de Marina N.º 5 Escuela, con asiento en Río Grande prov. de Tierra del
Fuego al cual nos trasladamos a principios del 1982.

El BIM 5 basaba su configuración operativa como la mayoría de los
Batallones de la época y en nuestro caso como Guardiamarinas fuimos
designados como Jefes de Sección de las Compañías de Tiradores

y yo de la Tercera Sección de la Compañía M (Mar)

con antelación al 2 de abril de 1982, se desarrolló la primera campaña
de Unidad, en proximidades del Cabo Peña, Tierra del Fuego, fue este
el primer contacto que tuve con los soldados a mi cargo; y es en aquella
fecha que nos anoticiamos de lo acontecido en relación al desarrollo
de la Operación Rosario y consecuente recuperación de nuestras Islas
Malvinas.

Comenzaron desde ese momento a circular rumores relacionados con
la eventual reacción que habría de tener el Reino Unido y en definitiva
también la aún no confirmada posibilidad que al Batallón le fuese
asignada la misión de desplegarse en el territorio de las islas.

No fue sino hasta el 8 de abril que tal posibilidad fue efectivamente confirmada.

Se nos indicó a partir de ese momento, el alistamiento perentorio y urgente, ante el inminente traslado de nuestra unidad, mediante la utilización de aeronaves de transporte de la Armada, efectivizándose en definitiva nuestro arribo el 09 de abril.

Mi indicativo como Jefe de Sección era AMARILLO la integrábamos un total de 37 hombres. Dos grupos de tiradores

un pelotón ametralladora, compuesto por dos ametralladoras pesadas MAG, con su dotación correspondiente, esto es, con su apuntador y servidor.

También a modo de refuerzo, nos fueron asignados y se incorporaron dos lanzacohetes, con el personal correspondiente a ellos.

En lo relativo a la tropa, se encontraba integrada por soldados conscriptos clase 1962, quienes estaban próximos a obtener su baja, en virtud de haber cumplido a ese momento su período de instrucción militar obligatoria, según el régimen vigente en ese momento.

Nuestros pertrechos de combate resultaron completos y adecuados al desempeño de operaciones de combate en zona Austral, cuyas características son muy similares a aquéllas correspondiente al lugar de asiento del Batallón.

Nuestra ropa de combate resultó adecuada, así como el calzado que es tan importante en la Infantería, armamento y munición, conforme a estándares asimilados por varias fuerzas armadas del mundo.

Particularmente la fracción contó con el siguiente armamento: , Fusil Automático Liviano FAL PARA 7.62, pistola 9 mm, granadas de mano MKII, Fusil Automático Pesado fusil FAP, ametralladora pesada MAG, granadas de fusil antipersonal y antitanque cuyas siglas son PDF y PAF.

Personalmente me fue asignado un fusil FAL de origen belga con mira infrarroja, más un dispositivo de visión nocturna, con un grado de eficacia muy elevado que permitía visualizar el terreno circundante durante las largas guardias nocturnas, con extrema claridad.

El avión que nos trasladó y al que habían despojado de sus asientos para aumentar la capacidad de carga del personal con sus equipos, luego de una breve trayectoria aterrizó en el aeropuerto de Puerto Argentino.

Inmediatamente comenzamos nuestra marcha en dirección hacia el pueblo primeramente, para luego en forma inmediata atravesarlo y continuar en dirección sur.

Esa primera noche nos encontró pernoctando en un galpón de esquila, próximo a Puerto Argentino.

Inmediatamente al día siguiente, con las primeras luces reiniciamos la marcha ya en dirección a la posición que constituiría nuestra línea defensiva y cobijarnos hasta el final del conflicto, esto es la Colina del Zapador ("Sapper Hill"), distante unos cuatro kilómetros al sudoeste de Puerto Argentino.

Los restantes componentes del BIM 5, en lo relativo a las compañías de tiradores, hicieron lo propio en los Montes William y Tumbledown, ubicados hacia el oeste de la posición propia. Particularmente mi Sección, se encontraba desplegada con frente a "Puerto Enriqueta" ("PORT HARRIET") es decir con orientación hacia el mar, y en las estribaciones de SAPPER HILL.

Ese primer día junto a los cuadros de la Sección, comenzamos a definir los lugares donde habrían de ubicarse las posiciones para cada uno de los tiradores y las armas de apoyo con las que contábamos.

Personalmente me ubiqué en el centro del dispositivo, compartiendo el pozo de zorro con quien se desempeñaba y cumplía la función de radio operador

El puesto de comando de compañía se encontraba en proximidades de la cima de "Sapper Hill" y las restantes dos Secciones lo rodeaban.

Por la propia ubicación de mi sección, bastante distanciada del puesto de comando de compañía gozábamos de una autonomía relativamente importante; Las comunicaciones inalámbricas se encontraban absolutamente vedadas es decir regía el silencio radioeléctrico por razones de localización enemigas obvias, contando con un tendido de comunicación telefónica relevante, aunque sumamente lábil, en cuanto luego de los intensos bombardeos a los que fuimos sometidos, tanto por fuego naval, aéreo y en última instancia por parte de artillería terrestre, este fue objeto de frecuentes y sucesivos cortes en su líneas.

Durante los restantes días del mes de abril, lo dedicamos a fortalecer nuestras posiciones, ello en la medida de lo posible debido a que las propias características del terreno, similares a las existentes en Tierra del Fuego, dificultaban enormemente ésa tarea. Se trató de maximizar la utilización de los promontorios rocosos, a modo de protección y teniendo siempre como objetivo principal la planificación de los fuegos cruzados.

El 1° de mayo a aproximadamente las 22:30 se produce un fuerte bombardeo naval británico realizado con cañones de 105 mm a nuestra zona, que se constituye en el bautismo de fuego del BIM 5 y que lamentablemente se cobra la vida del Conscripto Infante de Marina Hugo Daniel Caviglioli, siendo esta la primera sufrida por la Unidad.

Sapper Hill en las inmediaciones se habían instalado varias antenas como así también el Radar Antiaéreo de la Fuerza Aérea Argentina.

Estos bombardeos navales habrían de sucederse ininterrumpidamente durante la totalidad de los días hasta la finalización del conflicto, siempre en horarios nocturnos, con centro tanto en el aeropuerto con el objetivo de destruir la pista de aterrizaje, como así también gran caudal de ellos dirigidos a las posiciones que ocupó el Batallón, particularmente tal como dijera aquéllas correspondientes a "Sapper Hill".

También durante estos primeros días de mayo, desde nuestra posición fuimos testigos privilegiados del despliegue naval enemigo de varios de sus buques ya que se desplazaban frente a nuestras vistas primero en sentido sur-norte sin efectuar disparos y luego en sentido inverso, ya disparando sus cañones.

Observamos con incrédula emoción cómo los pilotos de la aviación propia, atacaban la flota a muy baja altura y proximidad absoluta respecto a sus blancos. Esos aviones literalmente se lanzaban sobre sus objetivos con la finalidad de concretar exitosamente su misión, en una demostración de valor admirable. Estas imágenes quedaron definitivamente gravadas en mis retinas, por el grado de temeridad absoluto demostrado

Tenía en mi posición una pequeña radio que me permitía escuchar en forma defectuosa radio Colonia, es así que por ese medio llega a mi conocimiento el hundimiento del crucero General A.R.A. Belgrano, ocurrido el 2 de mayo.

Transcurren los días y circula la versión permanente de abandonar las posiciones estáticas hasta ese momento adoptadas por la unidad, esto es movilizar el Batallón en dirección a San Carlos, pasando de una postura estrictamente defensiva a otra que habría de ser ofensiva.

En esta oportunidad, me ofrezco voluntariamente para ir a ese punto con mi Sección, siendo descartada tal posibilidad por el jefe de compañía.

En el transcurso de los días, el avance de las tropas enemigas, luego de su desembarco, es permanente como así también lo es el continuo asedio de la artillería naval, aérea desde muy baja altura, y ya en junio se siente la artillería terrestre, con un grado de precisión aún más certero.

Vimos igualmente con estupor en la madrugada del 12 de junio, el lanzamiento del misil exocet MM-38, emplazado en cercanías de Puerto Argentino, su luminosa trayectoria de más de 29.000 metros sobre el mar hasta impactar sobre el buque HMS "GLAMORGAN", unidad que si bien no fue hundida, quedó fuera de combate e inutilizada para atacar las posiciones propias.

Ya la noche del 13 al 14 de junio y durante la madrugada de este último día, observamos las líneas de fuego continuas del atacante, que fluían y convergían en "Tumbledown". Fue realmente un espectáculo dantesco que llegó a iluminar completamente la cerrada noche.

En las primeras horas del 14 de junio, somos violentamente sorprendidos por artillería terrestre, con una precisión hasta ese momento desconocida, los impactos ocurrían literalmente sobre la ubicación de nuestras posiciones, dejando a la vista cráteres de singulares proporciones y hacían temblar todo el terreno circundante.

Concluido dicho ataque, ya avanzada la mañana comenzamos a ver el desplazamiento de propia tropa encaramados sobre el camino principal en dirección a Puerto Argentino. Lenta pero inexorablemente vemos el pasaje de integrantes de diferentes unidades.

Con semejante panorama y ante la ausencia de órdenes concretas me dirijo hacia el puesto de comando de compañía, en horario próximo al mediodía; allí el propio Jefe, me impone la orden de replegar mi Sección bajo el concepto de establecer la defensa final en el perímetro de Puerto Argentino.

Con esa idea en mente, descendí de la colina en dirección a las posiciones propias. Allí el personal se encontraba fuera de ellas, expectante respecto a las órdenes a impartir, cuando encontrándome muy próximo, recibimos el alerta respecto a la proximidad de helicópteros enemigos; El primero de ellos, un "Sea King", se mantuvo prácticamente estático durante un lapso que pareció una eternidad, sin atinar su piloto el curso a seguir. Es en ése lapso que mis cuadros me preguntan qué hacer y es así que luego de cerciorarme que se trataba de un helicóptero inglés, ordené mediante la señal de rigor abrir fuego, orden que fue cumplida acabadamente por toda la Sección.

El helicóptero continuo suspendido unos breves segundos, hasta que tomó la decisión de caer hacia su estribor en dirección hacia el mar, y a unos pocos metros procedía a desembarcar tropa de infantería sin llegar a completar su aterrizaje. Luego de ello y ya humeante por los impactos recibidos, se puede observar su aterrizaje en dirección sur.

Esas tropas inmediatamente toman posición lineal, obteniendo una breve cubierta en un accidente del terreno y comienzan a disparar profusamente sobre nuestras posiciones.

En el momento de disparar mi fusil contra el helicóptero, él se había trabado, me arrastro hasta recuperar una mochila en la que había acopiado munición de todo tipo y me acerco a la posición de una de las ametralladoras MAG, para verificar porqué razón no se

Encontraba disparando; Resultó que su apuntador había sido herido y lo consideré muerto, por lo que instantáneamente decidí operarla con mis propias manos.

Comencé a disparar y percibí de inmediato la precisión de la respuesta del fuego enemigo, los proyectiles literalmente rozaban mi cabeza, por lo que decidí buscar una posición de tiro más cubierta, esto es simplemente más baja, ya que mayor protección no se podía obtener en la medida que el frente de la posición estaba construido con turba. También utilicé breves segundos en graduar el alza de acuerdo a la distancia que estimé se encontraba el enemigo.

El Cabo Segundo IM SINI, oficio de cargador. Fueron muchas las bandas que se utilizaron en un combate

La propia apreciación del tiempo que insumió la acción me excede, en cuanto a que se produce una total y absoluta pérdida de noción del mismo Sólo sé que dispare en forma continua, batiendo el sector de soldados británicos de izquierda a derecha y en sentido inverso en reiteradas, sucesivas y continuas oportunidades, de todas las formas posibles. Recuerdo que cambié la pieza para una mejor ubicación de tiro y me quemé la palma de mi mano derecha por la temperatura del tubo cañón, producto ello de su continua utilización.

Fue evidente en ése momento el impulso ofensivo atacante, en cuanto uno de los soldados enemigos se dispuso liderarlo logrando cruzar el camino que conducía a Puerto Argentino, llegando a una distancia muy próxima a nosotros, siendo abatido así, por múltiples disparos propios.

Esta secuencia continuó hasta que cesó el fuego desde el lugar que provenía. Es en este momento que me despego de la pieza y comienzo mi propio repliegue. Fui el último soldado.

; En mi retirada, encuentro yacente el cuerpo del soldado Robledo, que momentos antes había sido cargado por el Cabo Segundo IM Sini, en procura de trasladarlo hacia propia línea, adopto en el evento idéntica postura, lo cargo en mis hombros y comienzo a trasladarlo, A pocos metros percibo su cuerpo ya sin vida, con múltiples impactos visibles en su pecho y abandono el intento.

Continúo mi retirada, en busca del puesto de comando de compañía, para ello debía ascender por la ladera sur de Sapper Hill, en busca de apoyo mientras, en forma constante, soy objeto de disparos cuyos proyectiles me rodean ; se percibe claramente su impacto en la maleza que me circunda, ellos provenientes de otro lugar, esto es desde un rumbo más hacia el oeste, correspondiente, según me enteraría más tarde a tropas que habrían desembarcado de otros helicópteros en aquél sector.

Al retirarme de la colina, el helicóptero que primeramente se acercó a nuestras posiciones, aterriza humeante tal como dijera, algunos kilómetros al sur, otro helicóptero de similares características también fue alcanzado por el fuego de nuestras armas.

En relación a estos sucesos siempre tuve el interrogante, cuál fue el verdadero motivo por el que, el helicóptero o la infantería transportada en él decidieron trabarse en combate, ya que teniendo comunicación radioeléctrica, ellos sabían que las hostilidades habían cesado.

Fué muy evidente que el comandante de la aeronave dudó en abandonar el área al momento de percibir que su presencia era objeto de disparos y porqué se aproximó tanto a nuestras posiciones. Son todas incógnitas que aún subsisten en mis pensamientos.

Sin perjuicio de ello, hay una que con el tiempo pude llegar a clarificar y es la siguiente. El helicóptero inglés no se encontraba artillado, por lo tanto su proximidad en términos de ataque concreto no estaba perfectamente definido y en sentido estricto no representaba en ese contexto tampoco una amenaza y/o peligro inminente, no obstante ello, yo ordené abrir fuego sobre él; Fue eso correcto? Varios años me llevo asimilar la respuesta, pero hoy estoy convencido de haber actuado conforme la situación lo exigía y según la información con la que yo contaba en ese difícil momento.

Yo recibí una última orden de replegar mi Sección para constituirnos en defensa en un punto más hacia el norte;

Podría haber evitado el enfrentamiento con las tropas helitransportadas, seguramente sí, pero la decisión tomada era totalmente congruente con la orden previa impartida: DEFENDER y eso podía hacerse allí o en otro lugar.

De hecho fui el último hombre en permanecer en el campo de combate, esto como simple apreciación objetiva y sin pretender con ello atribuir mérito propio alguno.

Inmediatamente luego de dejar nuestro armamento, fuimos trasladados al galpón de la carpintería de las FALKLAND ISLAND S.F.I.P; para luego de dos días allí, el 16 de junio marchar a la península del Aeropuerto donde permaneceríamos hasta el momento en que fuimos conducidos al buque Hospital Bahía paraíso el 19/06 y de allí trasladados al continente, arribando finalmente a Puerto Belgrano el 24/06.

El respeto constituyó una nota distintiva del período que nos tocó vivir en calidad de prisioneros de guerra.

Ya ubicados en las inmediaciones del aeropuerto, construimos nuestro propio vivac mediante la utilización de las piezas correspondientes a la prolongación de aluminio de la pista de aterrizaje.

De regreso en el continente, nos fue otorgada licencia durante el mes de agosto; Reiniciamos actividades y se desarrolla en octubre la última campaña del BIM 5 en el año 1982, luego de pedir la baja voluntaria, me retiré de la actividad con el grado de Teniente de Corbeta de IM siendo mi último destino el Batallón de IM N.º 3 con asiento en La Plata Bs. As.

Con posterioridad estudié abogacía pasando a ejercer esa profesión a partir de 1989. En 1982 me encontraba soltero y sin hijos.

Concluyo este testimonio del accionar de nuestra fracción, permitiéndome la transcripción de una de las tantas e históricas frases del padre de la Patria General Don José de San Martín, que dijo: "honrar la patria, no es otra cosa que servirla desinteresadamente" y sin hesitación alguna puedo afirmar que quiénes tuvimos el privilegiado y altísimo honor de hacerlo, lo hicimos estrictamente bajo tal ideal superior.

Mi profundo reconocimiento y respeto hacia los soldados caídos, sus familiares, a todos y cada uno de los integrantes de la Tercera Sección, sin distinción alguna de jerarquía, que con certero valor supieron defender su posición hasta las últimas instancias, cuando todo ya estaba decidido.

Appendix B

Charlie Company Nominal Roll

Operation *Corporate*, 1982

Alphabetical order and no ranks. Drawn from an official list.

Allen A J H 'Ginge', Allen P R 'Paul', Arblaster D W 'Dave'.

Bannon A 'Alex', Barnes T V 'Terry/Tel', Barriball F A 'Andy', Bates J P 'Basher', Bates P J 'Paul', Beasley R R 'Dick', Beddall R 'Bob', Bentley P M 'Paul', Boyle P M 'Billy/Paul', Brooks C E 'Craig', Brown A W 'Adrian', Burden J D 'John', Burge S J "Sam", Burgess M A J "Mark", Bushby C J 'Carl'.

Cadywould N F 'Niel', Cahill T D 'Tim', Carter R J 'Rick', Carter S, Carvell S T 'Stan', Chesterton R D 'Ralph', Comb V I 'Vince', Comrie A R 'Sandy', Crowle P G 'Pete'.

Dolton D E 'Dean'.

Edmond B W 'Brian'.

Fitzgerald P T 'Fitz'.

Gallagher C J 'Skin/Colin', Garcia J 'Joe', Garnham M A 'Mark', Gaunt A 'Andy', Gibson M J 'Jim', Good P, Gouge G M 'Baz', Gray O K, Griffiths P 'Paul/Griff'.

Hall S J 'Simon/Sponner', Hare 'Brasso', Harper K 'Kev', Harris M P 'Matt', Hepburn A C 'Alex/Jock', Herd G 'Ged/Big Ged', Higley J A 'John', Hill G D 'Graham/Pusser', Hill M A 'Martin/Aubrey', Hobbs 'Brian', Holloway N 'Nick', Howe R N, Howie W M 'William/ Bill', Humberstone R K 'Roger', Hurn P R 'Ernie/Paul', Hames K 'Ken'.

Irving D F 'Damian/Dee'.

Johnson I N 'Ian/Jono', Johnson P G 'Paul', Joynes A N.

Kelly A P 'Tony', King A R L 'Andy', Kitcherside P C 'Paul', Kenney R P 'Ron'.

Leigh J 'John', Lewis V 'Vic', Lloyd B D 'Taff', Lucking C D 'Clive'.

Macfarlane N A 'Neil/Mac, Mackintosh R A J, Maloney M O 'Matt', Marshall J R 'Jim', Marshall J W 'John', McConville G M 'Gaz/Mac', McDonald P R 'Phil', McGovern M 'Mac', McGregor W J 'Wayne/Mac', McIntee J K, McLean S 'Mac/Steve', Miller R A 'Rick/Ricky', Mills A 'Ade', Mooney I J, Mudd C D 'Colin', Murphy S 'Spud/Steve'.

Naylor T 'Terry/Ginge', Nicholls M A 'Taff/Mark'.

Peters J S 'Pete', Pillar A R 'Andy', Pinches G R 'Gaz', Pleasance N R 'Pigsy/Neil', Poole S R 'Si', Porter 'Paddy', Porthouse D M 'George', Pretty C J 'Chris', Pritchard S G 'Steve', Purves C W 'Craig/Jock'.

Reed E C 'Eugene/Huwie', Reynolds A B 'Adrian', Roberts W V 'Wayne/Rocky', Rogers P W 'Paul/Buck', Rose P.

Salzano D C 'Salty', Sampson R N 'Sam/Sammy', Scarrott G P 'Jasper', Schofield D, Sinclair P 'Paul/Paddy', Smith G A, Smith I D 'Ian/Smudge', Stevens W I 'Bill'.

Thoburn M H 'Elvis', Truelove M J 'Mick'.

Walker D A, Walker M 'Mark', Watson P 'Pete', Webster I R, Western G C 'Gaz', White A, White R D E, Wickett A M 'Andy', Wilkins A 'Ginge/Alan', Wooding P 'Woody'.

Young C C 'Clark'.